# KNIGHT OF GERMANY

# KNIGHT OF GERMANY

## OSWALD BOELCKE, GERMAN ACE

### BY
### PROFESSOR JOHANNES WERNER

Translated by Claude W. Sykes

With an Introduction and Appendix
by Norman Franks

CASEMATE
*Philadelphia & Newbury*
A Greenhill Book

This edition of *Knight of Germany* is published in
the United States of America in 2009 by
CASEMATE
908 Darby Road, Havertown, PA 19083

and in the United Kingdom by
CASEMATE
17 Cheap Street, Newbury, RG14 5DD

 *A Greenhill Book*

ISBN 978-1-935149-11-8

Cataloging in publication data is available from the
Library of Congress and the British Library.

Printed and bound in the United States of America

Publishing History:
*Knight of Germany* was first published in German as *Boelcke der Mensch, der Flieger,
der Führer der deutschen Jagdfliegerei.* by K.F. Koehler Verlag, Leipzig in 1932.
    The first English edition was published by John Hamilton in 1933. It was reissued
in facsimile by Greenhill Books / Lionel Leventhal Ltd in 1985 and again in 1991
(this time with a new appendix by Norman Franks).
    This new Casemate edition has been completely retypeset but the original language
has been left unaltered.

# Contents

# *Introduction*

Born in Giebichstein, near Halle in Saxony, on 19th May 1891, Oswald Boelcke was the third of six children. By the time he was 25 years old he was the hero of Germany, being amongst the first of the successful air fighters of the Great War of 1914–1918.

What made Boelcke so remarkable, as well as his being an important fighter pilot, was that he was the first to try to study and to understand the new dimension in which he fought, the air. He was not a strong boy, but by the same determination that made him so great in the air, he overcame his weakness, and although more interested in sport, he had a fine mind for mathematics and physics. He was a very open and uncomplicated person, but with a flair for approaching any problem with an open mind and the desire to succeed in finding the best answer. It was these attributes that helped make his name and give him the title of the father of the air fighting arm.

Bent on a military career, he joined the Prussian Cadet Corps in March 1911, and was assigned to the No.3 Telegraphers' Battalion, at Koblenz, being commissioned the following year. During army manoeuvres he became interested in flying and in 1914 became a pilot. When the war started, he was posted to No. 13 Fliegerabteilung at La Ferté where his brother Wilhelm was an air observer. In the early

1

days of the war, the two brothers often flew together. Always eager to fly, Oswald received the Iron Cross (Second Class) in October 1914, followed by the First Class award in February 1915.

With the arrival at the front of the first of the Fokker 'Eindekker' single-seat monoplane fighters, one or two were assigned to each reconnaissance unit as escort machines, and Boelcke put in a request to be allowed to fly one. Owing to his flare for action and his aggressive attitude to it, this was granted, and he began to fly both the two-seater and single-seater types on the French battle fronts.

In April 1915 Boelcke was sent to Fliegerabteilung No.62, at Douai, flying the C-type LVG two-seaters as well as a Fokker. At Douai he met Max Immelmann, another young fighting pilot, who later became known as the 'Eagle of Lille'. It was now that Boelcke and Immelmann began to realise, as did their counterparts on the other side of the lines, the British and French, that there was more than just observation work to do. It was just as important to stop the other side from carrying out this reconnaissance work. Thus air fighting, although still in its infancy, began.

Boelcke may well have attacked or pursued any number of French machines in this early period of 1915, but his first recorded success came on 4th July, when he attacked a French Morane two-seater. In true style, Boelcke landed near to the crash site of his victims and arranged for their burial. He gained further victories during that summer, and by 30th October the German Air Service had recognised and confirmed six victories for him, most of them French. On 12th January, 1916, both men were awarded Germany's highest award for military action, the coveted 'Ordre Pour Le Mérite', known more popularly today as the 'Blue Max.'

His successes continued into the new year of 1916, and indeed he and Max Immelmann were soon vying to be the leading scorer among the early scout pilots. By the end of March, Boelcke and Immelmann both had 13 victories. In April each gained one, but in May, while Immelmann gained his 15th, Boelcke increased his score to 18. Immelmann brought his score to 17 on the day of his death in action on 18th June. Boelcke was to score just one more victory, his 19th, before the Air Service, fearful that he too might fall, took him away from the battle front and sent him on an inspection trip to the war zones of the south east, Boelcke soon found himself in Vienna and then in Budapest, Belgrade and finally Turkey. He went at a moment of great personal disappointment, for he was about to be given command of a small unit of Fokkers at Sivry, something he had been urging to have formed.

During his time at the front, Boelcke had learned much about air fighting and although he had tried to influence official thinking, he had not succeeded in putting his views forward. Now, following the bitter ground and air battles on the Verdun front, the German High Command were at last ready to listen. With the approach of the summer and an expected attack by the Allies in France, Boelcke had been ordered to help form the German fighting organisation.

It was now realised that rather than having fighting scouts attached to each reconnaissance unit, these nimble fighting machines should be bunched together into their own fighting units, both for escort work and to carry out fighting patrols to engage the Allied airmen, who seemed constantly to fly over German territory for observation and for bombing. Boelcke's skill and diplomacy now came to the fore in producing a scheme for the new concept of fighting units.

The new units would be called Jagdstaffeln (more familiarly called Jastas), and in the summer of 1916 the first twelve Jastas were, or were about to be, formed.

With the onset of the mighty Somme Offensive at the beginning of July, the air fighting over the front became intense. Boelcke was still in far-off Turkey, but as the weeks progressed, he was finally ordered to return to France and was given command of Jasta 2, flying on the British part of the front.

Oswald Boelcke led his Jasta with distinction and courage during the next two months, increasing his personal score from 19 to 40 by 26th October, almost all of his victories over the Royal Flying Corps. Jasta 2, with pilots such as Manfred von Richthofen, Walter Hohne, Erwin Boehme, Max Muller, Rudolf Reimann and Stephen Kirmaier, had brought the unit's score to over 50 in that same period. Their aircraft now were the Halberstadt biplane scouts and the nimble Albatros DIs, fore-runner to the successful Albatros DIII and DV, which his protégé Manfred von Richthofen was to fly so successfully, becoming known as the Red Baron.

Boelcke had returned to the front to meet his greatest challenge. He reached the zenith of his fighting career, met his destiny and forged his name into the annals of the world's great fighting airmen. He left his men, and the men who came after him, with an image to live up to. In his honour, his squadron was renamed Jasta Boelcke.

Oswald Boelcke left not only his spirit for others to live up to, but the tangible evidence of his farsightedness about air fighting and fighting tactics. His 'Dicta Boelcke' became the standard reference for all other Jasta pilots, and their basic principles applied to a new generation of fighter pilots during World War Two, for whom they appeared in printed booklet form.

## DICTA BOELCKE

1. Always try to secure an advantageous position before attacking. Climb before and during the approach in order to surprise the enemy from above, and dive on him swiftly from the rear when the moment to attack is at hand.

2. Try to place yourself between the sun and the enemy. This puts the glare of the sun in the enemy's eyes and makes it difficult to see you and impossible for him to shoot with any accuracy.

3. Do not fire the machine guns until the enemy is within range and you have him squarely within your sights.

4. Attack when the enemy least expects it or when he is pre-occupied with other duties such as observation, photography or bombing.

5. Never turn your back and try to run away from an enemy fighter. If you are surprised by an attack on your tail, turn and face the enemy with your guns.

6. Keep your eye on the enemy and do not let him deceive you with tricks. If your opponent appears damaged follow him down until he crashes to be sure he is not faking.

7. Foolish acts of bravery only bring death. The Jasta must fight as a unit with close teamwork between all pilots. The signals of its leaders must be obeyed.

When Oswald Boelcke was killed on 28th October 1916, in a collision with Erwin Boehme, he had achieved 40 victories in aerial combat. The war was to continue for a further two years and cover the most momentous months of air fighting on the Western Front, with machines far superior to that of the Fokker Eindekker or the early Albatros DI or Halberstadt Scouts. Yet in that time, only II other pilots were to better or equal his score. Of these, one was to exactly double it. Manfred von Richthofen, one of Jasta 2's young pilots, and a man hand-picked by Boelcke himself, brought down 80 Allied aeroplanes to make him the German, and the war's, Ace of Aces. It is certain that Manfred von Richthofen learnt well the teachings of his erstwhile leader and followed his 'Dicta' to the full.

Norman Franks
1991

# *Preface*

*A nation without heroes and hero-worship must perish.*
—Heinrich von Treitschke

SELDOM indeed has any star risen so swiftly and vertically from the darkness to lofty, glittering heights as the fame of our German hero of the air, Oswald Boelcke.

When the young lieutenant from a wireless telegraphy company, who had been seconded to the flying school at his own request, passed his pilot's tests in July 1914, shortly before the outbreak of the Great War, his success was a matter of interest to none but his narrow circle of personal friends. Yet two years later Boelcke was a national hero, whose name was known all over the world—the pride of his country and the terror of his foes. Aged only 25, he was the youngest captain on the active list of the German army; while still a lieutenant, he was decorated by the emperor with the 'Pour le Mérite,' the highest order bestowed for war services. When, barely six months later, an accident of blind chance put an abrupt end to the victorious career of the invincible airman, all Germany trembled and mourned, and he was laid to rest with princely pomp and ceremony. At that period the fame of Boelcke's victories and the lamentation for his loss brought forth a number of brochures and articles dealing with his life, but as most of these were based on their

writers' enthusiasm rather than any reliable sources of information, they had only a fleeting interest. We have far more
valuable material in "Captain Boelcke's Active Service
Reports," which the father compiled from his son's letters
from the front immediately after his death and actually published in 1916—another testimonial to the 'Boelcke spirit,'
as it shows that in spite of his new-found grief this parent
did not give way to useless repining against the irrevocable
but possessed sufficient energy to erect a literary monument
to his son. But although this little book received an enthusiastic welcome and reached a sale of a quarter of a million
copies, it cannot suffice for Boelcke's final memorial. The
limitations imposed a priori on its scope were too narrow,
firstly on account of the restricted choice of excerpts from
letters from the front as long as the war continued and secondly because the development of war flying was still in
process so that it was impossible to recognise and appreciate
the supreme significance of Boelcke in the history of aerial
warfare. The readers waxed enthusiastic over his daring
onslaughts and unbroken series of victories, but they could
not divine that the tactics he employed in those fights were
to furnish the basic principles for the operations of all scout
machines.

As we have now gained the necessary distance from those
events and a clear view over the history of air fighting during the war, as moreover Boelcke's parents have seen their
way to entrust me with the treasure of their son's pre-war
and war letters to them—a treasure hitherto jealously guarded from outsiders—together with all other documentary and
epistolary material they possess, I venture on an attempt to
give a complete picture of Boelcke's personality and significance. By setting this life-picture within the frame of the his-

tory of aerial warfare, we make the discovery that Boelcke was not only a very fine character and a model pilot, fighter and Staffel-leader, but also a leader of German scout flying in the sense that he pointed the way and exercised a decisive influence upon its development—even after his death.

# CHAPTER I

# *Nascent Forces*

TENACIOUS strength and a firm will, a cheerful temperament and a sunny nature—this is the happy blend of personality that Oswald Boelcke    owed to his ancestors. From his father, who was a native of Havelland, he inherited the vigour and homeliness peculiar to the province of Brandenburg, while he derived his charm, high spirits and sunny disposition from his Thuringian mother.

He had the good fortune to grow up in the house of true German parents, who were blessed with six children—five sons and a daughter. It was dominated by a spirit of piety and patriotism; simple, old customs held sway there, along with a true appreciation of all beauty and goodness and a broad outlook gained by many years of residence abroad. When Oswald came into the world as the fourth child at Giebichstein, near Halle, his birth took place only half a year after the return of his parents from the Argentine Republic, where his father had served his country overseas as headmaster of the German Protestant School in Buenos Aires for six years before taking the post of senior assistant master in the higher modern school at Halle. Five years later he

* *The various spellings of the name—Wilhelm, the elder brother, is entered in the Army List of 1914 as Bölcke, while Oswald appears as Boelcke—is due to the fact that the family wrote it with an ö. But Oswald, who always used Latin characters, wrote it oe.*

accepted a call to a similar position at the Antoinette School in Dessau, where he subsequently gained his title of professor.

Consequently Oswald Boelcke was four and a half years old when he arrived at the town of Dessau, which grew to be his real home. There he played as a child in the open spaces of the undeveloped Schillerstrasse, which is now named the Boelckestrasse in his honour. There he attended and matriculated from the DukeFrederick Grammar School. There also he found his grave in the war cemetery, where a beautiful memorial was erected to him. The aeroplanes from the Junkers Works often pass over him there, singing their droning song.

Oswald Boelcke was by no means a model classical scholar at the grammar school, but he went through all its classes and had no difficulty in passing his matriculation examination. His favourite subjects were history, mathematics and physics; he was interested in machinery at a very early age and showed his practical ability by rigging up his own telephone line across the street and the house opposite to the villa where his friend Haeslop resided, but he was not particularly attracted by classical languages.

The teachers always had a good word for the fairheaded boy with the sincere blue eyes and frank, open disposition, while his classmates liked him as 'a real good sort.' They also admired him as the best athlete in the gymnasium and their master at all boldily exercises and submitted willingly to his leadership in all games and 'rags.' He was a born leader.

His old headmaster expressed himself as follows in the oration which he delivered in his honour:

"His inclinations did not tend to book learning because he had too strong an impulse towards active work. He was a strong character who found it absolutely necessary to gain full occupation for his physical strength. In the essay on his own life which he had to write before taking his matriculation he designated rowing, swimming, diving, tennis, football and gymnastics as his favourite pursuits. To this list he might well have added dancing and skating, in which he showed particular proficiency."

When still quite a youngster Boelcke gave proof of his dexterity and instinctive self-confidence. His father took him to the swimming-bath in the Mulde river, where he demonstrated the motions of swimming to the little boy while he supported him in his arms. But a few moments later the lad suddenly slipped out of the paternal arms and swam about like a fish in the water—to the astonishment of all beholders. During his latter years at the grammar school he was a member of the Stillinge Swimming Club, where he made himself proficient in diving. He entered at a swimming meeting under an assumed name because pupils at the school were not allowed to take part in public competitions and returned home that same evening with a beaming face, carrying several first prizes to show the parents who were still blissfully ignorant of his participation in the various events. He also won prizes for diving in Madgeburg where he entered for a competition when he chanced to be on a visit to his brother Wilhelm, who was his senior by five years and a lieutenant in the Pioneers. During the war his proficiency in swimming gained him the life-saving medal for rescuing a French boy from drowning at Douai. He took a particular pride in wearing this medal alongside of the high decorations he won on active service.

His uncle, Pastor Karl Bölcke, wrote a memoir on his nephew, in which he gives an account of a gymnastic display the boys organised in honour of their parents' silver wedding. It took place in their garden, where they erected a steel horizontal bar they bought out of their savings. "The star turn came when eighteen year old Oswald did his huge vault. It almost took one's breath away, and yet it was a wonderful sight to watch his youthful, agile body swinging round the bar as if it was the easiest and most obvious thing in the world. I shall never forget this beautiful spectacle."

When Oswald was seventeen years old, he was taken to the Austrian Alps for the first time. Under the guidance of his father he became an enthusiastic mountaineer and developed into a skilled, fearless climber with the same rapidity with which he had acquired the art of swimming earlier in his life. His father relates that they made their headquarters at Lanersbach, where they accomplished many fine climbs on the mountains of the Tuxer range. The harder these climbs were, the greater were their attractions for Oswald; his youthful soul only found its full exultation when they reached the dangerous part of the expedition. His mother, who watched one of his exploits from the lower levels of Grieeralpe will never forget how after reaching the rocky summit of the Hollenstein he ran triumphantly in long strides down the steep, scree-covered slope and then stood on his head on the first level grassy patch he reached, while waiting for his father and his brother, Martin—following more cautiously—to catch him up.

Nature equipped Boelcke with inexhaustible strength and great agility. He was not tall, but yet not undersized; despite his broad shoulders, he had a slim, supple, graceful, well-proportioned body. His easy bearing and lithe movements gave a perfect picture of controlled power and harmonious beauty. From early youth he steeled his will and developed the assets Nature had given him by a course of systematic physical training. The only weakness he could not eliminate was an asthmatic tendency that remained as the legacy of an attack of hooping-cough; he was always liable to suffer from it if he caught cold or had to live in marshy country. This complaint, however, did not weaken him, but only served to strengthen his will. He fought against it from his earliest youth; for this purpose he went in for long distance running, at which he ultimately excelled to such an extent that in the spring of 1914 he won a prize at Frankfurt a/M in the 8th ArmyCorps Cross Country race that formed one of the preliminary trials for the Olympic games.

When discussing Boelcke's personal appearance, I cannot help thinking of his big, fascinating eyes of bright steel blue that charmed all hearts by their frankness and revealed his strength of character and purpose by their penetration. Those eyes must have made a similar impression on Field Marshal von Mackensen, who wrote to Boelcke's parents after his death: "I shall never forget the hour when your illustrious son was a guest at my table in Uskub and I was able to hear him tell of his exploits in his own modest way. I have never gazed into a finer pair of gleaming blue eyes. I encountered the eyes of a man who was absolutely fearless— a true hero."

Oswald Boelcke had no liking for a sedentary life and no inclination for any of the learned professions. He was an enthusiastic devotee of every form of athletic sport and liberally endowed with strength, courage and will-power; moreover he came from a family that might be termed conservative in the best sense of the word. Under these circumstances it is not surprising that he should have decided on a military career at a very early age.

In the essay on his own life which he wrote when sitting for his matriculation he mentioned only one of the authors he had read in the course of his studies. This was Homer, "who took me back into the wonderful heroic age of Greece." He then proceded to state that his favourite books were the works of Treitschke and the military histories published by the general staff. An even more characteristic sign of his early interest in military matters and—a remarkable fact!—in aviation, is his choice of subjects for the discourses he had to deliver when his class was instructed in elocution. In 1908, when Oswald Boelcke was in the second form,* his three themes were: "General Scharnhorst and his army reforms," "The first airship flights," and "Count Zeppelin's life before his earliest experiments in aeronautics!"

He took the first step towards a military career at a very early age and completely on his own initiative. One day, shortly after his promotion to the fourth form, he wrote to the Emperor without informing anyone; he stated in this letter that he was desirous of becoming an officer and solicited assistance in the form of a nomination to the cadet corps. His parents did not learn of this exploit until a considerable time later when they received a communication from Lieutenant-General von Schwartzkoppen, the commander of the cadet corps, informing them that the emperor had granted their son's request and asking them to forward the necessary papers. They thought, however, that it would be better for the boy not to leave his home so soon and decided to keep him at the Grammar school until he had passed his matriculation.

When Oswald Boelcke reached this goal at Easter, 1911, he jumped up from his school-bench with a triumphant

* *In German schools the first form is the highest (Translator's Note).*

"At last!" Then he set off on his journey to the Rhine, his destination being Coblence, where he was to join the Third Telegraph Battalion as an aspirant. The choice of this troop was occasioned by his particular interest in physics and mathematics.

# CHAPTER II

# *From Aspirant to Lieutenant and Pilot*

TO maternal affection we owe the preservation of all the letters and postcards which Oswald wrote to his parents between March 15th, 1911, the date of his admission to the army and the day of his death. This correspondence proved itself an invaluable source of information to me when I came to draw the picture of his life, because his indivdual characteristics and the development of his personality (which already begins to assume the traits of the later hero of the air) emerge clear to the eye from such unaffected and spontaneous communications.

Therefore the following mosaic taken from his pre-war letters may also be of interest and value, because it is the first example of biographical literature that gives us a really plain and reliable picture of the petty details of life in the old army, the joys and sorrows of an aspirant to a commission and the social and service life of a young officer. Consequently many who have known only the life in traditional regiments will receive a surprise when they learn how interesting and varied the service and life could be in one of these mere 'communications troops.'

## AN ASPIRANT IN COBLENCE

*19.3.11.* My dear parents, today being Sunday, I have my first chance of writing a letter; I had to scribble off the two

17

cards in the cleaning hour, and I expect they will look like it. I had no time to write a letter all the week, as we were hard at work every hour of the day—7 to 8 a.m., instruction, 8.30–11 drill, then clean out our room, make our uniforms presentable and dress for lunch at 12.45 in the mess. 2.30–5.30 more drill, 6–7 cleaning up again. Next week we are due for technical instruction from 5–7, with the cleaning up hour to follow.

Our barracks are situated near the Deutsches Eck, where the Moselle flows into the Rhine. We can see the Ehren-breitstein from our parade ground. There is ample space in the room I share with the other two aspirants; until we came in, it was a carpenters' shop—but we organised a big spring cleaning which would have delighted mother.

Yesterday I got my dress uniform, so that I do not need to go to the mess in working kit now. At present we find our time there rather boring, especially as they all eye us so inquisitively. Lieutenant Kröschel, our ensign 'father,' calls our attention to every little detail, but he is quite decent to us. We do not come into contact with the officers at all on duty, as the whole of our training is supervised by a sergeant.

*29.3.11.* It is 'quick march' for us all the time now; we hardly have time to eat our meals. When we line up for gymnasium, one of us three is certain to have his head, hands or feet in an incorrect attitude, which means that we must first execute a march through the riding school. Then we are put through our gym course in turn; while one of us is under instruction, the other two are supposed to do free exercises, such as knee-bends, with an occasional scramble on the 'wall' for a variation. Then comes drill and technical instruction; I have to copy out the Morse alphabet ten times for tomorrow.

Mother must not imagine it is so bad. The life suits me very well; I have not suffered from 'recruit aches' once yet, while one of our trio, who is not yet eighteen and a bit flabby, is always groaning about the pains in his thighs and has developed a knock-kneed walk. "He's got no energy in his belly," as our sergeant says. It's a good thing for me now that I was always so keen on gym.

You mustn't think the sergeant is so bad; he only puts us through the mill when one of the officers says we are too flabby. That does us no harm; it just 'takes the lazy flesh off us,' as the sergeant says.

Mother need not worry about the food, either. The meals in the mess are good and ample, though a bit dear (1 mark 30); also we aspirants always have to order drinks so as to have something in our glasses when anyone's health is drunk. I always take a glass of light beer ('the cheapest where you can get,' says the sergeant), so that lunch costs me 1.44 a day. But the meal keeps me going till the evening.

On Sunday we were allowed out of barracks for the first time; yesterday we were sworn in. We get four days leave at Easter, and the parents of my co-aspirant, Fey, have invited me stay with them at Darmstadt.

*28.4.11.* I enjoy the riding immensely. Pepita, my mare, is ten years old, but she has a bagful of tricks. Every riding lesson she rears up about ten times, and I have to keep a devilish sharp eye open, or else she would have me off. We are already riding in spurs; yesterday we had to trot and gallop sitting backwards. I was the only one of us three to keep my seat, and I have not felt at all stiff yet. I enjoy the hottest part of it all best.

Life has become much easier since we have been given

batmen (10 marks a month pay). This silly cleaning up after hard duty was often a really bitter business. But it is good schooling to learn to do everything yourself.

We have had some lovely walks in the Rhine and Moselle valleys in our free time. This glorious country would just suit father for a walking holiday; I believe he'd find somewhere fresh to visit every day.

*8.5.11.* On Friday we were taken out cable-laying for the first time, but were only allowed to look on. It was a night stunt; we set off at 8 p.m. and marched down the Rhine until we reached the spot where the cable was supposed to have been broken by the current and communications were being carried on by heliograph. It was most interesting, although we had to put in five hours hard marching.

The next day, of course, we had to carry on with our usual routine, beginning with stable-duty at 5 a.m. Yesterday, however, being Sunday, we had our compensation, as we went off to the fair at Kapellen with several officers. You can be sure I danced hard there.

*31.5.11.* Our inspection is happily over, and everything went off well so far as I was concerned. We are now in the company and do not have to wander about the barracks square by our three selves any more. Also our duties take us out into the beautiful country more often. On Tuesday we went to the range in the Mallandererbach valley for sharp-shooting practice; it is a narrow, lonely gorge, covered with fir trees, and we reached it by a two-hours march through glorious woodland valleys.

What a pity I cannot be with you at Whitsuntide! But we only get three days leave, which means that I could not be in

Dessau before Saturday evening and should have to go off again quite early on the Monday. I shall be the only one of the twelve Coblence aspirants to stop here.

*7.6.11.* My holiday was not as nice as it would have been in Dessau, but I had quite good fun. On Saturday I rowed up the Rhine with one of our lieutenants and then on through the Lahn valley with its lovely woods to Ems (through seven locks, all of which we had to work ourselves!); we did not get back to the boathouse until about eleven.

Yesterday I went to the castle of Eltz in the Moselle valley with several aspirants from the Engers War Academy. I spent a good part of the rest of the time on horseback; Lieutenant Lindner, who is in charge of our stables, allowed me to ride as many of our horses as I liked during our leave. I made good use of this permission, and was able to console myself to some extent for not being in Dessau.

*22.6.11.* We had a glorious trip last Sunday, by invitation of Fey's parents. We went by train to meet them at Mainz, and then went down the Rhine on a steamer from Mainz to Cologne. The trip lasted from 9 a.m. to 5 p.m.; it was glorious— I enjoyed it all from Niederwald to Cologne Cathedral.

To-morrow we start our great fortnight of field telegraph training. We are to set off for Limburg on the Lahn at 5 a.m., whence we start to lay our lines through the Taunus mountains towards Wiesbaden. We shall cross the Rhine at Eltville and then go on to Kreuznach, where we finish up on July 7th.

*8.7.11.* Our field training was pretty strenuous, but most interesting and always a jolly business. Never in my life have

I sung so much as during this last fortnight. I really mixed with our men the whole time, and thus gained genuine experience of a soldier's life—which I consider most important.

It was great fun being billeted on the peasants. In Heringen my host was a dignified old fellow with an embroidered cap on his head and a long pipe in his mouth; he was waiting for me at the mayor's office and took me straight off to his farm. He gave me the big family double-bed in an alcove of the living-room. There were no such things as plates, knives or forks; everyone, down to the smallest stable-boy, was served with a spoon and helped himself to bread and milk from a big bowl, meanwhile spearing potatoes from another bowl with his pocket-knife. No one spoke a word during the meal. There was only one wash-basin and one small mirror in the whole house. And yet it was not a poor household; they had three horses, sixteen cows and eight calves in their stalls. You can hardly believe it possible to find such a primitive state of affairs midway between two such world-famous watering-places as Ems and Wiesbaden!

I shall try to describe a typical day's training. On Monday, June 26th, my company had to lay a line from Kirberg to Langenschwalbach for marching troops. The idea was that our army corps was advancing; we, therefore, were detailed to lay our wires between the vanguard and the main body of the army so that the staff could remain in constant touch with the marching troops. It is strenuous work, because our wagon is never allowed to stop, which means that we have to be on the run the whole time to keep up with it. Our section was allotted the first sixteen kilometers out of Kirberg. We got through the job by 7.30 a.m., having taken about ten minutes per kilometer. We spent the rest of the day on a forty-eight kilometers' march to Eltville; as an N.C.O.

was told off to accompany our captain on a bicycle, there happened to be a horse free, and the lieutenant offered it to me. Consequently I rode through the loveliest parts of the Taunus range to the Rhine, while the others had to sit in the wagon. I particularly enjoyed the reconnaissance ride which the lieutenant and I made together when we had to discover the best roads for the wagons. We got into our billets about 7 p.m., but were called up at 10 for a night exercise, from which we did not return till 2. The next day the cable was laid through the Rhine, and the company crossed the river. We landed in Niederingelheim, where I had a fine billet. There was a lot of good wine there, as there is everywhere in Rhenish Hesse.

Now we are waiting every day for the 'buttons,' which we were supposed to get after our training. It is about time they made us lance-corporals at last; most of the aspirants who joined the field artillery at the same time that we started work are corporals already. But then we have to learn a lot more than the aspirants in any other troops.

*23.7.11.* Last Wednesday the major put us through our preliminary riding inspection—which went off splendidly as far as I was concerned; we are due for the big inspection by General von Lyncker on the 28th and 29th. Great importance is attached to riding now, because our troop is becoming more and more of a cavalry unit. Yesterday our officers started wearing spurs when off duty, while our morning and evening bugle calls are now the cavalry ones. All of which is very nice for us, because we shall be sent to the cavalry section in the War Academy.

If you can arrange your journey home so as to be in Nürnberg on Saturday, I shall present myself to you in uniform for the first time on August 5th. Our captain has given me two days leave on a red pass, which means that I can travel by the express trains.

*Kassel, 29.8.11. (postcard)* We are off for the imperial manoeuvres. At present we are on our way to Prenzlau. It means a forty-one hours journey, as we are shunted about all over the place on account of our horses, but it will be quite a comfortable trip, because we 'N.C.O.s' each have the whole side of a compartment to ourselves.

*Strasburg (Uckermark), 16.9.11.* I was in Detelow for the first week, where we laid our allotted portion of the neutral telegraph network. I was billeted on a clergyman, who treated me like an invited guest; as his wife is a sister of the lord of the manor, he was very much the grand gentleman.

On September 7th we were transferred to Strasburg, where the good people positively fought for the pleasure of billeting us; I was quartered on a dentist. We had practically nothing to do except stand by for an alarm. On Monday my troop was alarmed in the night. I had to establish communication with the village of Gross-Luckow, eight kilometers away from Strasburg. I was through with the job by 1 a.m. Luckily the clatter of our horses woke the village schoolmaster up, and he put his classroom at our disposal for a station.

That settled the first of our troubles. Then came the next of them: how was I to find accommodation in the middle of the night for our hot, tired horses when a whole regiment of uhlan guards was already billeted on this tiny village. After a long search I discovered a barn containing no horses and got one of our drivers to force the door open. The next morning I found our five nags munching away delightedly at the clover that was stored inside.

I stayed in Gross-Luckow for the entire period of the actual manoeuvres, swelling with pride at the thought of being supreme commander of all telegraphic troops quartered in the village. I had very little to do, because the manoeuvres took place to westward of Strasburg instead of developing in an easterly direction as was anticipated. My duties consisted solely of looking after my men, who were occupying the telegraph station, and I spent the rest of the time bathing in a neighbouring lake with the schoolmaster and giving daily exercise to my five horses. It was great fun riding the two led horses, because they had not felt a saddle on them for the past two years. As I had a luxurious, well-fed billet in the house of the estate manager and very good company every evening in the persons of a captain and two lieutenants from the Kolberg Field Artillery Regiment, these manoeuvres were as good as a summer holiday for me. The only thing I regret is that I did not take any part in the operations. I did not see any infantry at all until they came through on their way to the station when the whole thing was over; the officers and men were all covered with a thick coating of dust, which made my little lot look like drawing-room soldiers. This evening we marched back to Strasburg, where I found everything ready for me in my billet; the dentist's good lady made my bed every night in case I should turn up. Tomorrow we are going back to Detelow, to dismantle our station there; then we expect to return to Coblence on the 22nd and 23rd.

I gained one very striking impression during my first few days in Strasburg, as the airships and aeroplanes manoeuvering in the neighbourhood often flew over the town.

Monoplanes and biplanes flew close to the townhall tower, which I climbed to get a view of them. Flying is a fine game.

## AT THE WAR ACADEMY IN METZ

*22.10.11.* Although I would rather have gone to Hannover with Fey, I have settled down here very comfortably. The most interesting thing of all is that my life shared with so many comrades is just the same here as it would have been in Hannover. Metz is a very pretty place; not very far from the academy there are terraces and avenues along the banks of the Moselle, where you get glorious views of the neighbouring hills. The country round Metz is also supposed to be very beautiful.

However we certainly have not much time to see these sights. The so called War Academy is a real school, which fact first seemed rather humourous to me when fresh from the life of a gentleman at large on the manoeuvres. We were wakened at 6 a.m., with breakfast at 6.30; from 6.50 to 11 and from 11.45 to 1 we had theoretical instruction, with a warm meal in the interval. Then comes practical instruction from 1.30 to 5, followed by another meal at 5.15 and evening work from 6.30 to 8.

I have received all my practical instruction (gymnastics, drill, riding, shooting, etc) in the cavalry section, so that I learning a lot of other things, as, for example, how to use a lance. Representatives of all arms sit together in the lecture room.

I have struck lucky as regards my room (we have two, a bedroom and a sittingroom), because only one of us four room-mates is a smoker. The rooms are larger and far more comfortable than our room in Coblence.

I have been very lucky as regards inspections; almost all my comrades are nice fellows, with whom it is very easy to get on, and above all we have a splendid inspection-officer in the person of Lieutenant Giersberg, of the 12th Uhlans. Our commandant is not so popular; he rejoices in the nickname of 'the Owl.'

*19.11.11.* Last week we had our written examinations; it depends on these whether we get a dispensation from evening classes. The dispensation is not much use to me, as there is nothing much to do in Metz, and we have to be indoors by ten o'clock. Saturday is the only day (not even Sunday!) on which we can get leave till eleven. The only time we can go to the theatre is, therefore, on a Sunday afternoon; there is a very poor sort of audience for such performances, and the Metz stage is no comparison with our Dessau Court Theatre. I see no fun in running round the bars, and so I generally stop at home.

We make up for it on Sunday, however. A certain number of us who get on well together have formed an Arts Club, which is called 'the Clique' by the others. Representatives of all the arms are members. We meet in the 'Englischer Hof' hotel about 5 p.m., where we have supper, after which someone plays the piano. There is one fellow who can sing very nicely to a guitar accompaniment; we all enjoy ourselves and feel thoroughly happy. Then we toddle home again at 10 for the evening roll-call. One great thing is that no one splashes money about in the club. Generally none of us have any to splash, especially at the end of the month; usually I have the most and can help the others out, wherefore they all take me for a rich man in receipt of a most un-regulation large allowance. I let them go on believing—if they only knew how I manage to spin my money out!

We had a very nice inspection-evening lately, i.e. our inspection took the form of an evening meal in a beer-hall in the company of our inspection officer, with extra leave till 11. It was quite jolly; there is no stiffness about Lieut. Giersberg, who behaved just like one of ourselves. We finished up with a dance—this is quite the fashion here. If we arrive a couple of minutes too early for the evening roll-call, we always pass the time by dancing—ensign with ensign—in the messroom, just like they do in the cadet corps.

*13.12.11.* The instructors announced the first results of the examination on the 8th; fifteen pupils are dispensed from evening classes. I am one of these lucky fellows, which means that I am now finished at six every evening. But I am still more pleased about my success in riding. Only five out of the whole cavalry section have got better reports than 'satisfactory;' one of these is von Pentz, a 20th Uhlan and a member of our club, who has a seven, while four others, including myself, have a six. Our marks are the reverse of the usual; one counts as the worst, and nine is the best.

My reward was a glorious symphony concert, the ticket for which was sent to me by the parents of my room-mate, Hägert, whose father is a captain in the fortification department here. Another great pleasure for me is the view we get almost every day of the Zeppelin that is here for manoeuvres and constantly flies over our Academy. At present I spend every evening with von Pentz, as we are making preparations for our Club's Christmas party, which is to take place next Saturday. And then on the following Saturday, i.e. on Dec 23rd at 12.41 p.m. I shall start my Christmas holidays with you in Dessau.

*30.1.12.* The emperor's birthday celebrations were simply magnificent here. They begun with a most impressive tattoo the evening before, performed by eighteen military bands on an illuminated square in front of the military head-quarters; as Hägert's father took me into the enclosure reserved for officers, I was able to enjoy this fine spectacle at my ease. But the parade the next day, which lasted from 11 a.m. to 2.30 p.m., was still more impressive. We pupils had the best place to watch the parade-march, as we were directly opposite the general commanding the district. It was very interesting to see all the Prussian, Bavarian and Saxon troops march past; all arms were represented, including even the airship men.

At 6 p.m. we had to go to the banquet, which all the officers attended. We had quite a jolly time, however, as I managed to get into a congenial corner with all my friends. It was really good fun after the 'Owl' left the room.

*12.2.12.* This is the first time that I cannot be at home for mother's birthday. It seems an age since her last one. I have had so many new experiences that I simply cannot imagine I was still at the grammar school a year ago.

Last week I spent all possible time on the lovely ice-rink, where I learnt a lot from a gentleman whose acquaintance I made on the ice. On the whole the people here are a very poor lot of skaters, and consequently I cut rather a dash with my various feats and figures; I have even been photographed as an expert. A few days ago I had an opportunity for dancing at a party given by the Hägerts, and am glad to find I have not forgotten my steps.

We had a good time lately at the Academy, because the 'Owl' was laid up with a cold. He made his first reappearance outside his 'building'—as he calls his house—last

Saturday, and now runs about for hours in search of a victim to slaughter. All of us—officers and pupils alike—have to keep our eyes open. Not so long ago he punished von Pentz with a formal reprimand for leaving valuables lying about (which is strictly forbidden by the rules of the establishment) because he had a watch-sized alarum in a case on his table. Our inspection-officer complained to the authorities in Berlin and managed to get the reprimand cancelled. So now we are all afraid of the 'Owl's' revenge.

*22.2.12.* We have got through our written and viva voce intermediate exams successfully. To-morrow we start our practical course, which means that we are going to live quite a different sort of life. We shall be out in the country every day from 7 a.m. to 2 p.m. (reaching our destination by train, bicycle or horse), where we receive instruction in tactics, the art of fortification, scouting, map-drawing, etc. Lunch is at 2.30, followed by practical instruction (drill, gymnastics) from 4.30 to 5.30 and two hours of evening classes in the lecture room, where we discuss the morning's work and prepare our material for the next day. We are therefore on duty till 8 p.m., so that I hardly have any time to get about. That does not worry me, because I always preferred to stop indoors and read a good book; at present I am busy on Chamberlain's "Foundations of the Nineteenth Century." It is a nuisance, however, that we are strictly forbidden to leave the Academy premises during the daytime; previously we could always go out and buy anything we wanted in the intervals.

Last Sunday we had another lovely affair with the 'Owl.' Comrade Planck, who plays the cello very well, wanted to do a turn at the club that evening and sent his batmen—a fellow with a rather simple face, who is really a very tough customer—to the hotel with the instrument. The batman met our C.O. on the way; the 'Owl' promptly stopped him, because it is against regulations to be out in the streets with a large parcel, and told him he must take it to its destination by wheel. He naturally meant that it would have to go on the post hand-car, as the regulations prescribe, but what do you think our batman did? He went back, got hold of Planck's bike, tied the cello on it and rode past the 'Owl,' who was simply wild, but too flabbergasted to say a word. The whole Academy have been killing themselves over the business.

Aren't you surprised to find how nicely I have written this letter? I have been told in most forcible language that asa future officer I must acquire another handwriting because my old one looked like a specimen from an infant's school. Father always used to say the same thing

*17.3.12.* It has fallen to my lot to be always out in the country on interesting individual duties such as officers' patrols, etc., during this glorious weather. We were seven hours in the saddle today, with half an hour's pause for breakfast. It is funny to see the infantrymen when they get off their horses; they can hardly walk a step.

I cannot understand why so many fellows grumble at the practical course as being too strenuous. I like our practical service a thousand times better than sitting in the lecture room, to which I look forward with fear and trembling when the classes start again after Easter.

*18.4.12.* I have been back in dear old Metz for a whole week now; I still have grateful memories of the lovely Easter holiday with you, but also find much pleasure in my existence here and the gorgeous blossoms in the Moselle valley. The new summer timetable makes life far more agreeable, because I am finished at 4.30, which means that I can do something or other in daylight. I have taken up tennis again, but find I have forgotten a lot as I have not played for so long. But generally I go out to the big parade-ground at Frescaty, where there are several monoplanes and biplanes flying every evening. One monoplane makes particularly fine flights (glides, etc). I never get tired of watching and always stare at them with eyes of longing. It must be a wonderful sport—more beautiful even than riding! They are expecting more aviators here; there are to be fifteen of them when the emperor visits us on May 15th, as well as a Zeppelin, a Parseval and several captive balloons.

We shall soon have our big four-day inspection by the inspector of War Academies. Our instructors are getting busy already.

*3.5.12.* A sigh of relief went through the whole war academy last week; the 'Owl' has been transferred. Our new C.O., Lt-Col. von Drygalski, is a very nice gentleman; he is firm and authoritative, but always kindly and friendly—never petty or regulation-bound. His nickname is Mikosch; he can't escape a nickname at the Academy. He has made a lot of little changes already; for instance, we have no duty on Saturday afternoons and can get off lunch on Sundays, while riding instruction takes place in the country instead of in the school and we have gymnastic competitions for our afternoon work, etc.

*10.5.12.* We have got the big four-day inspection by the inspector of War Academies over successfully. His

Excellency, General von Falk, spoke words of praise about every-thing and was particularly delighted with our gymnastics, fencing and riding, in all of which our smartness gave him great pleasure. He was most impressed by the paperchase on horseback which the cavalry section organised and by the fact that all sections rode the obstacle course without stirrups, while the cavalry section even took it without saddles.

We finished off nicely with our 'ensigns' evening,' at which His Excellency put in an appearance. I took part in the gymnastic display there as well as playing a danseuse in our cabaret show, into which we naturally brought all the stale jokes from the classrooms, etc. But His Excellency sat through it all and was doubled up with laughter; when he bade us farewell, he said he wished he could always inspect such a nice, smart lot of pupils as we were.

There are lovely days ahead of us next week. The emperor is coming on the 15th to see the new fort that is being built, and on the following morning we start off on our five days' so-called 'instruction tour.' First we go to the big manoeuvre ground at Bitsch to watch the artillery practice, and then we paya visit to the battlefields of Woerth and Weissenburg. We finish up with a day and a half in Heidelberg—on pleasure bent.

Next Sunday we have part of the Upper Rhine Reliability Trials here, as the machines have to make an intermediate landing on the Frescaty parade-ground. I must see it all from beginning to end.

*21.5.12.* The emperor's visit and our trip were favoured with glorious weather. On the first of these occasions (last Wednesday) we were spectators of the imperial manoeuvres

which an army corps and a half carried out in the neighbourhood of Mörchingen—a fine spectacle which we followed
quite well from the so-called Cannon Hill. We were only
about fifty metres away from the emperor; later when the
public became too numerous and crowded round him so as
to block his view of the manoeuvres, we of the War
Academy were instructed to form a cordon, with the result
that we stood quite close to him for a long time. Several
papers, however, interpreted the incident in the sense that he
trusted his Lorrainers so little that he had to have his person
protected by a guard of his future officers. When the fight
was over, we marched to the parade-ground, where the
emperor inspected all the troops at 3 p.m. I thought the gallop past of the four cavalry regiments particularly beautiful.
We saw everything very well, as we stood next to the band
and straight opposite the emperor.

Our instruction tour was most interesting, both as
regards the artillery practice and the visits to the battlefields
of Woerth, Spichern and Weissenburg, where in each case
one of our instructors gave us a lecture. I particularly
enjoyed the Friday evening in Bad Niederbronn, where our
officers mixed with the pupils in most jovial fashion. The jol-
liest of all was our new commander, who actually enrolled as
a member of our club.

That came about in the following fashion: Lieut. Detring
toasted Gause and myself by our club nicknames of 'Gutti'
and 'Ossi,' and when the C.O. asked him what this meant,
he told him that all club nicknames ended in 'i.' Whereupon
the C.O. replied that he must positively jump into the club—
as he expressed in his genial Swabian—with his own name
of von Drygalski.

The whole Academy raves about him because he treats us

so decently. He has only to 'wish' something or other, and everyone will take care to see it done, which was certainly not the case with the 'Owl.' He gave us every possible freedom and relaxation on this trip, but not the slightest incident occurred, although more than a hundred pupils took part in it. Such discipline, born of proven confidence, seems to me far finer, firmer and more valuable than that which is merely superficial obedience to a command.

The best part of it all was Sunday (my birthday) and yesterday morning in Heidelberg, where we were free to enjoy the lovely town and its surroundings without any 'service.' On Sunday evening the Whole War Academy and its officers attended the concert in the Stadtgarten; yesterday morning we all went to Neckarsteinach, returning to Heidelberg by steamer after lunch. We landed back in Metz at one this morning.

Whitsuntide leave starts on Friday. I intend to have a look at Trier, then visit my old battalion in Coblence and spend the actual holidays with my room-mate, von Zengen, in Wetzlar. After this long series of happy days we begin to take life seriously again and cram up for our exams!

*16.6.12.* The written examination papers begin the day after to-morrow and last five days. We have no more practical courses, only lectures and classes; we start work at 6.20 a.m. and do not knock off till 8 p.m. Our instructors mean well, but the result is a minus quantity, because we. are all getting absolutely fogged.

Our 'reserve calendar' shows us that we have only twenty more days to get through. You know what I mean? We are counting the days to the finish of the exam on July 6th, and mark off every finished day with fervent joy.

*23.6.12.* I am writing to you on one of those sheets of official examination paper, on which I have penned my knowledge for the last week in Lecture Room D., and here-with
report that our written exams are now over! On Tuesday we
did the tactics paper, on Wednesday reconnaissance and fortifications. More fortifications on Thursday, as well as the
paper on arms, Friday the military correspondence paper
and Saturday map-drawing. None of the papers were particularly stiff, and I do not imagine I have been plucked in any
of them.

The viva voce exams begin on the 3rd and last four days.
They divide us up into groups of six, each of which is tested
for forty-five minutes in all subjects. The Higher Military
Examining Commission comes from Berlin to examine us; its
president is His Excellency, General von Oertzen, who is said
to be a very benevolent gentleman, but the same cannot be
said of the other examiners.

*Coblence. 8.7.12.* Back again in my dear old garrison, but
many of my thoughts are still at the war academy with its
fine comradeship and its happy ending for me. For, as I have
already told you briefly, I got all 'goods' and 'very goods' in
my viva voce. Unfortunately parts of my written exams were
only 'fair,' so that the final verdict was only a 'good.' But
that does not matter, because I came off best of the three
ensigns here, which means that I am now the senior in the
battalion. Also, as my commander told me today, I got a 9
(excellent) for 'leadership.'

At noon on Sunday we ate our farewell dinner, to the
accompaniment of two bands. Naturally we were all in high
spirits, even though there was a tinge of melancholy at the
thought that our coterie of comradeship was going to be

scattered to the four winds. Who knows when, where and how we shall meet again! All our club members have bought each other Indian smoking tables as souvenirs of their mutual association in the war academy, and everyone's name is to be engraved on their brass plates. Mine, however, can only serve as a tea-table.

I went off that evening to Coblence, where I found several of our officers in the mess and was received with much celebration. Today I reported to the major, who gave me a very friendly welcome. I have been appointed to the 2nd company, which is commanded by our very popular Captain Thaler. To-morrow I am joining in a company expedition—one of Captain Thaler's ideas—to the Siebengebirge, in which all officers, N.C.O.s and men of the company will take part.

To my great joy my application for leave has been granted; I can go straight off from St. Avold at the end of our exercises there, which means that I can be with you for the ceremonies at the opening of the Anhalt Hut. I am delighted to be seeing you again and having a chance to climb my beloved mountains again! I hope you have brought a pair of mountain boots along for me.

## AN ALPINE ADVENTURE

On July 23rd, 1912 Ensign Boelcke, clad in civilian attire, joined his parents and younger brothers in the little mountain village of Namlos in the upper valley of the Lech. There he was destined to face an Alpine adventure, which obtained a certain amount of publicity. It is included in this work, not merely because he risked his life on that occasion, but above all because it served to bring into prominence his sporting and ethical qualities, such as initiative, daring, endurance, inexhaustible energy and vigour.

On the day after his arrival he accompanied his father and brother Martin, who was then in the top form of his school, to the Heiterwand Hut on the southeastern side of the Heiterwand mountain. This hut was due to be formally opened on the morning of July 25th; like the Anhalt Hut on the north side of the mountain which was to be opened on the 26th, it was the property of the Anhalt Section of the Alpine Club, the chairman of which was Boelcke's father.

After the ceremony at the Heiterwand Hut Boelcke senior decided to walk round to the north side of the Heiterwand by a mountain path and join his wife at the Anhalt Hut. Meanwhile the two brothers started off early on the morning of the 25th for a climbing tour on the middle part of the Heiterwand's ridge, which is nearly seven kilometers long. They intended to follow this ridge as far as the Gabel Summit and then descend to the Schwarze Erd via the gulley which forms the only safe way down the otherwise sheer northern face of the Heiterwand. In this fashion they hoped to reach the Anhalt Hut in the afternoon.

They reached the Tarrenton Summit by 7.45 a.m.; then, still following the course of the ridge, they climbed the Heiterwand Tower and the two Alpeil Summits. When they stood on the western Alpeil Summit about 2 p.m., they saw two thunderstorms approaching—one from the Inn valley and one from the north-east—which forced them to leave the exposed ridge as quickly as possible. Their correct procedure would have been to look for a way down the easier southern face and then tramp to the Anhalt Hut via the Heiterwand Hut. This would have forced them to a long detour, so that they would not have reached their destination until late in the evening. But their parents were expecting them in the afternoon, and the thought of the anxiety they might cause them induced the two brothers to try a direct descent by the difficult northern face.

"And so, having made up our minds,"—the account is taken from a description furnished by Martin—"we dropped down into a gully, which seemed likely to take us down a good bit of the way. The rising mist prevented us from seeing its continuation, but we hoped it would bring us out on to one of the large expanses of scree. We crossed two snow-fields, covered with new snow; they were difficult and wearisome, but we kept our feet in them, with the exception of one small slip where Oswald lost his stick. Meanwhile it had begun to rain, and the mist was thickening. But there was now nothing for it but to go on, for the thunder rumbled threateningly over our heads. The further down we went, however, the longer and more frequent were the sheer drops we encountered in the gully. We hoped to find the fervently desired scree below each shelf, but we were disappointed every time. And the hands of my watch ran round as though they were in a great hurry.

"Our hopes sank when we saw it was eight o'clock, and we had to resign ourselves to a night in the open. I wanted to climb down one more shelf, just to see how far it continued, but the descent was so difficult and precipitous that I had to use the rope. When I got down, I saw that the gully broke off in a cliff of about three hundred metres; further progress was impossible. I wanted to get back again, but meanwhile a fresh downpour had turned the gully into a raging waterfall. I tried it, nevertheless, but slipped, although Oswald made superhuman efforts to pull me up, and fell back into the waterfall. As Oswald could not possibly get down to me unroped, we were separated for the night.

"Then we began to make our preparations for the night. We could only make ourselves understood by shouting to one another at the top of our voices. I was as drenched as if I had been in a river, but luckily we had a good supply of dry underclothing in our rücksacks. Oswald let a shirt and socks down to me on the rope, along with his spare coat. We had finished our provisions during the afternoon; Oswald still had a hunk of bread, which he shared with me. I had only a small packet of sweets, which I divided into two portions for our morrow's breakfast. The narrow surfaces on which we stood made sleep an impossibility; we called to one another every ten minutes to make sure that neither dozed off. I crouched under the overhanging rocks, which at least gave me shelter from the rain and the falls of stones that whirled down at very short intervals.

"The thick swirls of mist that rolled up from below, enveloping first my legs and then my whole body, were most uncanny. Suddenly I found a motionless figure standing beside me, clad in a white mantle, that stood out clearly from the wall of rock. It stood by my side the whole night. Not until grey dawn broke did this silent neighbour disappear—I had seen the spirit of the Heiterwand.

"When it was light, I resumed my efforts to reach Oswald; it was difficult enough, but I managed it, because I was not stopped by a waterfall, as on the previous night. I fell on my brother's neck with a shout of joy; then, after a breakfast consisting of five sweets apiece and rainwater that Oswald had collected in the night, we tried to find the way we had climbed down the previous day. But we soon went wrong and reached a point on the cliff where we decided to wait for help.

"We called out to a party of tourists passing below, but they took us for mountaineers out on an early climb and only replied with a joyous yodel. About 7 a.m. we succeeded at last in making our plight understood to a couple of gendarmes who were going up to the opening ceremonies at the hut. One of them hurried on at once to the Anhalt Hut to get help, while other remained below to mark the spot. According to his reckoning we were about three to four hundred metres up the cliff.

"From the point of view of morale, the morning hours that we had to spend waiting for help were the worst time of the whole period. Herr Roman Walch, an engineer from Imst, was the first to reach us about noon; he had a difficult climb up the cliff, somewhat to the westward of us, and then dropped down to our ledge—he is the best climber in the whole district. He then brought us up on the rope, being helped by the guides, Hermann Walch from Imst and Lechleiter from Boden, who came down to meet us.

"When we at last reached the ridge we had left nearly twenty-four hours previously, we made a huge meal off the provisions brought by the rescue party from the hut. Then we went on to the Gabel Summit and whirled down the gully and across the big snowfield; Federspiel, the gendarme, greeted us with a salvo of pistol shots when we reached the Schwarze Erd. Then we hurried—thrity-six hours had passed since we left the Heiterwand—along with Roman Walch to the Anhalt Hut, where we received a loud and hearty welcome from the assembled company. Unfortunately it contained a doctor, who ordered us off to bed at once, just when we were feeling ready for new exploits."

## WITH THE WIRELESS SECTION
## IN COBLENCE

*2.8.12.* This is an important day for me. Firstly I have been promoted to swordknot ensign, as my certificate has at last arrived, and secondly I have been transferred to the 4th, i.e. wireless company. It is something of an honour for me, because every telegraphy officer wants to be a wireless man. I hope I shall stay with this company, as the thing interests me. It will certainly mean a lot of work, because, although my enthusiasm is great, I have really very little notion of wireless. Already my table is piled up with fat copies of regulations and instructions that I have to work through. This afternoon we went up to the Karthause to get in touch with stations practising in Wurtemberg. I shall be on duty very soon again, i.e. at 11 p.m. to-night, because we are talking to Metz and Cologne.

*20.8.12. (telegram)* 2nd Lieutenant Boelcke presents his compliments to Herr and Frau Professor Boelcke.

*27.8.12.* Now that I have got my commission I must thank you from my heart, my dear parents, for having opened this career to me—certainly the only one that can afford me complete satisfaction and happiness. Fey's promotion and mine were gazetted on the 18th, but we did not get the news until the 20th. In view of my matriculation my officer's patent has been antedated to August 23rd, 1910.

Forgive me for not having written before, but as a student of wireless I have my time full. Last week we went out for a three days' course of training. It was most instructive for me, but fairly strenuous as well, because our operations are continuous, i.e. we are at work day and night when we are not on the march. Naturally we have to work in two shifts; the officers relieve one another as well. But I stuck to the station practically all the time because that is the best way to learn my job, and I am keen on getting to know it as soon as possible. I hope that a month will see one advanced enough to manage without being shown things by the N.C.O.s. Being dependent on one's subordinates to any extent is a bad business. I shall not be happy until I can do everything myself. To-morrow we are off again, to Bad Salzig, and this time I shall be in sole charge of the station.

*25.9.12.* "He's given up writing!" you will be thinking. As a matter of fact I am writing all day—not to you, unfortunately, but official correspondence. As our Captain Kopsch was in charge of all wireless stations during the imperial manoeuvres, he has to look through all their daily logs and write up reports on all their experiments, successes, etc. He has put this job on to Lieut Kohlhauer and myself, which does not please me at all. I would far sooner be breaking up stones.

*10.10.12.* My new flat (two rooms, batman's room, saddle room, corridor) is now ready, and looks wonderfully fine. It gives one a feeling of pride to have one's own home, with one's own things in it! Yesterday I had my housewarming, when I invited Baltzer, Kohlhauer and Leufgen to supper— but I did not treat them to caviar.

My house is, therefore, now in order, but I regret that I cannot say the same, of my finances. It is incredible how many funds (band fund, piano fund, shooting fund, reading room fund, mess fund, clothing fund, etc.) all want to get something out of a young officer. The worst of all is the one hundred and twenty marks for the silver fund, which is deducted from my pay in three monthly instalments. I shall get a minus quantity left from my one hundred and twenty-five marks pay that I draw on the 1st of next month. But the most idiotic thing of all is that the inland revenue officials want me to pay income tax on my allowance because father is assessed in Anhalt instead of in Prussia. They do not make things easy for a young subaltern who wants to lead a steady life. But all the same we are not downhearted.

I had to pay thousands of calls on Sunday. I did them all in one round as Baltzer put his Dixi car at my disposal, and only two lots of people were at home.

I went out hunting for the third time today. I nearly got the brush, as I was up with the first group. There was a field of more than fifty today; the officers that go out hunting are those belonging to the 23rd field artillery, the 8th army service corps, the 3rd telegraph battalion and any from the infantry and foot artillery who can get a mount. Siegfried, my service mount, a big dark-brown eight year old, is a splendid chap with a wonderful action; he can lift his legs quite thirty centimeters when he is trotting.

I am delighted to hear Martin has been accepted for the 5th telegraph battalion. My greetings to him as a very special comrade.

*21.10.12.* I drilled my telegraph recruits for the first time today. It is great fun for me to turn these civilians into decent soldiers. But father need not be afraid of me being too hard on my recruits. As soon as I see signs of good will I am satisfied—inwardly at least—even though I have to curse the clumsy beggars a bit.

My C.O. returned my call yesterday. It was very funny. I was sitting peacefully at my writing desk, —my batman had gone out to fetch something—when suddenly I heard some-one open the corridor door, which has not got a bell. Then there was a knock at my room; I thought it was an orderly and called out "Come in." But no one opened the door and I heard footsteps going away, so I yelled out: "Donnerwetter, why can't you come in!" The next moment the door opened, and Major Schroeder stood before me; he had only gone to hang up his overcoat. It was a somewhat painful situation for me, but the Major helped me out with a laugh and a joke. And so I have managed to curse my C.O., which is not a thing one often gets a chance to do.

I am now in the sign of the circles. First of all I belong to a reading circle, consisting of four lieutenants and four young ladies, which meets at each house of the latters' parents in rotation. Then I am in a dancing circle, consisting of twelve gentlemen (officers and civilians) and twelve ladies; it calls itself a dancing class, but no one can belong to it who does not dance well. So you see I am not afraid of either ladies or civilians. I particularly enjoy my visits to the house of a certain Dr Istas, although I must admit that the attrac-tions which draw me there are the doctor's son, with whom I have formed a friendship, and his daughter rather than the old people. There is such a cordial tone in one's association with these Rhinelanders—quite different from life at home. There is one young lady who calls me her 'golden lad'—nat-urally not to my face, but other people have told me she does.

*1.11.12.* My recruits are making capital progress. The only thing that causes me any difficulty is the technical instruc-tion, which I always have to prepare thoroughly in advance, as there is so much in it that is new to me. For that reason I

myself am the one that profits most by this instruction. But
I take an occasional squint at my one-year volunteers,
among whom there are several diplomaed and other engineers; they know far more about all this technical stuff than
I do.

I always put my recruits on to gymnastics in their last half
hour's drill. I arrange relay and individual races for them, in
which I naturally take part myself; we go through the riding-
schdol, over obstacles, under beams, etc. Not long ago I put
them to a competition of climbing over the barracks wall,
which caused sundry headshakings from military and civilian philistines. I did not worry about them; my men enjoyed
themselves thoroughly. The chief thing, it seems to me, is to
inculcate a liking and love for the service, and such enter-
tainments after the arduous labour of their drill are a great
help in that direction.

You thus see that I get much pleasure out of my recruit
school. The one drawback about it is that I get only an
hour's riding per day and have to renounce the greatest fun
of all, which is helping to break in the new horses. To-morrow is our last day's hunting—the so-called St. Hubert's
Ride, which is to be followed by a banquet in the mess of the
23rd field artillery.

Yesterday evening I made a meal off a fine hare that I laid
low myself. It happened like this; on Sunday morning I went
out to Neuwied to pay a visit to the sub-prefect, who had
invited me to a dance. I arranged to meet Baltzer at
Weissenturm, on the opposite side of the river to Neuwied,
as we were going to lunch with a family we had got to know
from the dancing class. We spent a very nice day there and
took Frau Professor Wattendorf and her daughter back to
Coblence in the car. The fine, moonlight night appeared to

have charms for a young hare. He danced about continually and of malice aforethought in the lurid light of our head-lamps; suddenly he stopped, and we ran over him. We pulled up sharp; I collected the unfortunate victim and handed him over to Frau Professor, who made him into a sumptuous roast and invited Baltzer and myself to sample it.

*5.12.12.* Please don't be angry with me because I cannot manage to write to you more often and so prefer to save up till Christmas all the many things I have to tell you about my lovely, gay, active life. If I tell you my programme for this week, I am sure it will serve as my excuse: Monday, banquet in the mess, Tuesday evening, an invitation from my captain, Wednesday the dancing class's Christmas party, today dinner and dance at the house of a government official, to-morrow, meeting of the reading circle, Saturday, excursion for the dancing class. How is one to write letters under those circumstances when one has to be looking after the recruits all day?

The worst of it is that they always put something extra on to me. Yesterday I had to be Father Christmas, dressed up in a chief forester's heavy fur coat and Fräulein Wattendorf's fur cap. That was not all—I had also to concoct the greater part of the rhymes to recite when I gave away the presents! You would be astonished at the amount of latent talent there is in your little boy! Then Baltzer and I are the committee for our Christmas festivities in the mess. We are such insepara-bles now that they have begun to call us 'Max and Moritz.' From all of which you can see that I am a very busy man and that I am not doing too badly.

*6.1.13.* Our social life continues in the new year with undiminished vigour. I have received an invitation from General von Ploetz, the general commanding the district, for next Thursday, while the 68th are giving a dance on Saturday, and next week I have three invitations for 'dinner and dance.' The 68th are Coblence's crack dancing regiment—perhaps I can learn a step or two there. This old traditional dance is a good ending to a week in which I have to undertake a somewhat unelegant job of stocktaking, i.e. I have to take stock of all the old worn-out boots, and other articles of clothing.

Many of my recruits have gone to pieces over the Christmas holidays, and I have to get them on their feet again. My captain turned up at drill on Saturday and cursed mightily. It is more or less a point of honour for him to do so before the inspection, and I am not going to let it worry me. To the great horror of my N.C.O.s I let my recruits play football ("But it's only a fortnight before the inspection, Sir!")

*20.1.13.* My recruit inspection went off without a hitch. Captain Kopsch was so pleased about it that he stood me champagne at Saturday's dinner in the mess. Afterwards we broke up at 10 o'clock and went off to a masked ball, the first of this year's carnival. I wore a red domino and Baltzer a blue one. I had a fine time there. It was a proper opportunity to see the Rhinelanders in a merry mood; I could not imagine anything like it in Dessau.

Yesterday our dancing circle gave a party at the civilians' club, with a theatrical performance in which I had to take a part. I always feel a bit awkward at such affairs; apparently I am not cut out for an actor. I look forward all the more to the gymnastic display that our men are going to contribute to the barracks show on the emperor's birthday; I shall take part in it myself—that is great fun for me, and the men like it; you can win their confidence if you associate with them naturally and do not try to play the high and mighty superior.

*13.2.13.* At last I have seen a real Rhineland carnival. That is something quite different from the affairs in Dessau, when the "Blue Cloud" smoking club or the "All Nine" skittles club gets up a masked ball in the "White Swan." Everyone celebrates Shrove Tuesday here. You can realise that from the fact that all our men had Monday afternoon and the whole of Tuesday free—except, of course, those that were detailed for sentry or stable duty. The fun in the streets began at three in the afternoon; everyone was in fancy dress, with or without masks, pelting each other with confetti and streamers. The quality appeared in their carriages and the very superior quality—like your son—in cars, i.e. in Friend Baltzer's car. When you have had enough of the row in the streets, you just drop in to some house where you know the family and drink a glass of wine. Rhineland hospitality lets you do anything you like at Carnival time. There was a big masked ball in the civilians' club on Tuesday; I appeared in turn as a clown, a pierot and a Turkish pasha—having borrowed the various costumes from brother officers. It was so jolly calling everyone "Thou," as is customary at Carnival; I can't get out of the habit.

As I have no more recruits, I am getting a decent amount of riding. In addition to my service mount I ride the horses we are breaking in. Riding is good for you when you don't get to bed till three and are on duty again at six. I like riding the raw animals best; they have absolutely no idea of the business, and then it is a pleasure to notice how they learn things from day to day.

We have formed a walking section from the members of our dancing circle; it consists of four men, including Baltzer, and three ladies, and goes off for long trips on Saturdays. Last Saturday we took the train into the Lahn valley and then climbed up a narrow side-valley known as the Rupperstal. There was an isolated crag, about one hundred and fifty metres high; the others went up it from behind, but alpine fever overcame me, and so I scrambled up its sheer front wall. I enjoyed that mightily; I hope I shall be able to go to the mountains with you in July, and for that reason I have not taken any leave now, as the other recruit officers have done.

*3.3.13.* Last Thursday we had a very jolly show—our riding display, i.e. after we had got the inspection over, our officers' riding course blued all the money collected in fines. After the meal Fey, Meunier and I slipped away to the stables and rode our horses on the snaffle and unsaddled upstairs into the mess room, where we gave three cheers for our riding instructor. When we rode down again, the other officers went to get their horses, and we had a lovely time riding in the mess garden in the darkness of the night.

Our service duties are very nice now. We have no more infantry work to do. Our main work is now driving practice on the big parade ground, where we have to work across obstacles and ditches. Then we are having some interesting experiments with the two wireless stations we recently rebuilt at Münster am Stein; I, however, have remained here at the main station.

*12.4.13.* I am going off the day after to-morrow for a three weeks' field training which begins at Lich and then goes from Oberursel via Langenschwalbach to Nassau through the most beautiful parts of the Taunus range. It is a pity, however, that it will stop me attending Fey's sister's wedding in Darmstadt, to which both Baltzer and I were invited.

*17.5.13.* The big field training brought a lot of hard work with it, but all the same it was a pleasure trip. We did a day's march and then stayed two or three days somewhere, practising wireless. I had a jolly break to this work, as I was able to get to Darmstadt for the wedding because we happened to be in Oberursel from the 25th to the 27th. It was a fine wedding breakfast, with eighty-seven persons present. The nicest part of it for me was that I found two ladies who could do all the old and new dances wonderfully.

We had hardly got back from the course before the Whit-week festivities began, which were trebly enhanced by the presence of Prince Heinrich Race. Friend Kohlhauer came over from Metz to see it; he was transferred there about a month ago. On Saturday Baltzer and I went to Bullay on the Moselle to meet him with the car, and then we took him for a wonderful trip over the Hunsrück to Boppard and back here alongside the river. We also spent Whitsunday in the car, or rather in two cars (Baltzer's and Fey's). We went via Ems to the Arnstein Monastery that lies in such a wonderful part of the Lahn valley and back through the Taunus range.

The next three days were devoted to the flying. All Coblence turned out to see it. As I had a job as umpire and timekeeper, I was able to see it all from quite close and made the personal acquaintance of most of the airmen. The first arrival for the Prince Heinrich trophy landed at 10 a.m. on Thursday, having flown from Kassel. It was a wonderful sight to see them drop down quite slowly on the landing ground, one after another. There was a flying display in the afternoon, at which I sometimes saw four or five machines in the air together. The rest of the Prince Heinrich competitors came along on Tuesday, and there was another flying display in the afternoon, in which Zeppelin 2 from Cologne took part. There were passenger flights (from fifty marks upward!). The next morning the fliers started off for Karlsruhe, and the Zeppelin "Victoria Louisa" turned up from Frankfurt a/M. All this flying made a wonderful impression on me.

Something new on again this week—a tennis tournament. My hand is quite shaky from strenuous practice, as you will see from this letter. The week afterwards I have to go to Bonn and Cologne on duty, to see the telegraph offices there.

You see, I am not doing so badly, and I get all the change I want.

*14.6.13.* Our party—a captain and five lieutenants—that visited the post office had a most instructive time. In Bonn they showed us a quite up-to-date telegraph office and explained that the good old Morse apparatus is hardly found anywhere now. One great joke was that each of us was detailed to a girl in the telephone department to learn how to connect local and trunk calls. And so it went on the whole morning: "Here, telephone office!" "2017, please, Fräulein!" No matter how deep a voice I used, the callers always addressed me as Fräulein. You have to be pretty smart, for by the time I had got one connection there were generally two or three others wanted. Everything was on a much larger scale at Cologne, which is the biggest telephone centre in western Germany. We visited the big cable-works at Mülheim on the last day; that was most instructive too, and it proved a nice finish to the trip as the director entertained us to lunch afterwards.

His Excellency, General von Hänisch, the inspector-general, was already in sight when we got back to Coblence, and so all the inspection fuss started again. Everything went off well; our battalion is said to have cut the best figure.

From Monday to Wednesday we had a nice practice in Bad Salzig; Baltzer and I managed the station. We were supposed to bivouac, but the director of the Kurhaus would not hear of it. He invited everyone—officers and men—to be his guests, just as he did last year.

We have another three days' practice next week, after which Baltzer. Leufgen and I are ordered to Metz to study the wireless station there. So there is always something going on somewhere all through the summer. All the same I hope to be able to join you at Namlos in my beloved mountains and shall do all I can to get there.

*16.6.13.* Once again I have had to leave a letter unfinished. But in this case it is all to the good, as now our new war academician, Brother Wilhelm, can add his greetings to mine.

Postscript by Wilhelm Boelcke: I am delighted with Oswald. He is positively swimming in health, happiness and comfort. He feels really happy here and enjoys many harmless pleasures with a very nice set of comrades; I like his friend Baltzer particularly. Coblence is also a delightful garrison town, where you get to know some very nice families, and lies in charming surroundings which they see a lot of in Baltzer's and Frey's cars. The garrison also seems to be a pleasant one from a service point of view.

*2.7.13.* The three days in Metz were particularly nice because Baltzer, Leufgen and I were practically the guests of our old friend Kohlhauer, who is at the wireless station. Also because I was able to refresh my War Academy memories and saw aeroplanes again. The wireless station was very interesting, but I should not care for service there.

At the moment I am getting ready for another trip. I am off to Württemberg for a big wireless practice with the 4th Karlsruhe telegraph battalion and the Bavarian telegraph battalion; it will last till the 13th. Then on the 16th I am off again to a reconnaissance course which will be carried out by the cavalry of the 8th Army; this goes on till the 26th. We shall be back in Coblence on the 7th, and on the 8th I hope to join you in Namlos. Quits a globetrotter, am I not? But one sees and learns a few things on one's travels. Auf wiedersehen on the Heiterwand!

*31.8.13.* I am sure you will have been surprised to get my card from Baden-Baden. It happened like this: several ladies and gentlemen from our dancing circle wanted to go to Baden, because the race week and the dancing tournament for the world's championship were on there at the same time. It sounded most enticing, and as I had nothing particular on in the service line, I suddenly decided to join their party. The races on Sunday and Tuesday were up to the mark from both a sporting and a social point of view. The battle of flowers took place on Monday; I found it very interesting because I have never seen anything of that sort before; I was amazed to see what a lot of money some people must have to spend.

But the dancing tournament was the principal attraction for me. It was just what I wanted to see; I have never come across such perfect dancing before. They only did the very

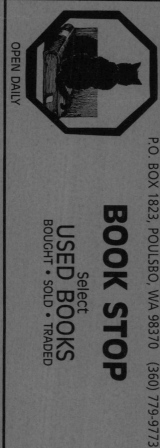

latest dances, such as the Boston, One Step and Tango. I only wished that all the philistines could have been there who write and preach so narrowmindedly about the licentiousness of modern dancing—then they would have seen what nonsense they talk. Everything about these new dances was full of beauty, grace and harmony—the perfection of art. Certainly these dances are so difficult that anyone who has no gift for dancing ought to keep his fingers—or rather, his feet—off them. It merely depends who is dancing these steps and how—some people can dance every waltz vulgarly.

I was there every evening from Sunday to Tuesday and learnt a lot, first by looking on and then by dancing myself. Apart from the sporting events—as a matter of fact dancing is a sport now—the evenings were most interesting on account of the various elements composing the society there. Firstly, there were all the types you find in a modern watering place, then there were the racecourse types (gentlemen jockeys, owners, etc) and finally the people from Paris and Berlin that took part or were interested in the dancing. I remained in the back ground as a silent spectator, as it would have been useless to try to compete with those plutocrats. I got through my money quickly enough as it was.

I went straight off from Baden to a three days' practice at Pfalzfeld in Hunsrück, from which I got back yesterday. I shall feel a bit lonely here in the near future, because all companies except mine are going off to manoeuvres and all the friends from my company are going on leave. My nice civilian friends and my horses must be my consolation.

Our people are somewhat excited about the number of transfers due to be announced on Sept. 22nd. These a redue to the order that every telegraph battalion is to have a fifth company added to it as a second wireless company on

October 1st. For the present I cannot get excited; I shall just wait quietly for Sept. 22nd. The only thing that would be terrible for me would be a transfer to the wireless station at Metz, which has already been hinted at. I should have to sit in a bombproof fort all day there, and my activities would be fifty per cent technician and fifty per cent clerk—I certainly cannot raise any enthusiasm for the last half of the job. I should be nought percent soldier there, and it is just a soldier that I want to be.

*16.9.13*. By chance I have managed to get to the 8th army's manoeuvres after all as a 'wirer,' i.e. I have to look after the trunk calls between the staff and the airmen who are stationed at Trier. As soon I have established the connection, there is very little for me to do, wherefore I go out riding every day with the staff of the 16th infantry division and learn a lot besides enjoying this glorious country (the deep, wooded valley of the Kyll). So I have got a nice job once more.

*22.9.13*. Now my days in my beloved Coblence are numbered. One of the seven possibilities—and by no means the worst of them—has materialised. My address from October 1st will be:

> 5th (Wireless) Company, 3rd Tel. Bat.
> Griesheim Manoeuvre Ground, near Darmstadt.

It will not be easy to say goodbye to Coblence, and I shall never have such a good time again as I have had here. But for that very reason it is a good thing for me to move—I was in danger of getting spoilt here. It is a wholesome education for a young officer to be continually transferred to new surroundings where he has to make position for himself anew.

Scenically Darmstadt is not be compared with Coblence. But in compensation I shall be able to wallow in the excellent Court Theatre—the theatre here is not much better than a superior booth. One very pleasant thing is the fact that our company there is practically on its own, as our battalion-commander is in Coblence. So I shall have no other superior in Darmstadt than my company-commander, Captain Nagel—a former lieutenant of ours, who knows me well. The other two officers transferred there are myfriends, Baltzer and Leufgen, with whom I have always got on very well. Leufgen and the captain are married, which means that we shall have some sort of social life, even in that camp of huts. Then we shall soon get into Darmstadt society, as four of our officers are natives of the town. I hope it will all turn out as nice as I picture it, and even if it does not, I shall still feel happy there,—for Mars—my saint—holds sway there as well as here!

## WIRELESS OFFICER IN DARMSTADT

*Griesheim. 7.10.13.*
"How can anyone ride such a horrible boneshaker!" mother will say when she learns that I have acquired a motorcycle. But it is a necessity here, because our camp is five kilometers out of Darmstadt and the light railway is not a very pleasant mode of conveyance.

The camp is in a pine wood at the edge of the huge manoeuvre ground which stretches before us like a sea of sand. It consists of nothing but huts, some of which are corrugated iron affairs. I live in the staff officers' quarters, with a lovely view of green woods from my windows. The company is quartered in a huge stone hut, with our horses stabled to right and left of it. We do not need any riding school buildings here, because the country is one large riding school. It is just ideal for a horseman—beautiful sand paths on which you can ride for hours. That is one great advantage over Coblence!

Besides us there is a section of the 84th field artillery and three companies of the 115th life guards, who are waiting for their barracks to be built. So we are not quite isolated here, and we see a lot of the other officers in the camp mess, where all unmarried officers have their meals. We get on particularly well with the artillery officers, with whom we join in riding instruction, lectures, war-games, etc. I have taken a special liking to a young artillery subaltern, named Thrän, and a Count Vitzthum of the 115th machine gun company.

Baltzer and I paid our first calls on Sunday—naturally on the Feys. Frau Fey has written out a long list of families on whom we ought to call. Then she gave us a lot of good advice in motherly fashion; we must always flirt a bit with some of the old ladies and we must not let ourselves be too much impressed by the dragoons, etc.—we had to roar with laughter at it all.

Our recruits arrive to-morrow—then my work will begin. So far only six one year volunteers have turned up.

*12.10.13.* I get even more pleasure out of my recruit service this year, because my captain has given me a free hand; I can do what I like with these recruits as long as I turn them into decent soldiers. It is very pleasant not to have anyone sitting on one's neck the whole time.

I paid my first visit to the theatre on Friday. An excellent performance! Everything there reminds me of the Dessau theatre. I have taken a quarterly season ticket; for us officers it is ridiculously cheap; it does not cost us as much as a mark a performance.

I took part in my first drag-hunt yesterday. This is how they work it: an hour before the hunt starts, a rider trails a fox-skin along a certain stretch of country; the hounds are laid on to this trail, and the field follows them. It is very interesting and amusing. Yesterday there was a field of more than a hundred, of both sexes. They have these hunts every Saturday; on St. Hubert's day we start hunting a living quarry, which is more interesting.

*21.11.13.* The lectures on wireless telegraphy which we attend at the local technical high school are very instructive and stimulating for us.

Last Saturday I went to Frankfurt to see Pégoud, the Frenchman, fly. You can hardly believe what that fellow can do—somersaults, vertical dives, turns over the vertical, upside down flying, etc.—and all with such confidence and assurance that you cannot for a moment feel he will crash. The man made a very great impression on me.

We have now received our first invitations to society functions. But we officers have been robbed of our pleasure in dancing by the emperor's strange veto on modern dances. Everyone here is shaking his head about it and especially about the disproportionately heavy punishment of instant dismissal. I should like to know what low 'dive' in Berlin was visited by the gentlemen who are responsible for it.

Last week I went to my two first balls; there were over one hundred people at each of them, and the grand duke appeared in person at one. Both were brilliantly staged, but nevertheless not to my taste; they were terribly stiff, and everything was done according to etiquette—quite apart from the fact that the wallflowers we had to partner danced more on my patent leather shoes than on the floor. The shortage of ladies made the few nice ones and good dancers almost inaccessible to us newcomers. Well, time will change all that—one must first get into the swing of things.

Last week Lt-Col. Schroeder, our C.O., came over from Coblence to inspect our company and my recruits; he was most laudatory. We used the opportunity to pour out our troubles to him. You have no idea how they stint the army. The money they allowed us to settle the company in its quarters hardly goes half the way. Our poor horses are almost artists in fasting. The rank and file are the only ones that come off slightly better, because food is cheaper here than in Coblence.

*17.12.13.* Baltzer and I were in Coblence on Saturday and Sunday to see our old comrades again and go to a party at the civilians' club, where I met all the good old friends again. It was a different kind of jollification to that of the stiff Darmstadt balls, and how differently our ladies danced to the Darmstadt ones. I shall have to teach some of the latter.

I look forward to our merry meeting at Christmas!

*5.1.14.* I have landed here safely with my 'son.' With the exception of two offences he behaved perfectly and always gave notice by whimpering, so that I could get him out of the compartment in time. He spent the rest of the time lying on the rack, where he was very snugly wrapped up in my rug. I have a childish delight in the animal. It is really strange that I did not get a dog long ago, seeing that I am so fond of animals. Do you remember how sad Herbert Haeslop was because his Tell loved me almost better than his master?

There is a splendid ice-rink here and lovely snow on the mountains. I went skiing from Cronberg on Sunday and got on to the Feldberg. Glorious!

*19.1.14.* I went to the court ball on Tuesday. There were quite a number of royal personages there, including Prince Waldemar of Prussia—so it was most interesting. This time I also had quite good fun, because I know a lot of ladies now, and they have already noticed that I am not exactly a bad dancer. I spend every possible free hour on the ice. Yesterday I went into the Odenwald, where I found very good snow. I was on my skis for six and half hours without a break.

My little Airedale terrier—he has not got a name yet—grows bigger and more impudent every day. He is very affectionate towards me and enjoys a universal popularity. He likes playing with Frau Nagel best, but also appreciates the woman who runs the canteen on account of the bits of sausage he gets from her. He has already developed certain dislikes; he bolts when my batman comes with his comb and howls dolefully when Baltzer plays the piano.

*2.2.14.* "Well, he's always got some new notion in his head!" mother will say when she learns that I mean to have a shot at getting into the officers' pentathlon for the Olympic games in Berlin. The five events are: four thousand metres cross-country race, three hundred metres swimming race, pistol shooting, fencing, five thousand metres obstacle race on horseback. The conditions are fairly severe and the competitors numerous—that means I must lead a steady life and go into strict training as soon as the weather is more favourable; in any case I have not yet taken to smoking, so that the only thing I can do is to drink milk instead of wine or beer. The competition for the officers of the 18th army corps takes place in Frankfurt, from which certain candidates are nominated for the Berlin army competition.

*28.2.14.* The period just before Shrove Tuesday was somewhat strenuous on account of the numerous social engagements and not at all the best preparation for my Olympic training. As the recruit inspection is now over, my duties are much lighter, and I can devote some time to breaking in the new horses.

I went to Coblence with Baltzer for the Carnival days, and on Ash Wednesday was the farewell dinner to our old C.O., Lt-Col. Schroeder, who has got a transfer. As he was very popular, it was a big dinner, and he was most touched. When it was all over we escorted him home in a carriage drawn by six horses ridden by officers; the rest rode before, beside or behind the carriage, carrying torches.

My little dog also went with me to Coblence; at first he thought it rather funny to be in a car, but afterwards he decided that it was a conveyance worthy of his rank and turned up his nose at all the pedestrians. He got his name at last on Shrove Tuesday; Wally Istas christened him with her brother's nickname "Ibi." Unfortunately he has not come out well on the enclosed photo. The horse with the saddle on the right is my service mount, the other is the one I am breaking in.

*30.4.14.* Our big three weeks' company course begins at Rüsselsheim on May 6th, goes on from there into the Taunus and finishes up in Rhenish Hesse. Ibi is naturally going too.

My training suits me very well. Mother need not be afraid of me overstraining myself. The competitions are to take place in Frankfurt on May 9th and 10th, so that I can easily get to them from Rüsselsheim.

I cannot have father thinking of giving up his beloved trip to the mountains because Martin's equipment costs so much—that won't do at all! My life in Darmstadt is much cheaper than it was in Coblence; as we have no mess life, I can even save a bit. Moreover I get an allowance of one mark fifty a day on account of the camp being some distance away from Darmstadt. So I beg father not to give me any allowance as long as I am quartered on the manoeuvre ground. Please accept this from me; I am glad to do it, and am not really making any sacrifice.

*Wörsdorfim Taunus, 12.5.14.* Yesterday we came to this place, which is four kilometers north of Idstein. We were four days in Rüsselsheim; I took the opportunity to see the Opel Motor Works.

I was in Frankfurt on Saturday and Sunday for the Olympic Games competition. I was easily the best of nine competitors in the three hundred metres swimming race with a time of five minutes, thirty and a half seconds; von Specht of the 116th infantry, who was second, took six minutes, fourteen seconds. In the cross country race I was second, doing the four thousand metres in fifteen minutes, thirty-four seconds against the fourteen minutes, fifty-one seconds of the winner; we were level for the first two thousand metres. I had less luck in the fencing and shooting, in which I came out 6th and 7th, so that I only got a third prize alto-gether. (Unfortunately the riding had to be dropped.) As usual, my prize was a smoking service for a non-smoker, but

I also got a plaque as a souvenir from the town of Frankfurt. So my training has not altogether useless.

The whole business was fairly strenuous. On Saturday afternoon we shot at 3, ran at 5 and swum at 8. The fencing began at 8 on Sunday morning and went on till 2, as all the competitors had to fence against one another, and I had to be on the ground again at 3.30 as I wanted to compete in the five and four hundred metre races. I could not get more than second in either of these, because I was tired with the pentathlon, whereas many of the competitors had not taken part in any other events.

We had a bit of a celebration in the evening, and the last train was just steaming off as we got to the station. Consequently I could not get away till 4.30 the next morning, reaching Rüsselsheim at 5.30, which was just in time to start a fifty-five kilometers' march with the company. We reached Wörsdorf at 4 in the afternoon, and I was on duty from 6 to 10—do you believe me when I tell you that I fell asleep as soon as I came off?

*Gau-Algesheim, 19.5.14.* Once again the course is simply a summer holiday; we spend the whole day in the open air in glorious country. Yesterday we marched through a wonderfully beautiful landscape, down the Wisper valley to Lorch and then in the Rhine valley as far as Bingen. Gau-Algesheim is also a marvellously pretty place, with a view on to the Rhine and the Taunus mountains in the background—a foretaste of the Alps. It is, however, rather uncertain whether I shall be able to join you this year, as we have so much on in July. Moreover we are going to put up military wireless stations in various towns. It is quite possible for me to be ordered off for a long period on one of these jobs. But the whole business is still supposed to be a dead secret—so please do not mention it to anyone.

*Darmstadt, 29.5.14. (postcard)* Having just got back from the practice, I received a telegram to the effect that I am ordered off to Halberstadt on the job I mentioned to you in my last letter. Fine! I shall be ever so much nearer to you there. But please do not mention the matter to anyone!

## FLYING

These last two communications probably contain the only untruth with which the honest Oswald Boelcke ever deceived his parents. There was never any question of erecting a wireless station at Halberstadt; his transfer thither was the result of his long desired and carefully prepared transfer to the Halberstadt Flying School.

But this deceit was a white lie which filial love prompted him to tell to his parents. To understand this we must remember that at that time aviation was considered a daring, neck-breaking affair that might well fill any parent's heart with dread. Moreover the elder brother had already been trained as an observer. Above all Boelcke desired to safeguard his parents' holiday in the mountains—which coincided with the period of his aviation course—from being spoilt by anxieties on his behalf.

Boelcke put in his application for a transfer to Halberstadt at the beginning of April. When it was granted at the beginning of May, he sought his elder brother's advice and received the following answer:

"As you have steady nerves, know something about cars and are untroubled by any unhealthy ambitions, I can only congratulate you on your decision. But—how are you going to break it to our parents? Yes, that is difficult. The best thing would be to say nothing about it, but that won't do, because you have to go to Halberstadt. Perhaps you might say you have been ordered there as a wireless officer, and that you are putting up a station there. The main thing is that you do not frighten them while undergoing instruction—when you have passed your tests and can fly, it will not be so bad."

Boelcke followed this advice.

In view of his hardy, sport-loving nature it is not surprising to find him attracted to the flying corps which was then in its earliest infancy. His letters show plainly the enthusiastic interest with which he followed the flying at the imperial manoeuvres in the Uckermark in 1911, at Metz when he was a pupil at the war academy, at Coblence when he saw the machines competing for the Prince Heinrich Trophy and at Frankfurt when Pégoud, the stunting pilot, gave his exhibition. But these letters do not reveal the influence that was the strongest factor in turning his thoughts towards the flying corps and inducing him to apply for his transfer.

Anyone conversant with the Army List of 1913 will wonder at Boelcke's letters mentioning no word of the fact that in addition to the units he enumerates as quartered on the manoeuvre ground at Griesheim the 3rd air battalion was there, in close proximity to the wireless company.

This noticeable omission in Boelcke's letters finds its explanation in the following statement, for which we have to thank his former friend and brother-officer Baltzer (now a major in the Reichswehr):

"When we were sent to Metz in June, 1913, on a three days' course at the wireless station there and took the opportunity to pay a visit to the aerodrome at Frescaty, we were taken up for our first flight in an aeroplane and were both enraptured with it. Afterwards we had plenty of opportunities to watch the flying at Griesheim; in consequence of the lack of observers we had the chance of making many short and long flights. We both enjoyed them immensely, but decided to say nothing about them in our letters home in order to avoid causing unnecessary anxiety to our parents. We saw much of the flying officers,—not only in the mess and on the aerodrome, but also at their reserved table in the Hotel Hess in the evenings."

Boelcke reached Halberstadt on the Whit-Monday of 1914 after a two days' ride on his motor-cycle through the Spessart, Kissingen and the Thuringian forests and began his flying career on June 2nd.

His letters to his parents are silent about his experiences during his course of instruction. In the June of that year, however, there was no occasion for him to write to them, because he went over to Dessau every Sunday on his motorcycle. In his letters to them in July, when they were in the mountains, he did not say anything about his flights, with the result that they only contain news of his walking and cycling tours in the Harz Mountains—in which he took particular pride in the fact that his N.S.U. motor-cycle carried him up the Brocken quite easily—, the prize he gained in a dancing tournament at Harzburg, Ibi's progress, etc. It is therefore all the more welcome to us that the letters he wrote to his friend Baltzer about his early flying career are available. Incidentally they give a not uninteresting view of the primitive conditions then prevailing at the flying school.

*Halberstadt, 16.6.14.* Our life out here—we are five kilometers away from Halberstadt and I have only been into the town once so far—is very pleasant. So are my brother-officers here, although so far I have only got into close contact with one of them (Kästner, a Saxon in the 68th field artillery) and he is nearly through his course, so that unfortunately he will be leaving soon. We are only on duty in the morning; we have all our afternoons free; we play tennis, lie about in the sun or make trips to the mountains. You could not imagine a more comfortable form of service.

If only it was not quite so comfortable and one was burdened with a bit more work. Certainly they wake us up at 3.30 if the weather is good for flying and we start business at 4, but if only there was not so much endless, aimless standing about and waiting! We have four instructors here, each of whom has one instructor's machine (you know the type with two sets of controls, one of which is worked by the pilot and one by the pupil) and three pupils, whom he instructs one after another. Our machines are 70 H.P. Bristol-Taubes, which possess one excellent quality for instructional purposes, i.e. slowness, but often, however, they also have the vice of refusing to do anything at all; if the weather is a bit warm or the engine not quite at its best, the brutes cannot get higher than five to ten metres when carrying two men, with the result that we do nothing but taxying, and so one learns nothing. It often happens that the pilot is fed up when he has finished instructing one pupil; consequently one can hang about for four hours and hardly get a turn—that always makes me wild.

Instruction generally consists of one round (six minutes) only, and then we drop down to land from a hundred or a hundred and fifty metres' height. I am now practising mainly landings—they are the most difficult of all. I am fairly well all right with simple flying and easy turns; my instructor has sometimes left the controls entirely to me for them. Today he took me up in a 100 H. P. machine for my first long flight (forty minutes) over Quedlinburg and Blankenburg; we got up to one thousand four hundred metres and then went down in a series of gliding turns—that was fine!

*Halberstadt, 3.7.14.* And now about my flying 'triumphs.' I put in the following report for July:

> Total flying time: 231 minutes, = 3 hrs, 51mins.
> Starts: 30—8 on a 70 H.P. Taube, 22 on a 100 H.P. Taube, all of which were instructional flights.
> Maximum height: 1500 metres.
> Breakages: none.

Today my instructor let me do my first solo on a 70 H.P. Taube, but I had bad luck. I tested the engine on the tarmac—faultless. It was doing fourteen hundred revolutions when I took off, but gradually dropped when I went into my first turn after a minute in the air. Although I pushed the stick energetically to give the machine a chance of recovering, the brute remained obstinate. 1300...1250.... 1200.....1150! the rev counter went back slowly but with consistent malice. As I came down to something like fifteen metres, I had to make up my mind to land. But there was nothing but cornfields all round me! I was not high enough up for a glide and so had to land with my engine on. I cut it when about five metres above the ground and put myself slowly down on to a field where the corn had grown a metre high. It came off fairly well; at least the machine did not turn turtle, but only went down slowly on its propeller. I sat quietly inside and had a look at the damage; the propeller and one of the undercarriage struts were broken. Well, at least I now have a propeller to hang in my room! But how damnable that it should happen to me! This evening I will see that I have better luck—I am going to get another machine as well.

I have been to Dessau every Sunday lately on my motor-bike: one hundred kilometres in two hours, ten minutes. Although I went through the villages like a gentleman, I have not been able to escape my first fine; it is not I who am to blame for it, but my N.S.U. that does not like to go down any slope under thirty kilometers an hour. To-morrow I am going to Clausthal via Schiercke to visit an old school friend, returning on Sunday by the Brocken. Ibi sends greetings to kind uncle Baltzer.

*Halberstadt, 14.7.14.* My flying makes progress; the first step on the ladder of fame is taken—yesterday I passed my pilot's tests. First came the so-called altitude flight. I got up to three hundred metres—wonderful, isn't it? You need a good quarter of an hour to climb that much in one of our old school machines. After that I had to fly two series of five figures of eight and land at a fixed point. When I came down thoroughly pleased with myself after the first five, my witnesses told me they were more like bretzels than figures of eight. I then learnt for the first time that I had to turn those eights over two fixed points. To my great joy this error gave me the chance of an extra take off.

It is a real misery that one gets so little flying here. I only did four solos before passing my tests. The factory has allocated only two machines for the use of us solo fliers, and every flight is counted so as to be sure you don't get too much.

Last Friday our C.O., Major Friedel, came along here and watched us flying. Thereupon I had a mighty slice of luck, for by chance I was the only officer to bring off two good landings. Consequently I got a devil of a good report, especially as I have been here the shortest time of all. I always have luck in the air—I have not damaged a machine since the day I landed in the cornfield.

I shall be finished here in about four or five weeks. Then I am to be sent to Cologne, because the only company of the 3rd air battalion that flies Halberstadt Taubes is stationed there. But I would rather go to Darmstadt and fly biplanes; so I have put in an application to the C.O. accordingly—perhaps my luck of the other day will stand me in good stead. So auf wiedersehen on Driesheim aerodrome! nf nf ddd.*

Boelcke's log book shows that he passed his second tests on the very day before mobilisation was ordered:

*31.7.14.* Second tests: Cross country flight Halberstadt—Wernigerode and back. Duration: sixty-eight minutes. Maximum height twelve hundred metres.

Another letter dating from July, 1914 contains the following passage. "My good parents are now in the Alps. Thank Heavens!

It would have been too ghastly having to keep up this farce and go on lying if they had started asking me about my wireless station, etc., when I was over in Dessau. If I could have guessed how one lie entangles you in others and how loathsome that is, I do not think I could have done it. But I meant well. As soon as I am finished here, I shall confess everything.

---

* *Wireless abbreviation: "Nothing more; finish."*

The outbreak of war brought this confession sooner than Boelcke had anticipated. On the evening of August 8th he had a brief reunion with his parents at Dessau railway station—too brief for him to go to his home—and said goodbye to them. Then he went forth into the night, to take his part in the war.

But Ibi went to the paternal dwelling, where he still stands at the entrance in a state of lifelike mummification to scare evildoers and welcome good friends, his poaching tendencies having brought him an honourable death from a gamekeeper's bullet.

# CHAPTER III

# *The Beginnings of War Flying*

QUARRELLING with his destiny because he could not go up to the front at once in charge of a wireless section attached to a reconnaissance squadron, as he would have done according to his original mobilisation orders as a wireless officer, Boelcke went off to Darmstadt to join a replacement section of the air service. He had the pleasure of meeting Baltzer and other old friends for a few days, but very soon afterwards he wrote:

"The whole garrison has left, but I, poor brute, must stay here and listen to the cheers they give when they march off. Four of our sections have gone already; they have left us all the old machines which they have no use for. On these I am helping to train our fifty new pupil-pilots; I myself fly Aviatik biplanes, which I like much better than the Halberstadt Taubes. All acquaintances here—especially the ladies—pet and spoil me, but what is the good of that if the war is over before I get out to the front!"

He even had to wait there after passing his third test (cross-country flight to Mainz, with intermediate landing at the Grosse Sand) and gaining his pilot's certificate on August 15th. "It is horrible to kick up one's heels here idly in these stirring times and go on motor trips to the Odenwald, when out at the front there is fighting going on in which I might take a hand. There is nothing I should like better than to go off there on my own."

At last his release came; he was ordered to report himself to the 4th base aviation park at Trier on August 30th. He remained at the wheel of the service car the whole day, (with the exception of a brief midday rest in Coblence which he spent with old friends) fighting his way though all the tunnels and across all the bridges of the Rhine and Moselle valleys that were carefully guarded by Landwehr detachments.

"The breeze blows more freshly here in Trier from the front to which we have to send up the reinforcements of pilots and machines that are wanted there. I am trying with all the power and guile at my disposal to get into the 13th section where brother Wilhelm is serving and am therefore practising on an Albatros biplane, which is the only machine flown in it. I have struck a fat slice of luck with my billet, for I am quartered in the villa belonging to a widowed Frau Kunz, who owns huge vineyards and wine cellars; I have a magnificent room and live like a prince. What a pity Ibi is not with me—he would have enjoyed all the many beautiful bones. Frau Maria Kunz treats and looks after me like her own son, and her two girls (about eleven and nine years old) stick to me like burrs."

This is one of the many examples that show how quickly all hearts went out to the 'golden lad,' as the ladies of Coblence called him. His relations with these friends he made during the week he was billeted on them blossomed out later. When he spent a day with the Kunz household in the late autumn of 1915 on the occasion of a service jounrey, he left his nightshirt behind. This was not sent on to him; it was kept as a relic by the little daughter and shown to his contemporary admirers for a fee of twenty-five pfennigs; with the proceeds she bought chocolate to send to the front. The mother always wrote to him as "dear son Ossi," the daughter as "dear brother Ossi," as shown in the following letter.

"Dear brother Ossi,
We were so delighted that you got the 'Pour le Mérite' order! I am as proud of you as if you were Hindenburg. Is it true, dear Ossi, that you are the youngest hero in the German Empire to get that order? But now you must send me a photo of yourself with all your orders. The one in the 'Illustrierte Zeitung' is not good. I am sending you a packet of chocolate for your valour; eat it reasonably, for it is very fine. If you go on winning victories, I shall have to put up the price of your nightshirt to fifty pfennigs. I cross my thumbs so that you will go on having luck.

　　With many hearty greeting from Ossi's little sister Mieze."

But even this domestic idyll on the threshold of war could not tame Boelcke's impatience to get to the front. How he succeeded in doing so,—not without some selfhelp—is shown in his

## FIRST LETTER FROM THE FRONT

*Chatel, near Varennes, in the Argonne Forest, Friday, 4.9.14.*
My dear parents, my card from La Ferté sur Chiers, dated 1.9.14, will have told you that I have got to the front at last and to Wilhelm's 13th section. If I had not acted somewhat impudently on my own account, I should still be sitting at the base, in the aviation park at Sedan.

　　It happened like this. You know I wanted to get away from Trier as soon as possible and join Wilhelm's section if I could. Then by chance word came from this section that two of their machines were missing, so that they needed replacements for them. Naturally I applied at once. As the commander of the park was not there, his deputy would not take the responsibility of letting me go, whereat I cursed mightily. All the same I quietly got my machine ready (compass, altimeter, armour-plates under the seats, etc.) and practically made up my mind to do a bolt. But as part of the park was to be transferred to Sedan and my machine happened to be serviceable, he allowed me to fly there at once with an N.C.O.

I fiddled about with all sorts of things on my machine, so that it was 6 p.m. before I could take off—as it gets dark now by 7.30 it was too late for me to do the one hundred and forty kilometers to Sedan. But this suited me very well, because I had made up my mind in advance to land at La Ferté in any case and offer my services there. If they did not want me, they could send me away again, and my visit there would count as a forced landing occasioned by darkness.

Having affixed the map to my steering wheel so as to prevent the N.C.O. from putting me off in any other direction, I flew over Luxemburg and northward of Montmédy until I sighted the tents at La Ferté about 7.10 p.m., whereupon I came down. Wilhelm had just gone off with his captain to H.Q., but his comrades gave me a jolly welcome and carried me off to their cheery mess. Wilhelm did not arrive back till late and could not get over his surprise and joy at having his 'little chap' here.

Next morning my fate was settled in the way I hoped; Captain Streccius, the commander of the section, refused to let me go and took the responsibility for my non-arrival at Sedan. No one was better pleased than I. From this incident

I learnt that one must not be too quiet and law-abiding, but take a risk sometimes to achieve one's object.

As I had brought no observer with me and Wilhelm's pilot Lieut. Maertens, had to give his nerves a rest, Wilhelm be-spoke me for himself at once. And so we two brothers are now united for life and death in an 'aeroplane marriage.'

On the afternoon of Sept. 1st—the anniversary of the battle of Sedan—I took off at 3.50 p.m. with Wilhelm for my first flight against the enemy. We cruised over the enemy's positions at a height of two thousand eight hundred metres for about an hour and a half, until Wilhelm had spied out everything. Then bolted back and landed about 6.10. As Wilhelm had reconnoitred all the enemy's artillery positions, he had to go off to see our various artillery sections and did not get back till 3 a.m. But, as we were informed yesterday by H.Q.—our section is attached to the 6th army corps— Wilhelm's report enabled our artillery to place their first rounds so accurately that the French artillery were forced to abandon their positions at once.

Yesterday—Thursday—we shifted our aerodrome forward a bit, because the French had bolted again. We flew out machine over to Buzancy in the morning; when we learnt there that we must move still further forward, we went on in a car to look for a new landing ground and found one here. On the way back I chanced to meet my Darmstadt wireless men in Landreville. It was a great joy to see Baltzer and Leufgen again. I stayed to lunch with them, but as the car did not turn up to fetch me at 3 p.m.—it had been requisitioned for a wounded man—I had to tramp the nine kilometers back to Buzancy on foot.

When I reached the aerodrome, I found that Wilhelm had gone off with Maertens. He had left written orders for me to ascertain the enemy's positions at certain points. Beside my machine stood Sergeant Menge, my passenger from Trier, who said that he was to fly with me. This seemed strange to me, because I was only supposed to fly with Wilhelm, but as I already knew the country from my first flight, I got in and took off. I had to cover a fairly large stretch of territory. I flew over certain roads and across the Argonne Forest, marking everything I saw on my map with a red pencil. Flying over Varennes at two thousand five hundred metres, I came under heavy shellfire. I made a good landing at 7.10 on our new aerodrome at Châtel.

And what were my thanks for swimming about above the enemy for two and a half hours? I got a ticking off. I had hardly switched off my engine before Wilhelm came running up and fired away at me: "Where were you? What have you been doing? Are you quite mad? You must never fly without my permission—and never unless I am with you." I could not make out what he meant at first—but at last I got to the bottom of it. Wilhelm had only brought Maertens as far as the new aerodrome; he meant me to fly there with the N.C.O. and then take him up for a reconnaissance flight. The mechanic misunderstood his directions; consequently I went off on my own, and Wilhelm was in an almighty funk that I would not turn up here. When the misunderstanding was cleared up, we went off peaceably in the car to our quarters. They are in a pretty château, where Wilhelm has also established the mess. But we shall probably not stay long in Châtel, as our armies are moving forward mightily.

I must tell you one thing that was a great joy to us; on Wednesday evening two of our missing men turned up again. They had to make a forced landing in enemy territory because their engine went dead. They had hardly got down before the French peasants attacked them from all sides with scythes and shot-guns; they could only save their lives by a speedy flight into a neighbouring wood—followed by the roars of the men and the screeching of the women. They managed to get into the Argonne Forest under cover of darkness, and wandered about for five days in territory occupied by French troops. They lived on roots and blackberries; generally they hid in trees during the day and wandered on at night.

They were very nearly starved into letting themselves be taken prisoners, but on the seventh day they heard the sweet sounds of that bugle-call: "Hurry along, you ruddy fool!" It was a German patrol, which then brought them back. Naturally they looked like bandits; now they have gone to Trier to recuperate.

By the way your son does not look much better than a banit, as I have not yet got my things. My batman was supposed to follow me to La Ferté by car, but owing to my many moves he has not yet succeeded in finding me—at present he is touring north-east France with my baggage.

And so, my dear parents, these are in brief my first war experiences. Take care of yourselves meanwhile—we shall soon come back. The French are getting a bigger thrashing than they have ever had before—the others will get their dose afterwards.

## THE ADVANCE TO BAR-LE-DUC

*Ste Menehould, 10.9.14.* I have to undertake the correspondence, as Wilhelm has no time for it. My last letter to you was from Châtel. As our army moved forward on the 5th, we received orders from H.Q. that same evening to move our section up to Ste Menehould. The next morning I took off with Sergeant Menge, because I have no regular observer, while Wilhelm always has to fly with Maertens when we move our position. I had hardly climbed up to five hundred metres before I was in the midst of clouds that grew continually thicker. It was a bit uncomfortable at first, because I have never flown in clouds before and was over the Argonne Forest at the time. But I said to myself that the clouds would have to come to an end some time and kept on climbing until I was above them.

I then flew by the sun and the clock: ten minutes with the sun at your back—that means you must be clear of the forest! I went down through the clouds again and lo—I was right! Then I found I could fly safely at five hundred metres to Ste Menehould, where I discovered that Wilhelm had already landed; he was delighted that I had found my way through so easily. Then we went straight off on a reconnaissance flight of two and a half hours' duration. I did not get any flying at all on the 7th. It is a misfortune that our section has fewer machines—only five now—than pilots; it means that we have to go in rotation, so that everyone can get a turn. I wiled away the time by trying a French racing car which we discovered here and practising my French on the local inhabitants.

We have found very good accommodation here. Our mess is in the house of a French curassier lieutenant. As Madame has preserved an incredible quantity of fruit, I am wallowing delightedly in such good things. Our meals are first-class, thanks to our excellent cook, who goes by the nickname of 'Adlon.' Our usual drink at table is champagne.

On the 8th I took off at 6.20 with Wilhelm for a very interesting flight. We got as far as somewhere to the south of

Bar-le-Duc. There we saw a French aerodrome, containing twelve tents. Two machines took off. As we were two thousand eight hundred metres up, we did not worry much about them at first, but when we noticed after a while that the fellows were chasing us, we cleared off hurriedly as soon as Wilhelm had finished. Unarmed as we were, we had no desire to find out whether it is true that some of the French aeroplanes are now equipped with machine guns. Once again Wilhelm had a whole sackful of things to report and made a rush for a car when we landed in order to get H.Q. as quickly as possible. The others ragged him by calling out: "Onecar, two, three, four cars for Herr Lieutenant Boelcke!" because they think he is trying to push himself and cannot understand that it is all well-meaning zeal.

Yesterday I saw the serious side of war for the first time. I went with Wilhelm and the captain to the 11th and 12th division and the light artillery in the morning—through shell-torn charred villages, with newly-dug soldiers' graves on either side of the road and dead horses lying about everywhere. Corpses lay still unburied round a churchyard which the Germans had stormed the night before; most of them were N.C.O.s, who had led the attacks. Then I saw the battlefield. That is to say, we saw nothing or very little. There were no troops visible, only isolated men on foot or horseback here and there. The only things one saw were the bursting shells from the artillery and burning villages. But in compensation we heard a lot—the dull gurgling of light artillery, the clearer cracks of the field artillery and the rattle of rifle fire.

We passed reserves when on our way to one of the staffs. They looked just like they do on manoeuvres; some were cooking a meal, others played about, but most of them lay on their backs, sleeping soundly in spite of the battle going on close at hand.

Finally we went in to H.Q. I naturally stood aside modestly. Then General von Pritzelwitz asked Wilhelm: "Is that your brother?" Afterwards he came over and shook hands with me; he patted me and said: "You two are doing your job splendidly."

As Wilhelm had to talk over something or other with the light artillery, we went on to Villelotte after leaving H.Q. The battle was very fierce at that time, because the 157th infantry were making a new thrust forward. Then I heard the whistle of bullets for the first time—they were a couple of stray ones that passed over our heads.

As we had a break-down, we did not get back to our place till 5 p.m., but we swallowed a hasty meal and were in the air by 5.30 because Wilhelm wanted to make a reconnaissance to which H.Q. attached much importance. Heavy fighting was still going on. I now saw from above what I had seen below. It was dusk when we landed again, guided to our aerodrome by star-shells. Wilhelm went off to H.Q. with the captain again.

We have a holiday today, as it is raining; I have had my sleep out properly. When I came into the mess for lunch, I found Wilhelm wearing the Iron Cross. The general decorated Captain Streccius and him last evening; he said a lot of appreciative things and embraced them both. I was delighted about Wilhelm's decoration; he has thoroughly deserved it.

The French evacuated their positions last night and so escaped us again. They understand the art of bolting so well that we cannot get hold of them. But we shall catch them one day!

## RETREAT!

*Buzancy, 16.9.14.* We left Ste Menehould early on the morning of the 13th and flew back here in storm and rain. Nasty rumours about a defeat of the 1st and 2nd armies were already creeping round the day before. You can imagine we were in very low spirits. We had been advancing all the time—and now, all of a sudden came the order: "Retreat!"

On the 12th troops and baggage passed through Ste Menehould the whole day, retreating. The G.H.Q. of the 6th army was also moved back. When the heavy clouds lifted a bit in the afternoon, Wilhelm and I tried to gain a view of the situation from the air, but were hotly shelled when over the enemy. We ascertained that the French were only following our retreating troops very slowly. Apparently they could not grasp what was happening—first they got a thrashing, and then their conquerors cleared off!

That same evening we made preparations for our own departure. As there was only a Landwehr battalion in Ste Menehould in addition to ourselves and we had, therefore, to count on the possibility of being attacked, we slept in our clothes, with our arms at hand. From 2.30 a.m. onward we heard artillery fire that lasted for hours, but the expected attack did not take place. Instead of it the storm howled in the chimney and savage raindrops beat against the window. We all wore long faces when we collected for coffee at 6a.m. But we had to take off—even if the heavens threatened to fall in on us.

We started at 7.10 a.m. in a twenty-five metre a second gale. Wilhelm went first with Maertens; I followed immediately afterwards, because we wanted to keep together if possible. My observer was Lieut. Jaenicke, whose nerves have gone to pieces completely. I was genuinely sorry for the poor fellow, because it was not at all nice aloft; the machine was badly tossed about by the wind. It was not so bad for me, because as pilot I have my hand on the stick and know what is happening, but that poor fellow must have had a bad time with his nerves. I soon lost sight of Wilhelm, as it is very difficult to follow another machine accurately in such weather. We all reached our destination safely, however, but as our tents had naturally not arrived, we had to peg our machines down and put a Landwehr guard over them to see the wind did not blow them away.

As Buzancy is on a main road, along which numerous columns had marched, there was not a house in it that was not packed from attic to cellar. We only found passable quarters after a very long search. Add to this the beastly weather that renders flying impossible and the retreat—our mood was not all too rosy.

The only nice thing is that my Darmstadt wireless people came here on the same day as we did and are staying for a couple of days' rest. Under the present circumstances it sounds most comic when I exchange Coblence dancing circle reminiscences here with Baltzer. I have also met my former inspection officer from Metz—Giersberg—here; he is leading a squadron of the 13th dragoons. One is always meeting old acquaintances on active service and derives much pleasure therefrom.

We are now sitting in a warm room. The open hearth-fire crackles away merrily beside me. My back will soon be brown. From time to time one has to shift one's position, so as to get the other side roasted. The wireless people are coming across later—we are going to play 'old maid.' C'est la guerre!

*Pontfaverger, 26.9.14.* We have been here since the 20th; our move was occasioned by the fact that our 6th corps now belongs to the 3rd army. I departed from Buzancy with a light heart, as it was inconsolably dull there—I did not get one flight in eight days!

Thanks to the better weather I have made some lovely long reconnaissance flights here with Wilhelm—always in the Châlons-Epernay-Rheims area. Yesterday we ascertained the departure of an enemy army corps. We flew three hundred and fifty kilometers, reached a height of three thousand one hundred metres and were in the air from 8 till 11.35 a.m., i.e. three and a half hours. Four hours is the longest that our machines can do on their petrol supplies; the others never fly more than two or at the most two and a half hours—their 'nerves' cannot stand more. If I only knew what sort of things nerves are! Luckily I know nothing about them, and it is all the same to me whether I fly an hour longer on not.

Generally speaking the situation has hardly changed at all. We are facing each other everywhere in trenches. Neither side attacks. Both sides are moving up their troops behind the front. When they have finished, things will start again. They are bound to get going some time within the next few days.

*Pontfaverger, 10.12.14.* We have been three weeks here now, but the situation still remains unchanged. The two sets of opponents have dug themselves in up to the teeth; every now and then one or other makes a push forward, but, taken as a whole, the present position at the front is a sort of fortress warfare. And so—for good or ill—we too have gradually accustomed ourselves to the idea that we must settle down here for some time.

It is no laughing matter for our troops; they are in the trenches day and night, and the nights are very cold already. One really feels ashamed of the good time we are having in contrast. So far I have always had a bed—we have only once used your sleepingbags—and we are better catered for than in peace time.

All of which would be very nice—if it was not for the horrible inactivity and boredom. I have not been over the enemy for the last ten days; the weather is bad, and there is hardly anything for us to reconnoitre since the war has frozen up. I had my machine taken to pieces during the last few days and thoroughly overhauled; it is as good as new now. Today I tried four flights over the aerodrome, taking a passenger up each time. First I took one of the general's adjutants, then a chief medical officer and a vet; finally I took Böhme, my mechanic, who was mad with delight—the poor fellows must always be looking after a machine and yet never get any flying themselves. You see that we are under peace conditions—passenger and demonstration flights!

Apart from that I kill time by going for walks, shooting partridges and hares, talking French with the natives, much reading and even more sleeping. When one of our cars went off to Trier lately, I asked Frau Kunz to send me something to read. My good vice-mamma send me a whole bookshop, together with a lot of presents and nice letters from herself and the girls.

Not long ago a French airman gave us a bit of a change by dropping a few bombs here. He was trying for the tents that house our machines, but only hit a couple of innocent Uhlans who were on their way to take their turn at sentry-go. I don't think much of this bomb-throwing business. The heavy things only slow your machine down, and the practical result is very small. But it may be that I underestimate the moral effect which such a bolt from the blue may have on funks, victims of nerves and the civilian population. Our H.Q. has mounted two howitzers near our aerodrome to fire at enemy airmen. But they have not hit any yet. That is not so easy, you know. The French have also shelled me a few times. It was certainly a bit creepy the first time that I saw the dainty little cloudlets—bursts of artillery shells—rise up from down below. Now I laugh at them, because they never hit you if you are flying high enough—about two thousand five hundred metres. Of course something might happen to anyone who was fool enough to fly below one thousand metres.

Father asked about Pontfaverger. It is a nest of a place, with a couple of thousand inhabitants. The better-off people have left, which is an advantage for us because we can occupy their houses. We get on very well with the part of the population that has remained here. The surrounding country consists of flat tablelands, with a fair number of woods, but, curiously enough, very few vineyards. There are châteaux with big parks all around us. Here in P. there is also a castle with a big and wonderfully pretty park. Our position is twenty-four kilometers north-east of Rheims. It takes from two to five minutes to fly direct to the front, and about a quarter of an hour in a car to our artillery positions.

We flying officers live all together in the house of a tax-collector, who was one of the fugitives. Wilhelm and I share the old grandmother's room, from which we have naturally banished all unnecessary rubbish, such as sewing table, sewing-machine, knick-knacks and family pictures. The other day our people wanted to put out flags to celebrate the fall of Antwerp, but there were none at hand. So they quickly made some, the materials being a black skirt, a white shirt and a red petticoat—I do not know whether the last-mentioned was grandmamma's. 'M. le recepteur' will not be very happy about our long visit. Although we have not done any willful damage—well, just imagine what it would be like if thirteen officers lived in your house for weeks and their batmen had to handle mother's plates, cups and glasses! C'est la guerre!

I enjoyed brother Max's amusing letter about Ibi. Don't spoil the rascal too much!

(P.S. The same evening) His Excellency has just sent me the Iron Cross by our captain, with some warm words of appreciation. And now I wish that Martin can also get it soon, so that you will have three decorated sons on active service.

*Pontfaverger, 5.10.14.* At last we have had something to do again in the last few days. The weather was so foggy for weeks that we thought we might consider ourselves temporarily pensioned off. It was difficult work to kill the time. We had decent weather again for the first time on the 22nd; we made good use of it. We were in our machines at 9 a.m. and kept at work till 5.30 p.m. I took off five times. First Wilhelm did a reconnaissance, and in the afternoon he directed our artillery fire. You see, there were several enemy batteries that our artillery could not locate. By arrangement with our own gunners we flew over the enemy batteries that our people had to shell, and Wilhelm noted whether their range was right, and then showed our artillerymen by means of various coloured lights whether their shots were too short or too far or too much to the right or left, until at last they got on their targets.

At first the business did not go at all well, and I had to make two landings at Nauroy, because Wilhelm had to go into the matter more thoroughly with our artillery men. But then they shot an enemy battery to pieces.

The next day the business worked splendidly straight off; we put our artillery on to three enemy batteries in three and a half hours. This kind of flying is strenuous work for both observer and pilot, because they must always keep such a sharp look out.

Wilhelm went off to H.Q. in the evening; when he came back, he was wearing the 1st class of the Iron Cross. He is the first to get it in our section. But he has already done six thousand five hundred kilometres flying over enemy territory, and I have done three thousand four hundred; Maertens, the next best in the section, has only done three thousand two hundred, although he has been much longer there than I.

### DIARY-LETTER

*Pontfaverger, 27.10.14.* From now onwards I shall write to you in diary fashion, i.e. a couple of lines each day and then send it to you as a collective letter when there is enough of it. If I only write occasionally, I always forget most of what I want to say.

Wilhelm has already located nine enemy batteries to the south of Nauroy and south-east of Rheims, and a heavy one in Rheims itself, quite close to the cathedral!!! We would particularly like to direct our artillery's fire on to this battery, but the weather is too bad—always deep clouds. Yesterday morning we had to give up our flight as hopeless after ten minutes. We tried again early this morning, but got into clouds at one thousand six hundred metres and had to turn back, because we cannot fly over the enemy at this height, unless we want to be shot down.

At noon today Captain Streccius called all the officers together in order to ease the tension that exists between us two and certain gentlemen of the section ever since Wilhelm was the only one to get the I.C.1. They complain that we pinched all the good, remunerative flights and so collected the laurels. The only true reason is their envy and annoyance at the fact that Wilhelm is the captain's right hand man and really runs the show here, although he comes only fourth in seniority.

*28.10.14.* No luck again yesterday, because the clouds obstructed us; our flight was not quite useless as we were able to locate three new enemy batteries.—The strained relations in the section still continue, although both parties are extremely polite to one another.

*29.10.14.* Dull weather the whole day, flying impossible. In the afternoon we paid a visit to Lieut. Schroeter, of the light artillery, with whom we work together. The name over his dug-out is "Wild Mazuria Villa." He is our special friend— a fine, racy fellow who looks really like a wild man himself with his huge red beard. He was mad with delight when we brought him a couple of bottles of Munich beer that had just come from Trier by car—a rare occurrence, because most of the stuff does not get any further than the staff and the columns, where it serves to fatten paymasters and camp-followers.

*30.10.14.* Bad weather. We had a nice beer evening; Schroeter and Captain Martini were there, along with Lieutenants Plaskuda and Delius from the local telephone section; Streccius also came in.

*31.10.14.* The weather is improving. We went off again at two to put our guns on to the French by means of our coloured lights. We could not pull off anything with Schroeter's battery, because the French had put up an anti-balloon gun on account of our frequent visits. We could not manage anything with our other two batteries either. We were furious at having tootled round for three and a half hours in vain. But our fight was not quite useless, because we located a battery near Rheims and another in the town when flying up and down the front.

*1.11.14.* We succeeded splendidly today where we failed yesterday; five enemy batteries have to thank us for friendly greetings from our own artillery. We worked from 8.30a.m. to 11.45 and from 3 p.m. to 5.45, i.e. six hours in all. Karstedt and Beckers (those are the two who were wandering about the Argonne for a week) flew to Paris with bombs today; they came back safely after a four hours' trip. There is not much sense or object in the business, as they will probably have only hit some old woman, but it is a nice, dashing sort of flight.—I have just received your news that Martin has also got the I.C.

*2.11.14.* The immediate neighbourhood of Rheims was the scene of our activity today. I had to take off twice, because I went off the first time with a huge flag flying behind me, to the amusement of all beholders—through an oversight I had caught the landing T. (four bed-sheets sewn together) in my brake. It must have looked extremely funny.

*3.11.14.* We really did not mean to fly today. But when we went out to our artillery at Fort Berru after lunch, we found that the French had fired at a neighbouring village with shells of heavy calibre, and by chance they managed to hit a number of our men who were assembled to draw their rations. That called for revenge. We pelted back to our aerodrome in the car, took off and flew to Rheims. Wilhelm found the guilty battery there, but—alas—our artillery could not reach it; they were just two hundred metres too short. When we got back at 4, the weather was so fine and calm that I got hold of that nice fellow, Jaenicke, who wants to get used to flying again, and took him to Sillery to drop four bombs. It was a nice little constitutional, in which I was boss of the show; all Jaenicke needed to do was to sit quiet and drop the bombs when I gave the signal.

*4.11.14.* We had a holiday today, because the enemy's artillery hardly fired a shot. I have sent father two hundred marks from my savings today; that will be one thousand two hundred marks since August—please put them into the next war loan for me.—There is peace in our section again; we actually play chess with one another, but a cordial, comradely feeling has not yet returned. We behave as though nothing had happened when we are with the others. As a matter of fact we spend more time with the telephone people than in our own mess—there is a nice friendly tone there—"Papa Martini" rules them like the father of a large family.

*5.11.14.* As the weather often gets worse in the course of the morning, we fly immediately after sunrise whenever possible, somewhere about 7.30. The enemy's artillery was active again in several spots and had to get a few smacks on the head. We were up soon after 7.30. Things went very well for us, so that we were finished in about an hour. Then we did another round for our artillery. As a matter of fact we are now flying for four of our batteries, which only shoot when we direct their fire. Whenever we put them on to a target, we find it masked the next time we go up. So we had to go up twice more today, making three trips in all, and we put four enemy batteries (three near Nauroy and one near Rheims) out of action. We are now doing this job on a large scale.

*7.11.14.* Thick fog yesterday and today. We utilised the time by going round to our artillery positions to ascertain what enemy batteries have been firing during the last few days. As the information was not sufficient for Wilhelm, we crept into the trenches today. Wilhelm tried to get a clear picture of the situation from the rather confused statements of a reserve officer—apparently a senior master (beg your pardon, father)—and several volunteers. As it took him a very long time, I amused myself on my own account. I scoured the country in front of me with field-glasses, because I wanted to have a shot at a Frenchman for once in a way, but none were in sight. But the enemy kept a much sharper look out. As soon as we put our thick heads above the parapet, they start-ed with a wuff, wuff, wuff, —I made an involuntary bow of acknowledgement to this attention, which amused our peo-ple mightily. Then the French artillery also obliged us with a few shots. Some shells burst right over our heads sss ... peng, peng—I made another bow of acknowledgement.

On the whole it is very quiet here. The men lounge about in the trenches and tell each other yarns; some read and most take a hand at 'skat,' while all are on the look out for the field kitchen, which comes along at 6.30 p.m. Some days the two sides hardly exchange more than a couple of shots. All our artillery fire is practically futile now; it could only acquire a purpose if the infantry advanced under its cover. But that does not happen, although the trenches are only three hundred metres away from one another in places. We do not know now what is happening or what is going to happen.

The most diverse suppositions are voiced: the decision will be reached in Russia—we must first capture Verdun, which threatens our rear—the authorities mean to save our men here until Italy comes in to effect a decision in our favour. In any case we are all prepared for the possibility of having to sit here idly for weeks and months, probably until the spring, and die of boredom. That would be terrible!

Week after week Boelcke wrote such letters to his parents. They are full of detailed descriptions,—proof in themselves of the amount of leisure time the airmen had on their hands—from which we can only quote drastic abbreviations. But if these further letters are generally so monotonous that it is superfluous to reproduce them in detail, the fault does not lie with the writer, but may be ascribed to the uniformity of his life. For his supposition that the section might be compelled to remain in Pontfaverger until the spring proved correct.

In vain the brothers made efforts to procure release from this empty monotony. "On 26.11. we went to Charleville with a wireless officer from my old battalion who had to go to G.H.Q. Wilhelm used the opportunity to have a talk with Major Siegerts, who is in charge of aviation affairs there, and see if we could not get a transfer to some place where there was a decent amount of work to do. But Major S. gave it as his opinion that this tedious trench warfare was going on along the whole western front, while he had no say in the affairs of the eastern front."

Flying suffered from the unfavourable weather. Again and again the diary-letter begins with: "Still this dismal fog." "It is snowing or raining all the time." Nevertheless the log book of the two brothers shows that they made no fewer than thirty-one flights over the enemy, with a total distance of about four thousand three hundred kilometres from Nov. 13th, 1914—the first day after the last quoted letter that they were able to fly—until March 27th, 1915 when they had to part company. The significance of such an achievement at this unfavourable time of the year is clearly shown by statistics contained in a latter of Jan 4th, 1915, wherein it is stated that of the various officers of Section 13 Wilhelm had made sixty-one flights over the enemy since the beginning of the war, Oswald himself forty-two—although he has the last to join the section—Sander twenty-seven, Karstedt twenty-two and Beckers twenty.

Both the log book and the letters show that only in November was artillery spotting the main purpose of their flights; later on reconnaissances and front patrols are always given as their work, with isolated bombing raids. The task of photographing the enemy's positions when out on reconnaisance flights is recorded as an innovation, while we also learn that from February onwards Boelcke often had to fly to the neighbouring 12th reserve corps.

On Jan. 21st he writes: "Our flights over the enemy since Christmas are: 24th, one and a half hours, 25th and 30th and Jan 6th, one hour each, 12th, four hours, and 18th, two hours. It was impossible to do any more flying on account of the persistent rain and gales. Whenever the weather was anything like possible, we made at least some sort of effort to have a look behind the enemy's lines. Our flying is not much use at present as our armies show no intention of wanting to make an advance. We have been facing one another for months, and each side knows the enemy's positions well. There is nothing to reconnoitre in the way of flank thrusts, outflanking movements, bringing up large bodies of reserves, etc., as in active warfare. The only purpose of our flights is to give the range to the artillery, but as we do not want to advance at the moment, our guns are not firing a great many rounds. In this phase of hostilities it is quite enough if a machine has a peep behind the enemy's lines every now and then, just to see if everything remains unchanged."

We see signs of the later Boelcke, who was always wanting the best and most modern machine, when Lieut. Parschau, a Darmstadt acquaintance, paid a visit to Pontfaverger on Nov. 11th, 1914, with his small Fokker biplane. Boelcke decided that he must have such a machine, and he went to Rethel on November 26th to obtain one. "I am sorry to say that I did not get my Fokker, because the only one there was reserved for another officer. But they have ordered me a new machine from the factory. I am delighted, as the Fokker's speed, climbing capacity and manageability make it very suitable for artillery spotting and short flights. Then we shall not be so dependant on the weather. When a favourable hour comes, we can use it, whereas we have to have at least two hours good weather with our old machine, because it climbs so slowly."—And in his entry of Dec. 9th: "I got my Fokker from Rethel yesterday. It is a monoplane, with a French rotary engine located forward; it is about half the size of a Taube. That is the very latest machine, and now I have flown every type of machine built in Germany. I got into it straight away in Rethel and flew here—it goes wonderfully in the air and is very easy to fly. So now I have two machines—the big biplane for longer flights and the little Fokker for artillery flights, etc. Both my children are now resting peaceably together in one tent—as it was difficult to make room for them both, the small one is dug in a bit, with his tail under the big fellow's wing. The Fokker is my big Christmas present, about which I am as delighted as a child."

*10.12.14.* Yesterday I gave my new Fokker a lot of exercise, so as to get accustomed to the machine. I made four flights above the aerodrome in the morning, and in the afternoon I took Wilhelm for a trip to Rethel, where I wanted to get some oil—the rotary engine is so particular that it will only run on castor oil. I also got a lot of practice today by running about energetically over the aerodrome. The band happened to be playing there, so that it was almost like a musical ride for me. First I took Captain Aulock (the adjutant of the munition column who always has horses for us when Wilhelm and I want a ride) up and then Plaskuda, the long fellow from the telephones, who was so delighted that each time I wanted to land he called out: "Another turn! Another turn, please! I'll stand you a bottle of champagne!"

Not only did Boelcke often take brother-officers up; his good nature prompted him to give a flight to his batman, to whom he thus afforded great pleasure, and he was ready to oblige total strangers. "Not long ago I took up a Landwehr man who always watched my flights with such longing eyes. He found it a bit uncanny when he got up aloft, but when he came down again, he pitched the tale to his friends, telling them that he would get a thrashing from his wife if she ever came to hear of it, but that he would not mind that because the flight was so lovely. The consequence was that about twenty Landwehr men told me they would like to go up, and they were quite sad when I replied: "No, boys, it can't be managed."

In November the two brothers looked round for a larger house, as their present one seemed too cramped for winter quarters; their house-warming took the form of a reception, at which their section commander was present. "It grows more and more evident that we are making arrangements for a long stay here. They are building expensive concrete hangars for the base machines in Rethel, and we are to have wooden sheds for ours instead of our tents." And again: "We are now arranging to get the exercise necessary to prevent us returning from the war with tummies like town-councillors. We are instituting hare-hunting, and almost every day we go for rides on the horses that Captain Aulock always has ready for us. That's what 'c'est la guerre' now looks like in our part of the world."

26.12.14. We had our party on Christmas Eve. It was very festive; we were all soldiers, with the exception of the nursing sisters, most of whom were so touched that they burst into tears. We arrived rather late, because we took off in the afternoon to do a reconnaissance round Sillery to the south east of Rheims. Everyone was rather excited, because they thought the French would profit by our Christmas holiday mood to make a big attack. They tried it on with a neighbouring corps. They gave us a lot of big gun noise on the

24th and 25th, but our people did not let it disturb their celebrations.

In the evening we had the men's party first; we distributed a lot of gifts that had come in. Then we officers had a
very nice party for ourselves. Jaenicke, who was Father
Christmas, composed some jolly rhymes. Unfortunately he is
leaving us to-morrow, to rejoin his regiment in the line.
Ledebur left us some time ago; he was transferred to a new
section at Antwerp. I am sorry about it; they were the two
nicest of our comrades. But our heaviest loss is our C.O.,
who is going to H.Q. as a staff officer. Streccius was always
very friendly to both of us, and we worked splendidly with
him.

We shall also have to part from our good friends of the
telephones; they are off to Warmeriville, which is, however,
only eight kilometers away. We found a good home with
them at the time when things were not too comfortable for
us in the section. But now there is a much more friendly
atmosphere in our section.

Yesterday we made an extra distribution of presents to
our four mechanics, two batmen and the workshop foreman
from the eight parcels sent by Dessau friends. It was not so
easy to get rid of the woollen things. All the men are so richly equipped with them that many of them simply refuse to
wash their stockings; they just throw them away when they
have worn them a few times. You have no idea what stupid
quantities of woollen things have been sent to the front.
There are two rooms in Nogent that are crammed full of
these things, because nobody wants them. I only hope there
will not be a revenge for this senseless squandering if the war
goes on for a long time, as it now almost looks likely to do.

We too have been overwhelmed with a profusion of presents from all friends and relations. We are now living just too uppishly, and our only worry is lest our stomachs may get too flabby. Please do not send me anything more at present—we are amply and richly provided with everything we want. The only thing you might send me is a few of mother's cakes from time to time—there is no one who understands the fine art of baking so well as our little mother.

Oswald Boelcke received the First Class of the Iron Cross on the Emperor's birthday, 1915. Decorated with it, he went home to Dessau with Wilhelm for his first war leave.

*14.3.1915.* While the 8th corps continues to be involved in severe fighting, deep peace still prevails in our part of the world. You will hardly be able to imagine that, but here are a few proofs: our men have started playing football—they have made a sports ground close to the hangars, with spring boards, parallel bars, etc.—a staff doctor has got a cinema put up so that the men coming out of the trenches can enjoy a hearty laugh and thus relieve their nerves—when we went off to a conference with the artillery a while ago, I saw a proper parade ground at Epoye, where the men were drilled in presenting arms and practised shooting at targets; not far from the village some drums and fifes were having a regular practice, just like they do at the 'Goose Wall' in Dessau. Everything is quite springlike here. I go for a lot of walks in the woods and fields, always accompanied by Wolf. Who is Wolf? I shall betray the secret to you, but please do not tell Ibi, as I do not want him to be jealous. Wolf is a lovely big sheepdog that Biebers gave me; my batman brought him from Berlin a week ago. We have a whole lot of halfstarved dogs that have taken up their abode with us, but that is not the same thing—my dog must be my friend, on whom I can rely. I shall now confess that when I was home on leave I firmly intended to take Ibi back with me, but when I saw how fond mother had grown of the dog, I could not bring myself to take him away from you.

*26.3.15.* Although we are now on very good terms with our brother-officers (with the exception of two or three who play up to our chief a lot and perhaps put him against us), our relations with the chief have grown continually more unpleasant. There was a sort of little war between us, but naturally we have resigned ourselves to the inevitable, for duty is duty. But when not so long ago the chief wanted to separate us brothers who have flown together successfully for six months (i.e. put Wilhelm with another pilot and me with another observer) and could give no answer when Wilhelm asked him: "Why?" (he only wanted to give us a demonstration of his omnipotence) we went on strike. We reported the matter at H.Q. and asked for a transfer to another section. His Excellency must have then said a few things to our Captain, because all of a sudden he caved in and now leaves us in peace. We did not want more than that. I flew with Wilhelm again today. But the situation is by no means pleasant, and we hope we can both get away from here soon.

*4.4.15.* A sad Easter Day for me! Wilhelm has been trans-ferred to the Aviation Reserve Section in Posen and has already left. Our C.O. managed to twist the business in such a way that Wilhelm alone was transferred, while I was left here. Naturally I put in another request for a transfer at once, although the captain threatened that he would have me sent to the infantry in the trenches if I did. I don't mind if he does—I only want to get away from here! I shall have to see how to manage it on my own account, as the captain—and H.Q., apparently—do not mean to let me go.

Meanwhile the doctor was kind enough to discover faint murmurs in my bronchial tubes and sent me to a convalescent home for three weeks. My address from Tuesday will be, Field Hospital 1, Château Porcien, near Rethel. My unexpressed hopes are that I shall find it easier to get to another section from there. At present I am only too glad to turn my back on Pontfaverger and the chief of the 13th section.

*Château Porcien, 7.4. 15.* It is silly and boring here. I continually go for long walks with Wolf and am delighted to see how beautifully he can scramble up a wooden fence—that is more or less my only pleasure. We have to simply fritter away our time here. My cure is supposed to consist of swallowing Ems Pastilles and inhalations, but I have not seen anything of the latter yet. The principal event of the day is the 'social gathering' in the evening, which means that the doctors, several officers from the column and 'we patients' swill beer together and talk more or less intelligently—I soon cleared off yesterday evening. As the post has already gone, I shall now play the postillon myself and ride over to Rethel (nine kilometres away) to post this letter there. I want to let you know at once that I am going on all right here.

The next letter, written by Boelcke from Warmeriville on April 24th, shows that he soon got over his bitterness at the change in his circumstances and finally felt himself quite comfortable in Château Porcien:

"Last Sunday I left Château Porcien quite suddenly. It was

really quite nice and jolly in the company of the doctors; on the day that I was discharged I flew straight across from here to the hospital and waved them a greeting from above. But there was no use in staying on there. I only went there because I hoped I should find an easier way to get transferred to another section. The assistant doctor wanted to send me to the Harz for a fortnight, but his chief made rotten excuses to keep me here. So I simply went to his room and asked him for definite information, whereupon it came out that he had orders from H.Q. not to let me go under any circumstances. General von Pritzelwitz had told him that it was bad enough having Wilhelm taken away from the corps and he wanted to keep me at least. So it was useless for me to remain there; I asked to be sent back to the section, and have been here since Sunday, because No. 13 was transferred to Warmeriville during my absence. But I hope I shan't stay here long! I am going on spinning my plans. The only nice thing is that I found my dear old telephone people here."

Boelcke had to endure only another week in the section. On Sunday April 25th he was able to announce to his parents triumphantly; "Hurrah! I have been transferred to Section 62, which is being reorganised in Döberitz. To-morrow I am off to Berlin to report to the flying corps' inspectorate. As I shall be there two or three weeks, I shall certainly be able to see you again."

An interesting supplement and confirmation of the above incident is furnished by a letter written by Staff-Surgeon-Major Arendt, who was then in charge of the hospital at Château Porcien, to Boelcke's parents after his death. "I made his acquaintance when he was sent to my field hospital in the spring of 1915. He was in low spirits because he had been separated from his brother, but even so he might well have been proud of the fact that the chief of the staff took the trouble to come to me and discuss his immediate future in the most appreciative terms. It was not easy to get on intimate terms with our 'little Boelcke,' as we called him, because he evidently had no great opinion of medicine men. But the ice soon thawed, and this silent, serious-minded young man became in his own fashion the cheeriest of all who shared those beautiful spring days and jovial evenings. Good music always put him in a happy frame of mind, and what a master of dancing he showed himself when he part-nered our chief dispenser! We gradually grew more intimate with him. A photograph that each of us will cherish shows him with Captain Przyskowski on one of his last evenings. Soon afterwards he left us, completely reconciled to his lot—so thoroughly reconciled, in fact, that he appeared over our little town in his machine that same afternoon and waved his greetings to us. That was on a Sunday; on the following Sunday he paid us another aerial visit and also came a long way round in a car to say goodbye because he was off to a new sphere of activity."

A leaflet that Boelcke had reproduced on the duplicating machine during those days of enforced idleness in Château Porcien and subsequently distributed to all troublesome questioners may be aptly adduced here as his contribution to the humours of the war.

It is impossible to pass over entirely the less pleasant facts of the temporary strained relations between the two broth-ers and the other officers of the section and the conflict with their commanding officer, even though I have omitted their unedifying details.

With regard to the first of these facts, the strained relations reached such a tension at one time that the Boelcke brothers preferred to associate with the officers of another corps. This is in itself a proof of the deleterious effect of the enforced inactivity and boredom during the war winter of 1914—15 on comradely relations. The men who stood by one another to the death in the days of battle wasted their energy in petty bickerings and jealousies. It seems truly ironical that Oswald Boelcke, who was always such a model of ungrudging comradeship of the air, should have had his irrepressible enthusiasm misrepresented as selfish ambition.

But in the second place the open conflict with his commanding officer and the way in which he severed his connection with the section he had served faithfully and successfully for seven months shows that Oswald Boelcke's star did not climb smoothly to its zenith. He experienced bitter checks and disappointments, past which he had to fight his way.

But from now onward his path lay free and clear before him. His rise to fame and victorious career began when he was sent to Section 62 in Douai.

PLEASE!!!

Do not ask me anything about flying.

You will find the usual questions answered below.

1.  Sometimes it is dangerous, sometimes it is not.
2.  Yes, the higher we fly, the colder it is.
3.  Yes, we notice the fact by freezing when it is colder
4.  Flying height 2,000–2,500 metres.
5.  Yes we can see things at that height, although not so well as at 100 metres.
6.  We cannot see well through the telescope because it waggles.
7.  Yes, we have dropped bombs.
8.  Yes, an old woman was supposed to have been injured and we put the wind up some transport columns.
9.  The observer sits in the front and can see a bit.
10. We cannot talk to each other because the engine makes too much noise.
11. We have not got a telephone in the machine but we are provided with electric light.
12. No, we do not live in caves.

AIRCRAFT DEFENCES AGAINST TROUBLESOME QUESTIONERS

# CHAPTER IV

# *The Development of War and Scout Flying: Retrospects and Prospects*

THE object of this survey*—which gives Boelcke's flying career its proper place within the frame of the general development of German war and scout flying—is to draw the attention of the reader who may be unacquainted with the details to the main points necessary for his comprehension of the letters adduced in the previous chapter and those quoted in subsequent ones. At the same time it should show to what extent Boelcke was dependant on this general development and to what extent he promoted it or exercised a decisive influence upon it.

The first eight months of his war flying career which have been depicted in the previous letters fall into the period when German war flying was in its infancy. We hardly know whether to describe this as a modest or a proud infancy.

It was certainly modest in regard to the equipment and organisation of the fliers as well as the tasks they were called upon to do. But there was also cause for pride in the esteem and value which the new air arm quickly gained when it far surpassed the modest expectations generally formed of it in military circles.

* The author acknowledges with gratitude the use he has made of Hans Ritter's work "Der Luftkrieg" (published in Leipzig, 1926).

In contrast to France, where the Ministry of War was not long in recognising the aeroplane as the 'fifth arm' for future warfare, the German military authorities were very sceptical of it. A 'provisional flying school' was indeed established at Döberitz in 1911, from which flying stations were formed at Döberitz, Strassburg and Metz in 1911. The pilots from these stations took part in the imperial manoeuvres, but when the big Army Bill of 1913 was passed, nothing further was done for the development of the youthful 'air arm' than the transformation of the flying stations—which had meanwhile increased in number—into four flying battalions. These flying battalions were under the inspectorate of flying, which in its turn took orders from the General Inspectorate of Military Communications. This body was utterly alien in its essentials to the new flying formations and consequently the newly created 'flying troop' was classed with the communication troops through sheer misunderstanding of its real nature.

The General Staff, however, contained a few farseeing men, such as Colonel Ludendorff and Captain Thomsen, who recognised the significance of aviation and prognosticated its developments, but they were unable to force acceptance of their views on the Ministry of War. Moreover in other military circles, the view continued to predominate that this new and purely technical creation could be utilised at the most as an aid to cavalry reconnaissances, but that for reconnoitring purposes the aeroplane was inferior to the cavalry for the reason that a cavalryman could ride by night and through fog, whereas the machine could only fly by bright daylight. Nevertheless they considered that aeroplanes might certainly have their use for long distance reconnaissances.

Thus the outbreak of war found the German air service still in the initial stages of its development. Its aviators went to the front for the sole purpose of supplementing the reconnaissance activities of cavalry patrols by acting as aerial patrols.

In view of this underestimation of the airmen at the outset the lucid reports they sent in during the German forward movement created such a surprising effect that the higher military authorities were inclined to treat them very sceptically at times and often deemed it necessary to await confirmation from ground reconnaissances. But the results of these aerial reconnaissances grew more copious daily and often proved of the greatest value, as, for example, when they were able to report the presence of bodies of enemy troops that had remained behind during a retreat. Consequently a complete change of opinion took place as regards the valuation of the new arm. What in peace had been deemed the impossible took place in the few weeks of mobile warfare—the airmen absolutely ousted the cavalry as a means for long distance reconnaissances.

When the transition to trench warfare took place, the strategic long distance reconnaissances carried out by the airmen came almost to an end as soon as the movements of troops behind the lines were finished and these reinforcements were immobilised in the trenches. They were replaced by tactical reconnaissances, the objects of which were to ascertain details of the enemy positions, such as the alterations they underwent when strengthened or extended, from which the enemy's intentions might possibly be deduced, etc. For this work the eye of the observer—who found it impossible to memorise all the details amid the confusion of the trenches and enter them accurately on his map—was replaced by aerial photography; the plate of the camera recorded everything, and the photograph revealed every detail when examined under a magnifying glass.

One of the most important tasks of a tactical reconnaissance was the location from the air of the positions of heavy masked batteries placed too far behind the lines to be discovered by ground observers. To this was soon attached the further task of directing the fire of the airman's own artillery on to the located positions of enemy batteries by coloured lights, as described in the letter of Oct. 25th, 1914. Subsequently this information was conveyed by wireless telegraphy. In any case artillery spotting was the chief activity of the Boelcke brothers during the winter of 1914–15 as well as the first collaboration of airmen with ground troops.

But although the fulfilment of all these various tasks (long and close reconnaissances, photography, artillery spotting) caused the air arm to be recognised as indispensable as early on as the first few months of trench warfare, it still remained a technical accessory for the ground troops. The first opportunity for active, independent intervention was afforded by the incipient bomb warfare, i.e. by the dropping of bombs from the machine. Boelcke practised this form of warfare on occasions at Pontfaverger, but the idea of an attack on defenceless victims from the security of the heights did not appeal to his chivalrous nature. He never liked bombing operations, and there is consequently no doubt that he underestimated their military importance.

His inclinations were for honourable, open combat. This was out of the question for the German airmen in the winter of 1914–15, for the simple reason that they were without any suitable weapons with which to fight their opponents. In the beginning their sole arms were the army pistols or carbines with which they could certainly defend themselves in the event of a forced landing on enemy territory, but it was impossible to attack an opponent of the air with them or even to defend themselves against him if he was better armed. Thus we read in the letter of Sept. 10th, 1914 that even a Boelcke was compelled to take to hurried flight when chased by two French aeroplanes over Bar-le-Duc.

The machine gun was the ideal weapon for the aeroplane. Even before the war there was a suggestion of arming aeroplanes in this fashion, but it was rejected on the grounds that an aerial patrol on reconnaissance flights was as little called upon to fight as a cavalry patrol.

The retribution exacted for this omission was increased by the fact that the French military authorities had made extensive experiments in this direction before the war, so that it was not long before they armed all their machines during the course of hostilities. It is doubtful whether the French aircraft actually carried machine guns during the initial period of active warfare or whether the German airmen who came under their fire mistook their self-loading carbines for such—but in any case all French machines were thus armed after October, 1914.

Even at such an early period as the winter battle of the Champagne in February 1915 the French possessed in addition to their heavy double-seater Farmans and Nieuports a number of light singleseater Nieuport and Morane scouts that carried a pivotable machine-gun mounted on a sort of balcony-like projection. A new invention enabled these latter to fire straight ahead without damaging their own propellers. Their superior speed and climbing capacity made these 'avions de chasse' fearsome opponents for the slower German machines, even when at least partially armed with the self-loading carbine, and the consequence was that the the German airmen fled precipitately as soon as ever such a well-armed foeman appeared. They were unable to carry out their reconnaissances, while the French machines were in a position to direct the fire of their batteries and drop their bombs behind our lines unmolested. Thus the German leaders were deprived of what was practically the only means of reconnoitring in trench warfare.

This intolerable state of affairs did not change until a firm hand took sole charge of military aviation and reorganised it completely. A cabinet order of March 11th, 1915, created the special post of a 'Chief of War Aviation,' who assumed authority over all flying and airship units in the field and on home service. Then only was the unnatural association of the air service with the communication troops abolished, while the inspectorate of flying in Berlin which had hitherto controlled the various flying sections on active service was now in its turn subordinated to the new chief. As far as their actual service at the front was concerned the flying sections still remained under the orders of the generals commanding the army corps or armies to which they were allotted, but for each of these commands an 'Aviation Staff Officer' was appointed. He was the immediate superior of the flying sections and acted as an advisory expert to the general in command when questions of their utilisation were discussed.

Thomsen, who was then a major on the general staff, was appointed chief of war aviation. General von Hoeppner, who was subsequently* appointed general commanding the air forces, characterises this man to whom German aviation owes so much in his work, "Germany's War in the Air," as follows: "He was well acquainted with the essential features of aviation through his peace-time service and cherished a deep inner conviction of the importance of the new arm and its vast possibilities of development. His imperturbable, clear outlook was directed presciently into the future. He carried out with a most unusual energy the measures he recognised as necessary; by nature he was a fighter who loved activity and shrank from no obstacles, and his steelhard resolution proved a driving force to all personalities who collaborated in his work."

The first effects of the new epoch now opening out for war aviation began to make their appearance just at the time when Boelcke went to Douai to join Section 62.

One of the first endeavours of the new chief was directed towards the evolution of a new machine with a more powerful engine (150 H.P.) and a machine-gun to replace the defence-less B. machine, which Section 62 were using when they first went to Douai. The result of his efforts was the so-called C. machine, which was also differentiated from all previous types by the fact that the pilot occupied the front seat instead of the observer. Its pivotable machine-gun was built in to the observer's seat; it could be fired backward, upward and sideways, but not forward because the pilot's head, the engine and the propeller blocked that line of fire.

This new machine represented a long step forward. Its inmates were no longer weaponless; they did not need to break off a reconnaissance at the appearance of an enemy, but could remain to fight a defensive battle. Not only were they in a position to carry out all their own reconnaissance work, but they could also obstruct enemy aircraft's reconnaissances and prevent them from dropping bombs behind the German lines.

Yet the C. machine was not a fighting type in the true

sense of the word. It was unsuited for aggressive tactics because its machine gun could not be fired in the direction of the line of flight; this meant that when attacking an opponent the machine had to be put into a turn before its observer was able to fire. The turn was bound to widen the distance from the enemy to some greater or lesser extent, so that its fire was only effective for a short period, after which contact with the enemy was lost.

Boelcke was given the first of the new machines allotted to No 62. In it he won his first victory on July 4th, 1915, his gunner being Lieut Wühlisch, of a hussar regiment. Boelcke's wonderful skill in the air enabled him to offset the machine's clumsiness in attack.

Meanwhile success had crowned the efforts of the new air chief to produce a fighting machine that should be a match for the 'avions de chasse.' Fokker, the aircraft designer, who was in Schwerin at the time, contrived to solve the problem of how to fire a machine gun in the direction of the line of flight (i.e. through the circle made by the propeller) without damaging the propeller. His solution was, in fact, far more perfect than the French device, because he brought out an invention which enabled the pilot to use a rigid machine gun mounted in the line of flight and thus did away with the necessity for a special gunner. Consequently Fokker designed a light single-seater monoplane that was far superior to all other machines (including the French types) in speed, climbing capacity and agility.

In May, 1915, Fokker paid a visit to the front with two of these machines—the so-called E. type. He first demonstrated them to the Crown Prince at Stenay, near Verdun, after which he made a long stay at Douai with Lieut Parschau, who flew the second machine. There he was daily in the company of Boelcke, whose quick mind soon grasped the fact that this was the first machine really suitable for agressive action. When Fokker departed, he left the machine he had been flying (E. 3) behind for Boelcke, who was therefore the first pilot to fly the new Fokker single-seater as a fighting machine.

A new era in war aviation began when this novel fighting single-seater first made its appearance at the front. The historical importance of the letters of Boelcke which we reproduce in the later chapters of this work is that they depict the history of scout flying from its inception to the formation of the Jagdstaffels. The rest of this survey may therefore be limited to giving a brief exposition of the facts necessary to an understanding of those letters by summarising the main outlines of the development of scout flying that is described in them and Boelcke's share in the same.

When the new E. machine first took the air, it came as a complete novelty in the art of warfare. No one had any experience of the best means to exploit it advantageously, but with the instinct of a true flying genius Boelcke was the first to sense the art of aerial warfare. Having made this discovery, he developed it to such a pitch of perfection that his tactics became the standard ones for aerial duels and remained so until the end of the war. In this fashion he made his mark on scout flying in general.

At first the Fokker single-seaters were distributed among the various sections, their task being to keep the air clear over the German lines and obstruct the enemy's reconnaissances and bombing raids. Their scope was soon extended when they were given the further duties of acting as escorts to our own reconnaissance and artillery machines that worked over the enemy's lines. But at the beginning of their activity these Fokkers were actually forbidden to fly beyond their own lines for fear of the secret falling into the enemy's hands if one of them was brought down. As shown in his letter of July 16th, 1915, Boelcke defied this veto and went to look for opponents over their own lines when the spirit moved him. From his habit of going off at random to hunt the enemy we derive the term 'Jagdflieger' (scout flier), which was taken over for official use when the Jagdstaffels came into existence at a later period. Boelcke was, however, the first 'Jagdflieger' because he deliberately sought out his opponents, whereas other pilots only fought the enemies they chanced to meet. Thus he anticipated the offensive aerial warfare for which this new weapon was predestined.

Gradually the distribution of the Fokkers among flying sections that were stationed a long way behind the lines came to be recognised as unpractical. At the beginning of the Verdun offensive Captain Haehnelt, the first staff officer of the air units attached to the 5th army, decided to employ a portion of his Fokkers as independant advanced forces in the east (Arvillers), centre (Sivry) and west (Bantheville) of the Verdun front. These machines did not use temporary aerodromes as they had done on former occasions such as, for example, during the counter-attack on Tahure (see Boelcke's-letter of Nov. 2nd, 1915, page 154) but were quartered at permanent stations. The new formations, consisting solely of scout fliers, were known as 'groups' at the time—a designation which may easily lead to confusion because an amalgamation of several Jadgstaffels were also termed a 'group' at a later period.

In a historical sense the groups of scouts formed at the Verdun front may be regarded as a preliminary step towards the later Jagdstaffels. As soon as they severed their connections with the sections and obtained release from the essentially defensive duties they performed in them they were employed for offensive action against enemy air forces. Their mission on the Verdun front was not merely to keep the air free over our lines, but to fight for the entire supremacy of the air.

It cannot be ascertained with any degree of certainty whether the three scout groups on the Verdun front were formed successively or simultaneously. From a statement by Lt-Col. Haelnelt it is, however, certain that the group at Sivry came into existence at Boelcke's urgent request and that the aerodrome in a meadow on a bank of the Meuse (chosen by Boelcke himself) was the nearest to the front of those used by the three groups. In any case Boelcke was one of the first to be entrusted with the leadership of an independant group of scouts.

The next stage in the development of scout flying was reached when the groups began to take shape as more permanent formations. In June 1916 Boelcke received orders to form his own Staffel at Sivry (see the letter of June 12th, 1916). He could not lead it himself, as a special order from the emperor, issued at the end of June, forbade him to fly personally until further notice because he was recognised as irreplaceable for scout flying purposes. He was sent on his mission to the east instead.

The first regular Jagdstaffels were not formed until after Boelcke's return from the East at the end of August, 1916. The latter portion of this book will show what he achieved— not merely as a fighter, but also as an organiser, instructor and example during his leadership of Jagdstaffel No. 2, on which the honourable title of 'Boelcke Staffel' was bestowed by the emperor not long after his death. Boelcke did not survive to witness the further development of scout flying, which reached its pinnacle when four Jagdstaffels were merged together into a squadron under the leadership of his greatest pupil, Manfred von Richthofen. But his fighting tactics remained in force until the end of the war, while the spirit and example of their pastmaster inspired all future heroes of the air in the sense of the vow that Lt-Col. Thomsen laid on Boelcke's grave for all of them: "I will be a Boelcke!"

# CHAPTER V

# *The Beginnings of Aerial Warfare*

THE beginning of May, 1915, saw the mustering in Döberitz, under the leadership of Captain Kastner, of the new 62nd section, which was originally destined for attachment to the 12th Reserve Corps. "Our captain," Boelcke wrote from Pontfaverger on May 16th, "is very sympathetic to me by reason of his personality and knowledge; the difference in our ages and ranks will certainly be an obstacle to any near intimacy, but it is of great value to have such a man as my superior."

Among the pilots of this new section there was also a certain Lance-sergeant Immelmann, a reserve N.C.O. He had been a cadet in Dresden, but when he entered the railway battalion he passed into the reserve before obtaining promotion to commissioned rank in order to prosecute his technical studies. Although accepted for the air service at the beginning of the war, he did not pass his third set of tests until March 26th, 1915, after which he served in the Champagne, where he won the reputation of being a specialist in the art of crashing his machine on landing.

Boelcke paid a visit to Dessau on his first trial flight in the L.V.G. machine B.308, which had been allotted to him. As all the meadows were flooded at the time, he was unable to

119

land and could only circle round his home, where Ibi sat in the garden, staring up at the aeroplane humming overhead and blissfully unconscious that it contained his master. His observer on this flight was Lieut. Aschenborn, who subsequently flew with him on all his flights from Douai until the middle of June.

Boelcke was in need of a new batman. He chose a trusty Hessian, whose face he liked, from the ranks of the men called up to form a new reserve regiment of guards in Döberitz. This man—a certain Ludwig Fischer—was reluctant to enter his service at first, but Boelcke simply thrust Wolf's leash into his hand, and therewith the bargain was concluded. This chance meeting led to a fine, firm bond between man and man, of a type that is not often seen. Fischer looked after his 'lieutenant' and later his 'captain' with a devotion such as only a mother lavishes on her child; he accompanied his coffin from Cambrai to Dessau, subsequently serving until the end of the war as batman to Martin Boelcke, the younder brother who was destined to gain honourable mention in despatches of August 28th, 1918 for his leadership of a battalion of the Schwerin Grenadiers. Fischer still remains on terms of faithful affection with the Boelcke family, and this book owes much to his vivid statements.

On Ascension Day, (the day after Boelcke had obtained a newer type of machine (B.712) from Johannistal to replace his old one which proved unstaisfactory) the new section set off for the front, reaching its destination on May 15th. This, to Boelcke's surprise, proved to be Pontfaverger!

But on May 7th he was able to write to his parents: "Hurrah! My section is going to the 8th army corps, probably to Douai. I am delighted,...a new district, where there will be something doing!"

*Douai, 22.5.15.* We have now been three days here, after an eighteen hours' railway journey from Pontfaverger. I hope we shall soon have plenty to do here, but so far the weather has washed us out—fog and low-lying clouds every day. So we have had time to settle down comfortably, practise in our machines, etc.

Life here is quite different to what it was in Pontfaverger. The town reminds me of Zerbst; there is a modern residential quarter and an old part with the houses of the former gentry, ruins of a wall, an old town hall, etc. It is undamaged, and the greater part of the inhabitants have remained. They have a very good time, except for the fact that they are not allowed outside the town on account of espionage.

All shops are open, as well as the hotels, public houses, etc. But we have to pay for everything in cash; requisitioning is forbidden. So far I have been in a café every day with two comrades, Ensign Immelmann and Lieut. von Teubern, both of whom are Royal Saxons.

Generally speaking, one would hardly realise here that the heaviest fighting is going on twenty kilometres away. The French have gained a lot of ground in the sector occupied by our corps. A couple of days ago all the inhabitants were brewing coffee for the refreshment of their liberators, but now they are singing small again. We have now such strong forces here that it is absolutely impossible for the enemy to break through.

We have a fine aerodrome, which we share with Section 20. It is about half an hour from here in a car. Our men live on the aerodrome; we officers are quartered in jolly little villas in the town—always two or three of us together. I share a house with Lieut. von Wühlisch, a little fellow from the

Stolp Hussars; we have two nice rooms apiece, and our quarters are quite close to the mess.

## A FIGHT IN THE TRENCHES

*Douai, 25.5.15.* The day before yesterday I was by chance witness of a grand military spectacle, of the type that I as an airman never get an opportunity to see. As I was off flying duty in the afternoon, I went to the artillery observation post with our captain. About 4 p.m. we reached Vimp le Petit, whence we had a walk of about half an hour to the post. We had only just arrived there when a red light went up from the French trenches to signal: "Shorten the range of the fire from the trenches." I was then able to watch the following events through the telescope from a distance of eight hundred metres away.

Very soon after the signal the Frenchmen came out from their trenches all along the line—massed more thickly than I could have possibly imagined—about a brigade, I judged. We could only admire their pluck. They came on in a thick line, headed by their officers; there were some coloured troops among them, which I recognised from their baggy trousers. They all went forward in step. Our people held their fire while they advanced four hundred metres of the intervening seven hundred; then our first shrapnels started. As our artillery had the range exactly, they scored hits at once; then the first shells from our heavy artillery came along.

The fire was now beginning to be murderous; the din was such that we could not hear each other speak at two paces distance. Again and again the shells burst in their serried ranks and tore holes in them. Nevertheless they carried on their advance with the same courage, closing the gaps at once.

Now our infantry also came into action. Our people stood up in their trenches, exposed right down to their hips, and shot like mad. After three or four minutes the attack was checked in several places, i.e. several groups and columns came on while others hung back. A quarter of an hour later the French reached our trenches on the left wing (which I could see), shot and stabbed downwards and then jumped in. Now we saw the scuffle quite plainly: heads bobbing up here and there, butt ends of rifles swung about (apparently they were smacking away at each other all the time) and gleaming bayonets. On the right wing the attack seemed to proceed at a slower pace and almost came to a standstill. Here and there in the centre we saw oncoming groups, at which the artillery blazed away mightily. We also observed figures running about distractedly, but they could not get away from our artillery. All the ground was covered with dark dots—dead or wounded that had remained behind.

One battery of our field artillery showed up particularly smartly. There were four guns in covered positions about one hundred metres behind our trenches. As soon as the attack started these fellows lugged their guns out of their positions and blazed away in the open, although they were under heavy fire. In a little while two of the guns got it so hot that they were out of action, but the other two fired away vigorously until the end.

After a quarter of an hour of hand to hand fighting the French started to retreat. First one, then two and three climbed out of the trench, stared about distractedly and then bolted. As soon as some of them had got away, between ten and twenty others came out, then a whole lot more. Finally the rest climbed out and fled. Again and again the French officers tried to rally their men and resume the attack. But in vain—more and more broke away and sought salvation in flight. Many of them fell, more, I imagine than in the attack because our infantry came out of the trenches and picked them off at their ease.

In the centre the French had got up to within fifty metres of the trenches and could now advance no further. When the retreat began on the left wing, several of them noticed it and scuttled back like scared hens. But nearly all of them were caught. I saw six fellows running—bang! a heavy shell came down close to them. They all disappeared; the smoke cleared away, and there were only four of them—bang! another shell plumped down. Only one was left, and our infantry got him.

How complete was their defeat is shown by the following incident. Suddenly four fellows got up, waved their caps, swung their arms about and ran to our trenches. They were hardly inside before about another fifty of them did the same and started to run. That made the rest of the French angry; they must have been afraid that there would be a general surrender. Bang! four well aimed heavy shells came down in the midst of the deserters—I was quite pleased to see these cowardly curs shot by their own side. But the retreat was now general; at 6.45 the main action was over, and afterwards we only saw isolated stragglers running or crawling back. It was vastly interesting for me to experience all this from quite close—one never sees anything of the sort from the air. But it is a great pity that we airmen cannot take part in such fights from above!

But now we have enough to do in any case. Our standing orders are to conduct reconnaissances and photography of the lines, which alter from day to day; we also put our artillery on to the positions of the enemy batteries we have located.

*Douai, 8.6.15.* Things are lively here now. Last week the French attacked almost every day and ran their heads up against us. I flew every day; Aschenborn, my observer, is very smart and takes a lot of trouble. But we hardly notice any signs of war in Douai—we see civilians going for walks, the boys coming back from swimming and the girls from tennis. I go swimming almost every day with several comrades; my batman and Wolf naturally come along too. The chief fun is when we both dive in off the springboard together and Wolf 'rescues' Fischer.

I get on excellently with all my brother-officers here. I am very satisfied with Fischer; it is quite touching the way he looks after Wolf and myself. The former has great need of his care, as he was run down by a car a few days ago; he is hobbling about again now, and barks and growls whenever a car comes along, as he is furious with them all. Ursfeld, my former batman, is now leader of my squad, and is mightily proud of it.

*Douai, 19.6.15.* The devil is still loose on our part of the front. Yesterday the French and English staged a huge attack along a space of thirty kilometres, but they only captured a stretch of about six hundred metres of our positions; the rest of their attack broke down. Our 93rd Dessauers are in the thick of it here.

Our flying activities are also naturally very lively and remunerative. For the last few days I have been flying with Wühlisch, the little hussar fellow, instead of Aschenborn; he is very smart, and his nerves are unimpaired.

*Douai, 24.6.15.* The 8th corps, to which we were attached, has sustained such heavy losses that it had to be withdrawn and allowed to recuperate, but we airmen are stopping on here. My old 6th army corps has come in its place, so that I shall be flying for my old corps under General von Pritzelwitsch again. My old section 13 will be at our aerodrome in a few days—isn't that funny? Unfortunately none of my old acquaintances are with it except Karstedt, but I am very glad I have not to see the old C.O. again; he was transferred some time ago. I am delighted at the idea that my old telephone friends from Pontfaverger will have to come here too.

Yesterday afternoon our commanding general, the Crown Prince of Bavaria, inspected our aerodrome. We now have a collection there of practically every type of machine that our aviation technique has evolved—two sections, (20 and 62) and a squadron of fighting machines. The two sections fly the ordinary biplanes, but we now have a novelty in the form of wireless apparatus, with which we direct our artillery fire instead of the coloured lights formerly employed.

The squadron of fighters has come along because there is more going on here than anywhere else on the western front. They have the most cunning sorts of buses, e.g. a huge fighter with two engines that carries three men and a special bombdropping device—a most colossal ship. Then there are five other fighters armed with machine guns; they are much bigger than the ordinary machine. Besides those there are some little Fokker monoplanes, also with machine guns—every sort of machine that you want, in fact. The squadron has only been up once so far, but the French have never shown themselves since; they have got cold feet apparently.

Here the chronicler must intervene once more. The above enumeration of the machines is correct, but what Boelcke concealed from his parents was the fact that he himself had been flying one of the C. fighters for the last twelve days, wherefore he had chosen for his observer the dashing hussar officer who had already learnt to handle a machine-gun. He likewise hushed up the fact that Fokker himself was then in Douai for the purpose of demonstrating his new single-seater fighter, that he was daily in Fokker's company and already burning with desire to fly the new single-seater.

The obvious reason for this silence is that he did not want to alarm his parents, preferring to give them time to get used to the idea that there were such things as fighting machines.

In reality Boelcke's career of fame commenced on June 15th, 1915, after he had practised with the new machine, C.162, on the 13th and 14th. His log book reports the following fights, all with von Wühlich as observer:

*15.6.15. Fought Condor Biplane near Arras. Enemy went down in glide. Two hundred rounds.*
*16.6.15. 10.20–11.20 a.m. Fight near Neuville. French machine broke away. Engine trouble; returned. Forty rounds.*
*16.6.15. 5.10–6.30 p.m. Fought English Avro Biplane near Lens. Gun jammed after eighty rounds; went down. Four holes in wings.*
*16.6.15. 7.35–8.50 p.m. Fight near Lens. French machine went down.*
*Fight near Arras. French machine went down.*
*Fought five French biplanes near Neuville. One went down, but other four attacked us. Retreated.*
*Eight hundred and eighty rounds.*

Here the log for the second day's flying shows five fights on three flights. This is a proof of the fiery zeal with which Boelcke applied himself to his new work. The log for the following days gives similar reports; moreover the entry for June 24th records for the first time: "Trial flight in Fokker E."

His letters of June 19th and 24th say nothing about these events. Not until the next letter, dated June 30th,—the latter portion of which merits particular attention as shedding light on the improvement of his status and growth of his self-confidence—did he consider his parents sufficiently prepared to receive the whole truth. Then the following letter of July 6th brings the report of his first victory.

*Douai, 30.6.15.* You may perhaps have read in the official communiqué that the German airmen have won the upper hand over the French airmen round Arras way. I helped a bit towards it. The fact is that I have been flying a fighting machine since 14.6.15. It is a biplane with a 150 H.P. engine; the pilot sits in front, while the observer is behind and handles a machine gun that can shoot backward or sideways. As Wühlisch is a smart chap and has been through a machine gun course, I took him as my observer.

As the French tried to obstruct our reconnaissances round Arras by means of fighting machines, we have now got a few of them to protect the section machines when out reconnoitring. When the others take off on artillery flights, etc., I go up with them, fly about in their neighbourhood and protect them from enemy attacks. So if a Frenchman comes along, I pounce on him like a hawk, while our other machine goes on calmly flying and observing. Meanwhile I whack the Frenchman by flying up to him and giving him a good hammering with our machine gun. Those chaps bolt so quickly that it is really glorious. I have whacked about a dozen Frenchmen in this way. It is great fun for me.

My position in our section is quite different from what it was in No 13. There I was to a certain extent overshadowed by Wilhelm; I hardly worried my head about the locality of the flight, the observations or the results of the reconnaissance—Wilhelm did all that, and I seldom had anything to say about it. But everything is quite different here. My former observer always fitted in with my arrangements, and Wühlisch also relies on my greater experience. In conversation I often give advice which is gladly taken by the other observers, who are mostly novices. On occasions, e.g. on our way home I even tell my C.O. that this or that would be better, and he generally realises it. Moreover I feel much more comfortable in this new section as regards my relations with brother-officers, because there is a complete lack of that envy and jealousy of junior pilots that there was in No. 13, and no accusations of selfishness or ambition are brought against any of my actions.

## THE FIRST VICTORY

*Douai, 6.7.15.* On Sunday I succeeded for the first time in carrying a fight through to complete victory. I had orders to protect Lieut. Porr, who was spotting for the artillery, against enemy aircraft. I had hardly started on my way to the front before we saw a French Parasol Monoplane over Liétard that was approaching us from a greater height. As the lower machine is at a disadvantage, we got out of his way; he did not see us, but flew onward and downward. We were delighted to see him, because the French machines have seldom crossed our lines lately and an opponent cannot get away in a glide if he is over our territory.

As soon as he was past us, we started to chase him, but took quite half an hour before we came up with him over Valenciennes. It would seem that he was very late in sighting us. We started to engage him near Valenciennes, where I tried to cut him off. Luckily we were the speedier, so that he was unable to get away from us by turns. As soon as we got close enough, Wühlisch began to pepper him with the machine gun. He defended himself as well as he could, but we remained the aggressors and kept him on the defensive; we were higher and faster, while he was lower and slower, so that he could not possible escape us. He tried to increase the distance between the two machines by all sorts of manoeuvres, but did not succeed—I sat on his neck all the time. It was a glorious business. I hung on close to him, so that Wühlisch could shoot steadily from short range. We could see all the details of his machine quite clearly; we could almost spot every wire on it. The average distance was about one hundred metres, but sometimes I got up to within thirty and forty metres of him, because the great speed at which aeroplanes fly affords no prospects of success except from a very close range.

The whole fight lasted from twenty to twenty-five minutes; in its course we came close to Marchiennes. There were brief intervals in our fire, occasioned by the enemy's turn, jams and reloading of the machine-gun; these I utilised to come up with the Frenchman and get close to him. Our superiority became more and more evident; at last I gained the impression that the enemy had stopped defending himself and nearly given up hope of escape. Shortly before the machine crashed the observer made a typical gesture with his hand, as if to say: "Let us alone; we are beaten and will surrender." But who can trust an aerial opponent in such cases?

Thereupon he went into a glide—I followed close behind. My observer fired another thirty to forty rounds, and then the machine suddenly vanished. I went into a steep glide so as not to lose close contact with him, and then all of a sudden Wühlisch shouted: "he's falling, he's falling!" and whacked my shoulders in his joy. I did not quite trust that Frenchman, because those monoplanes can go into a steep dive that looks very like a fall, and so stared round in astonishment, but could see nothing more. I went down in a glide, and meanwhile Wühlisch told me that the other machine suddenly heeled over and fell vertically into the wood below us.

We dropped down to one hundred metres and scoured the wood for the fallen machine, but could discover no signs of it. Then we decided to land on a meadow close to the wood and look for it. But already soldiers and civilians were pouring into the wood from all sides. They told us that the machine crashed down vertically from a huge height, turned over twice and vanished in the wood. This news was confirmed by a cyclist who had already been on the scene of the crash and said that both inmates were dead.

We climbed out to go and see. On the way we met Captain Bieler, whom I knew from Pontfaverger times; he took us in his car and told us that everyone in the district had followed the fight from below. They were all very excited, especially as the great height at which we flew made it impossible for them to tell which was the German and which the Frenchman.

We found officers, doctors, soldiers, etc., already on the scene of the crash. The machine must have come down vertically from a height of one thousand five hundred to one thousand eight hundred metres. As both the inmates were strapped in, they did not fall out. The full weight of the machine struck a tree; it was smashed to bits, while the inmates, a hussar lieutenant named Tétu and a certain Comte Beauvicourt, were naturally dead—strangely enough the latter was the owner of the wood into which he crashed. The sudden fall is to be explained by the death or mortal wounding of the pilot. The pilot had seven and the observer five bullets wounds. I firmly believe that both died in the air. We found important papers and photos on them, including one of their own machine.

Captain Bieler took us off to lunch, along with four officers from our section who had come along by car in response to a telephone call. In the afternoon we flew several triumphal rounds above the scene of our victory and then went back to Douai. The two Frenchmen were buried in Marchiennes cemetery yesterday with military honours; Wühlisch and I were summoned by the Crown Prince of Bavaria and had to give him a report of our victory. We went to Marchiennes today; the grave is covered with flowers, as is also the scene of the crash, where we found a large red, white and blue bouquet.

I am delighted that Wülhisch has got the I.C. 1st class. He fought and shot splendidly, firing eighty three rounds in all, twenty-seven of which got home on the enemy's machine.

The orders of the day issued by the H.Q. of the 6th army dated July 3rd, 1915 concludes with the words: "I congratulate our valiant airmen on this fine success and hope that their skill and daring will succeed in gaining further superiority and sweeping the air free above our army. Signed Rupprecht, Crown Prince of Bavaria & Royal Bavarian Colonel-General."

The orders of the day from the corps, dated July 5th, 1915, first confer the Iron Cross, 1st class, on Lieut. Wühlisch and then conclude: "I herewith express to the pilot, Lieutenant Boelcke, my special appreciation of the vigour and prudence he has shown once more and grant him a commendation. Signed; von Pritzelwitz."

The continuation of the letter written by Staff-Surgeon-Major Arendt from which we have previously quoted affords a welcome completion to this incident: "Then there came another Sunday on July 4th, 1915. We were in Marchiennes. The radiant summer's day found us in the streets, watching the inhabitants who were proceding to their huge place of worship, dressed in their best Sunday attire. Then—a rattle of firing—somewhere. Machine-guns here, thirty-five kilometres behind the front? And again—where does the firing come from? Our eyes looked upwards—a fight in the air! Two aeroplanes hurtle by at frantic speed, one obviously fleeing from the other—which is the German? They pass over the town at a height of two thousand metres. Then the fugitive goes down in a steep glide to one thousand four hundred metres, with the other hard upon him and firing all the time—the first machine dips and goes headlong down in a vertical dive, revealing the tri-colour on its wings when the sun gleams on them. Hurrah!

"So now to see it! Captain Bieler took me in his car. When we reached the meadow where the victorious German machine had landed, a dapper little red hussar came to meet us, accompanied by—our Boelcke. Lord, what a pleasure and what congratulations! But all the talking was done by us; as usual, Boelcke was silent in his proud modesty. He lunched with the captain, took coffee with us afterwards and then flew a farewell round over our garden, nodding a waving to us—the dear, splendid fellow!"

The triumph of the 4th of July, 1915 was considered the first victory for German aviation, and is still deemed so by many people. That is not literally true. Spirited German airmen who thought it stupid to encounter opponents in the air without means of defence often equipped themselves with suitable fire-arms, such as automatic loading carbines and even in some cases with machine-guns from vanquished French machines; shortly before obtaining his C. machine, Boelcke also mounted the machine-gun from a French machine, that was forced to land near Douai, on his B. aeroplane. Many successes were achieved with such weapons before Boelcke gained his victory. For instance, the papers in the official archives show that a C. machine belonging to Section 12 and lent to Section 20 at Douai forced an enemy aircraft to land behind our lines on May 26th, 1915. No further particulars of this feat are known. It may be assumed, however, that such victories were due rather to fortuitous successes than to any aerial duel fought out according to plan. Otherwise such early victories by the young air arm would not have remained unknown in wider circles when Boelcke and von Wühlisch became heroes of the day through theirs. The essential fact, however, is that Boelcke deliberately sought battle and won his victory with von Wühlisch after an obstinate fight of twenty to twenty-five minutes' duration, having anticipated the tactics he employed in his later fights in spite of the clumsiness of his machine in attack. In this sense we are justified in regarding the victory won by Boelcke and von Wühlisch as the first complete success scored by German airmen in a fight that was deliberately sought and waged according to plan.

We may close this incident with a quotation from

Boelcke's characteristic words in his letter of July 16th, 1915: "Father asks whether my report may be published in the papers. You know that I do not think much of publicity in the press. Moreover I consider that my victory does not afford the proper style and scope for a paper. The good readers want a more poetic and awesome description, with psychical tension of fear-tortured nerves torn to shreds, followed by exultant glee, clouds that tower like Alps or the blue sky of heaven full of whispering zephyrs, etc. If, however, it would give you great pleasure to see it published, I shall not object. But naturally no names must appear."

The victory of July 4th was due to the joint efforts of Boelcke and von Wühlisch. The latter fired the decisive shots at the target given him by the airmanship of the former. But this first victory was also Boelcke's last in a double-seater. Shortly afterwards he obtained the single-seater fighter E.3 left behind for him by Fokker and became a solo flier.

On July 10th we find him writing to his parents: "I have been flying my Fokker single-seater since last Wednesday. I shall seldom fly biplanes now. I am sorry to part company with Wühlisch—we worked splendidly together. On the other hand I am highly delighted, because I believe in the saying that 'the strong man is mightiest alone.' I have attained my ideal with this single-seater; now I can be pilot, observer and fighter all in one."

## BOELCKE AS A SCOUT

*Douai, 16.7.15.* In addition to its technical points my little single-seater possesses the advantage of giving me complete independence; I can fly when, where, how long and how I will. I have not yet caught anyone else over our lines—the event of 4.7 has given the French a mighty scare and they treat my single-seater with a holy respect. As soon as I appear on the scene, they bolt as quick as they can. As I cannot catch any of them here, I go to look for them on their side of the lines where they think they can spot for their artillery in safety. I have to prowl about stealthily and invisibly, using every trick and wile I can manage. In this fashion I have succeeded in shooting at four of them, but as they always make a dive for home at once, I could not get any of them because I cannot chase them too far behind the enemy's lines without exposing myself to their artillery fire.

Most of the other gentlemen flying Fokker fighters— there are only eleven all told so far on the western front— think differently and do not intend to attack anywhere but behind our lines, because they can fight to a finish there only. That is certainly true, but the consequence is that they do nothing but go for joyrides round our lines and never get a shot at the enemy, whereas I have the pleasure of getting a good smack at the fellows over yonder. One must not wait till they come across, but seek them out and hunt them down.

*Douai, 31.7.15.* I have just moved in to a very nice new house with a bathroom; my batman likes it so much that he said to me yesterday: "We'll never get anything as nice again, Herr Lieutenant. It's much finer than anything at home." It is close to our mess, which we have shifted to a big villa looking out on to the canal. Yesterday I had as my guests two old friends from Pontfaverger, Lieutenants von Brixen and von John of the 11th Grenadiers. So then we heard something about the real war again—they have been in four attacks in the last few days. I always fly over their trenches and only see the same general picture from above.

My main activities consist in disturbing and chasing away the French artillery fliers between the hours of 7 and 9 in the evening. As they get the sun at their backs at the time, there is a favourable visibility that lures them out of their holes. When I have a few quiet moments, I naturally take a peep down and locate the enemy batteries by their flashes which I can see very plainly in the twilight. Therewith I am certainly running into competition with the observers, but can book a positive achievement in addition to my negative ones of chasing the enemy away.

So Max would like to know how I can shoot forward in spite of the propeller. It is quite a simple business: the gun is mounted rigidly on the machine's bonnet and points forward. It has a catch, which is connected with the engine by a rod. The safety catch acts on the machine-gun automatically through this rod whenever a propeller-blade passes in front of the barrel; as soon as the blade is clear, the machine-gun is automatically released again and can fire whenever I press a button that is connected with its trigger. Have you grasped it? Naturally I cannot aim with the gun, because it is mounted in a fixed position, but the art of shooting is to fly in such a way that the machine is in a direct line with the target whenever I shoot.

Not long ago Colonel Thomsen, who is chief of the air service, came along here—he seemed to take a special interest in me.

## IMMELMANN'S FIRST VICTORY

*Douai, 11.8.15.* You asked in your last letter whether I did not take part in the air fight of 1.8. 15. Naturally I did!

Early on the morning of 1.8.15. —it was a Sunday—the clouds hung so low that the officer on duty telephoned it was no use going out to the aerodrome. So I was lying quite happily in bed when Fischer suddenly woke me and said there was an Englishman about. I jumped out and ran to the window. But as the Englishman was making for the front and so I had no chance of catching him, I crawled back under my bedclothes, cursing. I had hardly got warm once more before Fischer rushed in a second time; the Englishman was coming back again. Well, if the fellow is so impudent, I thought, I'll get up quick and have a go at him. So all unwashed, with my nightshirt still on, but no puttees, I shoved along to the aerodrome on my motor-bike and came just in time to see those chaps—there was not one but four of them—amusing themselves by dropping bombs on our aerodrome. I jumped into my machine and took off. But as the Englishmen flew home as soon as they had dropped their bombs and had very fast machines, I did not manage to get within range of them. I turned back sadly.

When I got over the aerodrome again—I could scarcely believe my eyes—there were another five machines that had come to pay us a visit with their bombs. So I went for the nearest, a French monoplane. I got to grips with him nicely and peppered him well, but when I was close enough up to think that the next shot must send him crashing—Lord, my gun jammed! Oh, I was wild. I tried to removed the jam up there and used so much force on the lock in my rage that the obstructing cartridge broke in half. So there was nothing for it but to land and get a fresh supply of ammunition.

As I went down I saw our other monoplane coming up and felt pleased that those English machines would at least get their tails twisted by it. While I was loading with new cartridges down below I saw Lieut. Immelmann attack an Englishman in grand style and send him bolting. I climbed up again quickly to help Immelmann against the others. But they cleared off again as soon as they saw me arrive on the scene a second time, and I had only disappointment for my trouble. Meanwhile Immelmann had forced his Englishman to land; he put a bullet through his elbow, so that he had to come down as quickly as he could.

Immelmann was extraordinarily lucky over the whole business. I only gave him his first lesson on a Fokker three days before, i.e. I went up with him in his machine and let him help handle the controls. The day before he did his first solo and had great difficulty in pulling off his landing. He had never flown against the enemy in a Fokker and had never fired his machine gun before—and then he had the luck to catch a defenceless biplane over our aerodrome, because the Englishman had left his observer at home to save weight for his bombs. All the same Immelmann did his job beautifully and I congratulate him sincerely on his success. But I really am annoyed at my own bad luck; it was the first time for four weeks that I got an opponenty bang in front of my gun, and then it must go and jam! That was my share in the events of 1.8.15.

But you can see from the enclosed snap that not all my flights are made with warlike intent. Lieut. von John, who is in hospital here with an injured knee, came along to visit me with two nursing sisters. As they were both so longing for a flight, I took them one after another for a jaunt above the aerodrome in my little monoplane, to the great joy of all beholders. But now, in order to prevent mass visits to the aerodrome, our C.O. has forbidden us to take any more nurses up!

## THE SECOND VICTORY

*Douai, 23.8.15.* I had another stroke of luck on 19.8.15. When I was out on my usual evening flight for the purpose of chasing French artillery fliers away, I found a lively traffic in the air. First I got to grips with an English Bristol Biplane. He apparently began by mistaking me for a Frenchman; at any rate he came flying towards me in a comfortable way that my opponents are not generally accustomed to do. But when he saw me shoot, he made off quickly. I followed hard behind and gave him a few shots. I must have hit either him or his machine, for he suddenly cut his engine and vanished in the depths. As our fight was over the lines, he unfortunately succeeded in landing on his own side—in the enemy artillery positions, according to the statements of our own gunners. That is the second fellow I can positively assert to have gone down to a forced landing because I hit him and not merely because he was scared of me.

The same evening I attacked two others; both bolted and went down in glides. But I cannot really say whether I hit either of them, because the fight took place behind the French lines.

On Saturday morning I was summoned to our Prince Aribert, who comes here as the representative of our Grand Duke to visit the 93rd occassionally; they are in the front line here. As the prince wanted to have a flight, I took him up in my biplane in the afternoon — my Fokker is too narrow to contain such big men—for twenty minutes and showed him Douai and the surrounding country. So as to prevent him saying afterwards: "Oh, there's nothing much in this flying!" I gave him a bit of a shaking up intentionally and went into a few turns, but he stuck it splendidly. Then I flew with his adjutant, Captain von Oheimb. Both the gentlemen were very edified with their flights.

By the way I met our Pastor Vahlteich recently; he is an army chaplain here—but he did not seem to have any desire to fly.

This morning I had a great sorrow. As I was on duty on the aerodrome, I took Wolf out with me and tied him up because he always wants to attack and bite any quickly moving object he sees. Early in the morning our armoury master tested my machine-gun with the engine running. Wolf, who had managed to get loose, charged up, attacked the propeller before anyone could stop him and was naturally killed at once. I am terribly sad at losing such a beautiful, clever, faithful beast. It is a good thing that the war prevents us from mourning for our dogs!

*Douai, 29.8.15.* Not much flying with this bad weather about. So I have been able to go in for more sport. As we have discovered some fine rowing boats here, I row very often, either alone as a dashing sculler or in a pair with Eckstein. It is good fun and healthy for the lazy body.

Yesterday I was also able to give a proof of my swimming arts. Our mess faces the canal, which is about twenty five metres across and two and a quarter metres deep. There are said to be fish in its water, and consequently half the population sits on the banks and angles; I have never yet seen anyone catch anything.

In front of our mess there is a kind of jetty where the boats unload. Yesterday afternoon I was standing at the front door with von Teubern after lunch—then I saw a boy (about fifteen years old) climb over the railings with his angling tackle and jump down into the water. I ran across to see what he was up to, but could not find any signs of him. As I could not assume that he was practising dives,.. I had not much time for reflection—I took a header and in I went. It all happened so quickly that Teubern only just saw my legs disappearing and had no idea what the trouble was.

I came to the surface again, but saw myself still alone in the water. Then I caught sight of some bubbles not far away, and down below them was the fellow—drowning. So I swam across, dived, managed to get hold of him and came up again. Meanwhile Teubern and our chauffeur had arrived. Teubern thought I was drowning too and was about to jump in after me, but I shouted to him to push out to us in a boat that was moored nearbye. I made the boy hang on round my neck and swam to the boat, where Teubern pulled him out; then I climbed inside.

Meanwhile our other gentlemen and a large crowd of civilians had arrived. The first thing the rescued boy experienced was a good spanking from Captain Ritter and Teubern. He was so surprised at it that he did not say a word, but slunk off scared and was taken in charge by his mother, who came running up and uttered her thanks in a big torrent of words. The rest of the civilians also gave me an ovation. I must have been a fine sight, because I was in full uniform when I hopped in and stood there like a dripping poodle.

P.S. A letter has just arrived from the families of Delplace and Dutercq, in which they express their thanks to the 'sauveur du jeune Albert Delplace agé de 14 ans.'

*Douai, 9.8.15.* Yesterday I called on the parents of the boy I hauled out of the canal. He got dizzy when looking down from the high quay and so tumbled in. They were nice people and extremely grateful; they want to try and get me the French 'Legion of Honour.' That would be a joke. But I should set greater store by our Life-saving Medal, for which Captain Kastner has sent up my name.

Last week I was able to make an interesting trip as I had to get a new Fokker in place of my old one, which has already been sent away. First to Ostende: it was glorious bathing in a high sea, but otherwise the place seems dead— this Ostende without its summer visitors. Not a civilian to be seen, only persons in uniform are allowed on the beach, the whole of the promenade is fortified with trenches and barbed wire entanglements, all the hotels are shut, there is a huge search-light on the Kurhaus, and one sees gunboats patrolling off the coast. Then I went to the old town of Bruges, where I saw submarines (with torpedoes) and minelayers along the quays, as well as the torpedo boats stationed there—it was all new to me, and most interesting. Then came Ghent, Antwerp with its desolate docks and Brussels that is full of life. It was a nice change.

Now I have my new Fokker E.37 with a 100 H.P. engine; the old one had only 80. It is much faster and climbs more easily. I have already done a couple of war flights on it. So now to new deeds!

Please subsribe to some more war loan for me; the money I have sent home from time to time must amount to quite a decent sum.

## THE "THIRD"

*Douai, 18.9.15.* I was invited to dinner with Prince Aribert, but unfortunately did not get much of the sumptuous dinner—or rather, fortunately I should say, because I had a very happy experience that evening.

As you know, I always go off to the lines in the evening with Lieut. Immelmann to hunt the French there—as they they are usually there in force between 8 and 10, we both get enough to do. On the 9th we succeeded in getting on either side of a huge French fighting machine, so that it did not know what to do and only escaped us by a hasty dive. The French were very cross with us about that; when the pair of us arrived at the front in the evening for a peaceful bit of hunting, practically all the French aircraft in the neighbour-hood went for us. And suddenly those fellows really got megalomania and attacked me; among the assailants was a new type of biplane (with a cockpit and very fast). They appeared to be very astonished that we calmly let them attack us—on the contrary we were very pleased to run up against someone who didn't bolt at once. After several futile attacks they retired, but we—being far from lazy—went after them, and each of us forced an enemy machine down in a glide.

As it was fairly late, we were satisfied with this success and flew off, side by side, in the direction of Douai. But when I happened to look round, I saw two other machines circling about behind their lines. As I did not want to give our people in the trenches the impression that we were bolt-ing, I signalled to Immelmann that we would fly round a couple of times, just to show that we were cock of the walk. But Immelmann misunderstood me and attacked one of the Frenchmen (Farman type, without a cockpit), who was not going to be drawn into a fight and so sheered off. But while Immelmann was busy with the Farman, the other Frenchman (a Morane-Saulnier Biplane) swooped down on him from behind. So then I had to turn back to help

Immelmann, who could not see the second French machine. When the Morane saw me coming up, he turned round to meet me. I peppered his nose a bit, so that he got in a funk and turned back. That was his greatest mistake. I sat on his neck, and as I hung on and came up fairly close—up to about fifty metres—it was not long before I hit him. I must have mortally wounded the pilot—suddenly he threw up both his hands and the machine went down vertically. I watched it fall, and saw it turn over a couple of times and crash about four hundred metres in front of our trenches. Our people ascertained that it was smashed to bits and both inmates dead.

Meanwhile it had grown fairly late and was high time for us to fly home, especially as our petrol was running out. Finally we had to land about eight hundred metres in front of our aerodrome; as the corn has already been cut, we succeeded in making good landings in spite of the growing darkness.

There was much joy in the section over my new victory. Our infantry had already rung up from the trenches to announce the crash. The fact that the fight and victory occurred within view of the trenches has done much to inspire confidence in our airmen. Naturally it has just the opposite effect on the French. Since then none of their machines have trusted themselves in the neighbourhood of a Fokker; they make a wide circle to dodge us now. Also our biplanes are not molested so much, because no Frenchman comes across if there is a Fokker flying on our front.

So now you know why I missed my meal, i e. a part of it, at Aribert's table. The prince was delighted with my success; after dinner I had to sit by him and tell him all about it. After three quarters of an hour's conversation I got away from him

(it was a big affair) and obtained an introduction to the lady
of the house in which he is stopping—a very nice mamma
with a still nicer daughter of about fifteen and a half years,
named Ninette. I made friends with her at once and and call
there almost every day now to practise my French on her—
naturally that is the reason!

As Aribert now knows me and all my evil deeds, the
Anhalt Bear and Swords Order is likely to come along for me.

My log book records seventy six war flights since I have
have been with No. 62 in Douai; it has long been too much
bother to count up the kilometres I have flown.

On Sept. 19th, 1915 Boelcke was suddenly transferred to
the pigeon postal section at Metz. It is not clear from his letters whether he was informed of the real reason for his transfer. In any case all persons not in the secret were puzzled why
this renowned scout should be sent to a fortress some distance behind the front. The military laymen among our readers will be even more surprised; they will wonder what a
fighting airman was to do in the company of the peaceful
'pigeons.'

In reality the sections comprised under this cover-name
were the strongest fighting organisations. The first 'Pigeon
Post Section' was formed in Ostende in November, 1914, for
the purpose of bomb raids on England, which proved impossible at that time; in August, 1915, a second section was
established in Metz. Up till 1916 these two sections formed
the only German bombing squadrons; in December, 1915,
they received the names of Fighting Squadrons 1 and 2.
Their main distinctive feature was that they were not allotted to individual army corps, like the field sections, but
remained at the disposal of the Higher Command for special
service anywhere. For that reason their members did not live

in quarters, but where accomodated in railway trains so that they could be despatched anywhere at a moment's notice.

Boelcke's transfer to the 'pigeons,' however, did not imply that he was to take part in the special missions (bomb raids); his real task was to act as escort to the heavy bombers. A number of the best scouts were sent to the 'pigeons' for this purpose when new enemy offensives were expected.

# CHAPTER VI

# *The Master of Aerial Warfare*

THE chapter dealing with the period between the end of September, 1915 and the end of June, 1916 will show how Boelcke developed his airmanship and the tactics of aerial warfare in his fights in the neighbourhood of Metz, in the Champagne, in Douai once again, and especially on the Verdun front, until he became a master of his art,

Through his relations with the chief of the air service he exercised a growing influence on the development of German scout flying, while by reason of the various orders bestowed on him and his rapid promotion to lieutenant and captain (at the age of 25!) he found ample recognition and became 'the famous Boelcke' and a national hero.

## IN METZ

*Metz, 22.9.15.* On Sunday evening I suddenly got a telegram that I was transferred to Metz. I was not too pleased with the move. There were many farewells on Monday—Mlle Ninette was very unkind about my sudden disappearance; in the evening there was a farewell dinner in the mess to myself and Teubern, who is transferred with me as my observer, because I have always flown with him whenever I had to take the biplane up for long distance reconnaissances ever since Wühlisch was wounded in August. Kastner was very loathe to let me leave his section.

148

We arrived here yesterday, bringing our batmen and mechanics with us, but no machines; I am to have a biplane and a Fokker as well. The new section is much larger than those in the field—there are twenty machines here already, but more are expected.

Unfortunately the fine life we led at Douai has come to an end. All the officers are quartered in a sleeping car on the Frescaty aerodrome which I know so well, while a dining car caters for our meals. We have two compartments each; rather cramped quarters when one comes from such a princely mansion as mine was in Douai, but on the other hand it is quite comfortable and practical to be always on the aerodrome. Strangely enough, my new C.O.'s name is also Kastner.

## FIRST MENTION IN THE OFFICIAL COMMUNIQUÉ

*Metz, 27.9.15.* You will certainly have been surprised to suddenly find my name in the official communiqué that is printed in your paper—I was just as surprised when wandering through the streets by chance I studied the latest reports and found my name in them.

It was on the third day of my sojourn here. As my machines had not yet arrived, the captain gave me a Fokker for the time being and told me I must be ready to take off at any time from 9 a.m. onward because the emperor was lunching at a near-by castle and we had to protect him from bomb attacks. The emperor was expected at 10 a.m.; our machines were therefore to take off at 9.15. As I wanted to give mine a trial first, I took off at 8.45. After I had been in the air for four minutes, perhaps, I saw shell bursts; immediately afterwards I sighted not one but three or four enemy machines flying towards Metz. I therefore tried to get up quickly to the height of the enemy airmen, but that naturally took time, and meanwhile the enemy were already over Metz, where they dropped their bombs on the station at the very moment that the emperor was about to step out of the train. The French knew the exact time of the emperor's arrival at the station—luckily they did not hit anyone.

When those fellows had unloaded their bombs (meanwhile they had increased in number; I counted seven Farmans and Voisins and three of the cockpit type), they flew homeward. But now I was gradually climbing up to their height and drawing closer. Then one of the cockpit biplanes—which, so it seemed, were protecting the others— saw me and dived down to attack me. Now one can only shoot upward very badly—practically not at all. I exchanged a couple of shots with my opponent and then bore away. That satisfied the Frenchman, and he flew on with the others. But I hung on to their squadron again, and, as I was faster, I soon succeeded in getting within range of the lowest of them. I did not shoot at once, because I did not want to draw the attention of the others to me too soon. So I did not open fire until I was within one hundred metres. My opponent got scared and tried to bolt, but I hung on to him and chased him along with well-aimed shots from behind.

Then I had trouble with the other brethren, who heard my shots and turned round to help their comrade. So I had to act quickly. I knew I had scored, because the Frenchman finally tried to escape me by going into a glide; we therefore both went down from two thousand five hundred to one thousand two hundred metres, and all the time I was shooting at his back to the best of my ability. Meanwhile two of his comrades arrived and were kind enough to send me some greetings. That is not particularly pleasant, but what was most unpleasant for me as well was the fact that I was tossing about without a map in territory that was completely new to me, and so did not know where I was. As my first opponent went down deeper and deeper and his companions also closed in on me, I had to finally assume that I was over the enemy's lines. For that reason I broke off the fight; as I had the superior speed and the Frenchmen promptly sheered off from me, I was soon alone once more.

But now I had to find my way back. So I flew due north and then soon got over country that was familiar to me from my time at the War Academy. When I landed, I only knew what I have described to you; I could only report a fight, not a victory. With the help of maps I ascertained that I had been somewhere near Pont-à-Mousson. Reports came through from the front in the afternoon; the infantry posts had seen a biplane 'fluttering' down on to Hill 368. The artillery were more definite; they reported that the biplane I had fired at was on the ground behind the enemy's barbed wire entanglement, the pilot had been dragged into a neighbouring trench, dead or badly wounded, while the machine was hit and destroyed by our artillery. Now I piece the story together as follows: I wounded the pilot severely in the fight; he tried to get down in a glide and land behind his own lines, if possible; shortly before landing he fainted or lost control over the machine and then 'fluttered,' i.e. crashed. Voilà, c'est le quatrième!

As pilots are needed on account of the great offensives in various localities, part of our section has been sent to the 6th army at Lille and another part to the 5th at Stenay. Unfortunately they have left me here, because they only want biplanes with observers, and mine has not yet arrived.

It is a great pity and an awful bore, because there is nothing doing in the air here.

## IN THE CHAMPAGNE

*Rethel, 11.10.15.* We have been here for a week—just four machines from the Metz pigeons to reinforce the Ostende pigeons, who are all here. Flying activities have been very much curtailed by persistently bad weather.

If Max is really determined to volunteer for war service, I can get him into my battalion as an aspirant—thanks to my present status my requests are not lightly refused. I went to my present C.O., Major Seelmann-Eggebert, in Stenay; he will gladly take Max, but at present aspirants are not appointed by the commanding officers but by the general inspectorate in Berlin. I therefore rung up Major Thaler (my former company commander in Coblence) at G.H.Q. immediately, and he will take the business in hand.

Besides that I got on to No. 62 yesterday on the phone—Immelmann brought down another Englishman yesterday.

The Berlin Illustration Company will manage quite well without my photo—I beg you not to send them one. I don't like all this publicity—I find quite enough articles in the papers about myself to be sick of it all. I am told an English paper lately announced that I bolted to America before the war because I could not pay my debts as a lieutenant and worked as a liftman in a New York hotel.

*Rethel, 17.10.15.* Yesterday I brought down a French Voisin Biplane at St. Souplet, which is quite close to Pontfaverger. It happened like this:

I got my Fokker from Metz several days ago and flew it

daily—to the great sorrow of Teubern, who consequently has nothing to do. Yesterday morning I patrolled a stretch of the front from Rheims towards the Champagne. Just as I was over Pontfaverger, I saw a machine rumbling about behind the enemy's lines. I kept my eye on him and was highly delighted when I noticed the fellow coming across—apparently he had failed to spot me. For a fight behind our lines is something different from one on the other side, because the enemy cannot make a bolt for the ground.

The Frenchman circled round our territory and then wanted to go home. But I barred his way; he came slanting across to me and was cheeky enough to shoot at me. I calmly let him fire away, for the combined speed of two opponents meeting one another reduces the chance of a hit to practically nil—as I have already found by frequent experience. Besides, I wanted to get behind my man as quickly as possible.

As I was a few hundred metres above him, it worked very well. At the moment that I was directly over him I took my machine round and dived on him. Now things began to get a bit uncomfortable for him, so he tried hard to get away and flew round in circles.

But as the fellow shot up at me in a slanting direction, I quickly dropped down a bit deeper and came at him from behind. In air fights it is absolutely essential to fly in such a way that your adversary cannot shoot at you, if you can manage it. Owing to my superior speed I soon came up quite close—within twenty to thirty-nine metres of him—from which distance I put about two hundred shots into him. That was too much for him, and he preferred to dive head-long.

The pilot lost control of the machine and dropped straight down; the machine caught itself once and spun round like a piece of paper. I went down in a glide, ready to attack him again if he should regain control of his machine. I was following him at a distance of several hundred metres—then all at once I saw the machine go down vertically into a plantation of young trees. I have just seen that I am in the official communiqué again—so you will have learnt all about it in the quickest possible way.

## THE HOHENZOLLERN ORDER
## FOR THE SIXTH VICTORY

*Rethel, 1.11.15.* The day before yesterday I sent another Frenchman crashing. Today I received the following two telegrams:

The first from General von Falkenhayn, Chief of the General Staff: I am delighted to inform you that H.M. is pleased to invest you with the Knightly Cross of the House of Hohenzollern, with Swords, in recognition of your magnificent achievements against enemy airmen."

The other from our chief of the air service: "I herewith express my appreciation of the magnificent achievements, whereby you have put the strength of an enemy flying section out of action, and congratulate you on the high distinction bestowed on you by His Majesty. All comrades of the air service look up to you with pride."

*2.11.15.* Today I shall give you further particulars: Our men were due to carry out an attack in the neighbourhood of Tahure, which was to start at 4 p.m., on Oct. 30th, the object being to recapture a portion of the positions previously lost to the French, who were threatening our flank severely. All enemy air reconnaissances had to be obstructed in

*Original oil painting by Hans Schultze-Görlitz.*
*The caption reads: "To the parents of our unforgettable Boelcke. Wilhelm,*
*Crown Prince, Christmas 1916."*

Photograph of painting by Emil Theiss, Dessau-Ziebigt

*Boelcke as an Ensign.*

Photograph by Heinz
Bensemann, Metz.

*The north face of
the Heiterwand.*

*With Lieutenant Baltzer in his Dixi Car.*

*With the Wireless Company.*

*The animals' friend at the practice ground in Darmstadt*

*With his brother Max, summer 1916.*

*With his brother Wilhelm at Pontfaverger.*

*French airman Lieutenant Tétu in his Parasol.*
*This photograph was recovered from the wreckage of his aircraft.*

*With von Wühlich viewing the*
*remains of the Parasol.*

*Aircraft designer Anthony*
*Fokker riding a horse for the*
*first time at Douai aerodrome.*

*With Nurse Blanka in a Fokker at Douai Aerodrome.*

*Flieger-Abteilung 62 in Douai, January 1916.*
*In the middle: Boelcke, Captain Kastner, Immelmann.*

*Boelcke's first Fokker single-seater.*

*The Crown Prince with the three youngest knights of the "Pour le Mérite" order: Boelcke, Rackow and von Brandis.*

*Boelcke onboard the S.M.S. Goeben at Constantinople.*

*In the sea at Cordilio near Smyrna with Buddecke.*
*3rd from the right is Buddecke, 5th from the right is Boelcke.*

*The Dragon Machine.*

*The squadron's stork with his jackdaw friend.*

*Boelcke and von Richthofen studying a captured British Vickers machine "for instruction purposes."*

*Boelcke reporting on his 34th victory.*

*Boelcke as Staffel-Leader.*
Photograph by Julius Müller, Dessau.

Boelcke and
Captain Wilson.

*The last
photograph.*

*The last start.*

On His Majesty's Service.

*An das deutsche Fliegerkorps.*

TO THE MEMORY OF CAPTAIN
BOELKE, OUR BRAVE AND CHIVALROUS
OPPONENT.

FROM, THE ENGLISH
ROYAL FLYING CORPS.

*The letter from the Royal Flying Corps.*

*The funeral service at Cambrai Cathedral.*

*Boelcke's grave and memorial in Dessau.*

Photograph by Emil Theis, Dessau-Ziebigt.

order to ensure secrecy for all our preparations and the positions of our storm troops, reserves, etc. All the seven Fokkers of the district were assembled as a fighting Staffel on a temporary aerodrome at Monthois, south of Vouziers, with orders to fly barrage patrols. But it was a very difficult job that day because the clouds hung down to below one thousand five hundred metres and one doesn't like to fly over the lines at less than two thousand five hundred on account of the enemy's anti-aircraft artillery. One can easily keep watch from a low height over one's own lines and prevent any enemy from coming across—which the French never do in any case if they see us in the air—but it is almost impossible to chase away an enemy who is flying behind his own lines at a low height which just suffices to let him reconnoitre the procedings on our side. But I risked it because today it was really a matter of great military importance.

I was due to fly a barrage patrol along our lines from 11.30 to 12.30. Then I saw three Frenchmen mucking about behind their own lines for observation purposes. As it was urgent for us to stop those fellows, I decided to go across and make it hot for them. The low clouds were a great help to me for this purpose. I therefore kept my eyes open until one of the chaps on the other side was flying alone; then I climbed into the lower cloud layer so that neither the French airmen nor anti-aircraft guns could see me and hurled myself down on the emeny. The first one I attacked saw me in good time and escaped—but at least I gave him a good dusting up and spoilt his little observation game.

Thereupon I retreated speedily to the clouds once more and lurked there. Just before 12 one of them came quite close to the Tahure positions. I got to within one hundred metres of him unseen this time and then opened fire. He promptly turned away southward and tried to bolt. But I was much faster and pounced on him like a hawk. Now he went down, and I had to follow if I did not want to let him escape.

The following incident was very funny. I had hardly opened fire before the head and upper body of the French observer appeared above the top wing—do you know that the pilot and observer in a French machine sit in a kind of forward balcony, with the engine behind them?—and in spite of his leather helmet and goggles I saw the fellow was in a blue funk. Then he vanished quickly and reappeared a moment later with an old blunderbuss in his hands. Owing to my great speed I was so close to him the next moment that he got a thorough fright and popped his head in again—perhaps I hit him, as I was blazing away the whole time.

But the pilot was quite a tough fellow. His machine turned this way and that and refused to fall. Then I headed straight for my opponent until it looked as if the two machines must collide; when I was only three or five metres away, I pulled mine to one side and saw the Frenchmen go down by the right wing at the same time. The whole business only lasted about a minute, during which I fired five hundred rounds at the enemy. What helped me greatly was a visit from one of Fokker's mechanics a few days ago; he fixed my machine-gun up with a patent novelty which enables me to fire from four hundred and fifty to six hundred shots a minute instead of the former four hundred.

But now it was high time for me to get back! I was heavily engaged and had dropped down to one thousand metres in the course of the fight. The artillery was blazing away like mad, but their shells were far too high, because they could not believe anyone would be impudent enough to fly over them at one thousand metres. Two Farmans that pursued me naturally could not catch me up. So I reached our lines without being hit once.

Then I went on flying my patrol until 12.30, but without any further incidents; the French appeared to have had such a strong dose that not one of them came to the front. When I landed on our aerodrome, I was met by news from our front line—from the 5th Bavarian Infantry Division—that a French machine was seen to fall vertically into the enemy positions about two hundred metres from our lines to the south of Tahure—that was my patient.

I have written you an exact description so that you need not imagine it is all much worse in reality. As long as one keeps one's head and judgment, my fast, nimble Fokker makes a fight in the air hardly more dangerous than a motor trip. So don't worry about me! Promise me that.

By the way, in two or three weeks I am going to have a brand new Fokker again, with a more powerful engine (160 H.P.) and two machine guns.

*Metz, 9.11.15.* As the French offensive in the Champagne has been squashed, I arrived back here a couple of days ago—but not for long, I expect.

Yesterday I was ordered to G.H.Q. at Charleville by the chief of the air service, who made a speech and decorated me with the two new orders, which, by the way, look very handsome. In the afternoon I was introduced to the other officers of the general staff as 'the famous Boelcke,' got some nice cakes to eat and had to tell them a frightful lot of things. In the evening I was invited to dinner with the chief of the air service, where I was the guest of honour; I sat at the chief's right hand at table, had to go in first, etc., and heard a very nice, kind paternal speech about myself.

Probably I shall be able to spend a little time with you soon in the course of a service journey, and on the way back I can visit our little Max, the new aspirant, in Coblence.

Obviously the dinner on Nov. 8th was not the sole purpose of the visit to Charleville; important discussions on technical questions of aviation also took place. As soon afterwards as the 11th Boelcke went on an official mission to Fokker at Schwerin by order of the chief of the air service, proceding thence to Berlin. In all probability this journey had something to do with the new Fokker type with two machine guns that Boelcke mentions at the end of his letter of Nov. 2nd.

This is the first of the many instances in which the air authorities entrusted Boelcke with special missions to Germany—a proof of their high appreciation of his technical knowledge, quick perceptive faculty and trustworthiness. "Boelcke possessed my complete confidence in a high degree," writes his former chief of the air service. "It was the natural consequence of his character that these confidential relations were continually strengthened."

Discreet as he was on all service affairs, Boelcke said as little to his parents about the important reports based on personal experience that he delivered to his chief in writing or by word of mouth as he did about the particular purposes of these missions.

The following judgment on the significance of these reports we owe to Colonel Thomsen:

"The reports on tactical, technical and organisation questions—sometimes briefly couched, sometimes at great length—which Boelcke continually gave me, formed a unique and valuable basis for the official battle orders drawn up by my staff, firstly for the scout-fliers, then for the groups and finally for the Staffels. Boelcke's early death indeed prevented him from gathering further experience for the methods of warfare applicable to larger scout formations, but the basic principles that he evolved for the tactics of aerial warfare retained their value for the later battle orders issued to the squadrons, whose attacks generally resolved themselves into series of single combats."

It is a matter for regret that these reports were not preserved. They should have been deposited in the state archives at the conclusion of the war, along with the papers of the chief of the air service, but in spite of all the efforts made by the staff of the archives—for which I am as truly grateful to them as for the other help they have given me in the preparation of this book—they were not to be found. Presumably they were lost in the confusion of the retreat and the revolution. Taken in conjunction with the battle orders issued to the scouts, they would have given us detailed proof of the importance attached to Boelcke's judgment in competent circles and the influence he consequently exerted on scout flying.

## BACK IN DOUAI

On Dec. 12th, 1915 Boelcke writes once more from "old, familiar Douai. Everything is just the same in the little town, but there are many changes in the section; with the exception of Captain Kastner, Immelmann and Gusnar are the only two of the former comrades still there. Kastner was particularly pleased to be able to welcome me yesterday with the Life Saving Medal; by chance it had just arrived, and he considers it a very good omen."

In his letter of Dec 21st. Boelcke complains of the unfavourable weather ("so far only two good flying days") and
his troubles with the new Fokker, occasioned by the fact that
his mechanics were not yet familiar with this latest type.
At the Christmas celebrations the section commander handed him a silver cup, the gift of the chief of the air service,
which bore the inscription: "To the victor of the air."
Immelmann received a similar cup.

Not until New Year's Eve was Boelcke able to report
another 'joyous scrap:'

*Douai, 31.12.15.* The day before yesterday we had another
merry day after the long spell of bad weather. In the morning I chased away the fellows who came across from Arras,
and when flying home I saw shell-bursts to the west of
Cambrai. So off I quickly went to look. I came just in time
to see another Fokker—it was Immelmann—start a scrap
with two Englishmen. I dived on the one nearest to me,
but then saw that Immelmann had already taken him on
and given him enough, so that he was bound to go down
soon. So I promptly went for the other, who was ready for a
tussle.

That was a fine fight. I had to deal with a tough fellow,
who defended himself stoutly. But I forced him on to the
defensive at once. Then he tried to escape me by turns, etc.,
and made an effort to get at me on my weak side. He did not
succeed, but the only success I scored was forcing his
machine ever further down—we began at two thousand
metres, and in a short time I fought him down to less than
one thousand. Finally he could defend himself no longer,
because I had mortally wounded his observer. It was now a
comparatively easy job to shoot the fellow down, but when

we got to eight hundred metres I ran out of ammunition because I had previously used some of it on two others. That was his salvation. We now circled round each other, but neither could do the other any harm.

Finally Immelmann came to my aid, and the fight began all over again. I kept on attacking merrily, so as to confuse the Englishman. We managed to force him down to one hundred metres and waited for him to land, but he went on flying about like mad all over the place, with the pair of us behind him. I tried to cut off his further progress by flying at him, etc.; then my engine gave out, and I had to land. I could just see my opponent disappearing behind the next row of trees and thought he would land there; I was delighted and, arming myself with a Verey pistol—I had no other weapon at land—I rode across on horseback to take the fellow prisoner. But he had flown on. I made enquiries everywhere and rang up—no definite news obtainable. Then in the evening there came a report that the Englishman actually flew over the trenches at a height of one hundred metres and got home. Smart of the fellow; he won't have many imitators! Immelmann could not go on shooting at him because his gun jammed.

That was no victory, but a joyous scrap.

*Douai, 7.1.16.* Did you read my name in the official communiqué again yesterday and rejoice with me?

On the morning of the 5th I took off at 9 a.m. to chase a couple of English biplanes that were reported from Lille to be on their way home. I managed to catch them up north east of Henin-Liètard. I attacked the hindermost of the pair at once—the other flew on steadily; apparently he did not notice me. There some joyous shooting began. I potted away at that fellow's hide, so that he went down deeper and deeper in the course of the fight. At last I noticed that he wanted to land and surrender—he made me understand that quite clearly by waves of his hand. Having grown wise through my recent experience, I sat tight on his neck and let off a couple of shots every now and then, just to show him that I was ready to start again if he did not go down quickly. Then he landed somewhere north of Harnes, still waving his hand to me. His machine went to pieces when he put it down—as I afterwards learnt, I shot away one of his controls. I fired about eight hundred rounds in the course of the fight.

I chose out a landing place close by. When I reached the enemy machine, I found it surrounded by a crowd of our men. Both the airmen had already been bandaged by two ambulance men—the pilot had a flesh wound on his head and the other a nasty shot in the shoulder. I went straight up to the Englishmen, shook hands with them and told them I was delighted to have brought them down alive. I had a long talk with the pilot, who spoke German well. When he heard my name, he said with a grin: "We know all about you!"

I then saw to it that they were both taken in a car to the hospital, where I visited the observer today—the pilot had already been sent off—and brought him some English papers and photos of his wrecked machine. When they had gone, I rode over to Harnes with an artillery major to telephone for my mechanics and fresh ammunition. After a short stay in Harnes I rode out to the machine again, and found my mechanics had already made it serviceable. I soon took off again and waited up there for fresh work. As none came along, I flew home an hour later.

The sky having clouded over meanwhile, I drove into the

town. I had hardly sat down to lunch when ten enemy aircraft appeared over Douai. I jumped into a car and drove out to the aerodrome. When I got there, all ten were just unloading bombs on our aerodrome. Consequently all the mechanics had crawled into the dug outs—I bellowed like a bull until at last one came out. Unfortunately Immelmann, who stayed on the aerodrome over lunchtime, had taken off in my new 160 H.P. Fokker—he could not get the hang of its gadgets—so that I was left with an old 80 H.P. reserve machine. Consequently I could not overhaul the enemy squadron, but only got near a single machine that lagged behind the others. But this was already picked off by another Fokker—our Lieut. Hess.

The pair of them were doing gymnastics all round each other. To help a bit, I dived on the Englishman and put about one hundred and fifty rounds into his machine. Then the fellow saw he could not do anything against the two of us and preferred to make a quick landing at Vitry—with the both of us at his heels. The Englishman was alone in his machine, and still had his fat bombs with him. As he was unwounded, he must have come down because he was scared of us; he certainly said his engine went dead, but we could find no sign of trouble there. This valiant man was then taken to H.Q.

So on the 5th I brought one machine down alone and helped to get the other, which will be credited to Hess. A little while ago a telephone message came for me from G.H.Q.:

"On receiving the report of the air fighting on the 5th His Majesty paid a further warm tribute of praise to your ability, as I have great pleasure in informing you. von Falkenhayn."

## THE 'POUR LE MÉRITE' ORDER
## AND BOELCKE'S ANSWER

*Douai, 15.1.16.* Events have now followed so hard upon one another that I cannot catch them up in writing.

First I will tell you what happened on the 12th. I took off at 9 a.m. and flew to Lille to go hunting round there, but had no luck to start with; I flew about for more than an hour without seeing anything. At last I saw firing round Ypres. I flew off—such a far flight that I could see the sea—but unfortunately could not find any signs of the machine.

On the way back I saw two Englishmen come across the lines to the west of Lille. I went for the first of them, but he did not appreciate my attentions, for he turned round at once and flew back. I left him alone, because I wanted to give the other one, whom I saw flying eastward to the north of Lille, a bad time for reconnoitring on our side of the lines. Thanks to my speedier machine I gradually overhauled him. When I got within four hundred to five hundred metres of him, he appeared to have seen all he wanted in our territory, for he flew—or tried to fly—westward. I flew on steadily behind him until I was near enough. The Englishman seemed to know the game, for he quietly let me come up to him without shooting. He only started when I did. I flew directly behind him and could take aim very nicely and steadily because the enemy was flying ahead on a straight course. Suddenly, after a very short time, the enemy machine went crashing down—I must have hit the pilot. It hurtled into a garden in Mouscron village, to the north east of Turcoing.

As I could find no landing place there, I flew on to the aerodrome of Section 5 at Lille. There I reported my fight over the telephone—and what did I hear to my astonishment? At the very same time Immelmann had shot down an Englishman near Bapaume. I could not help laughing.

Then I went off at once in a car to Mouscron to see how things looked from below there. The machine, a B.E. Biplane with an American engine, had whirled into an apple-tree. Both the inmates were already removed; the pilot was dead and the observer severely wounded. I was delighted to see the position of my shots—they were almost all in the cockpit of the machine. Then I flew back from Lille to Douai in the afternoon.

As the chief of the air service chanced to be in the neighbourhood, he came along and congratulated Immelmann and myself personally on our successes. But the greatest surprise came in the evening. We were just sitting down to dinner when I was called to the telephone. There the chief's adjutant announced himself and congratulated me on receiving the 'Pour le Mérite.' I thought he was having a joke with me, but he informed me that the order had been bestowed on Immelmann and myself by a telegram from His Majesty. Great were my surprise and joy. Then I went in to the diningroom, but said nothing and just sent Captain Kastner to the telephone. He came back and made a public announcement about our decorations; at first everyone was very astonished, then there was great rejoicing. Various congratulations arrived that very same evening, and all the next day I could not do anything but receive congratulations. They are all off their heads with delight. An old general simply would not let me go, and I only got away when I promised to pay him a visit. Congratulations poured in from everywhere by telephone and telegraph. The King of Bavaria who happened to be in Lille with the Crown Prince, asked us to dinner on the 14th.

And now comes the best part of the joke. On the 14th, i.e. yesterday, there was good flying weather in the morning. So I took off about 9 a.m., all fresh and lively again, to see after my customers. As the sky above Lille was clouding over, I shifted my hunting-ground to the south of Arras. I had hardly been flying for an hour before I saw shell-bursts round Bapaume way. While I was flying there, the Englishman seemed to catch sight of me, for he flew back. But I soon overhauled him. When he noticed that I was going for him, he went into a sudden turn and attacked me.

Now began the hardest fight I have had up to now. The Englishman tried all the time to get on to my back, and I tried the same with him. So we whirled merrily round each other, but as I had taken to heart my experience of Dec. 29th (when I shot away all my ammunition) I only fired when I had him well in my sights. Thus it came about that we went round each other for several minutes without my firing a single shot. The merry-go-round did not worry me, because we were over our territory; I said to myself "Sometime or other he'll have to fly straight to go home." Then while we were circling he continually tried to work his way nearer to the front lines, which were not too far distant. On one of these occasions I succeeded in getting on to him and shooting his engine to pieces—I noticed that because after I attacked him he tried to reach the English lines (which were now quite near) in a long glide, with a column of oil vapour trailing behind him. I had to stop that.

His glide had brought him fairly low down, and so I had to attack him again. I caught him up just by our trenches at a height of one to two hundred metres and pounded him from close quarters with both my machine-guns—I did not need to save ammunition now. We were both just above our trenches at the moment when I caught him. I then turned away; I could not find out where the other machine was, because I had to clear off myself as I had not much petrol left.

(In the copy of this letter which Boelcke sent to his brother, Wilhelm, there is a footnote drawing his attention to an important addition at the end which was a piece of private information for him: "For you alone! The real reason of my retreat was that the Englishman shot my tank to pieces; I had only some petrol from the emergency tank. Moreover the machine had been hit several times; one bullet went through the bonnet on to my chronometer, while another penetrated the sleeves of my overcoat and jacket. I must have got it from close range when we were about eight hundred metres up—it felt like a blow on the arm.

When I saw that arm and engine were both in working order, I set about the fellow with both guns as a punishment. As I also came into the propeller wind at the moment when he hit me and and the machine side-slipped a bit, that chap must have certainly thought I was done for. But afterwards he was able to convince himself to the contrary. You don't need to be afraid I'll be too rash; I'm looking after myself all right.")

I therefore landed at Flers village, where I received very kindly attentions from the divisional staff and, much to my delight, learnt at once what had happened to the Englishman. After I turned away, the enemy machine landed at once close to the English trenches—at this spot the trenches are only one hundred metres away from one another. One of the inmates—the pilot, apparently—climbed out of the half-wrecked machine and escaped into the English trenches in spite of the fire directed on to him by our infantry. Our field artillery then shelled the machine. One of the first shots was a direct hit, so that the machine took fire at once; the other inmate, probably the observer, who was already dead or badly wounded, was burnt with it. Only the skeleton of the machine remained.

By chance the quartermaster general of the forces on the western front was in the trenches occupied by the 109th Infantry at the time and watched the whole of the fight—he was most enthusiastic.

As it was fairly late and my mechanics had not yet arrived, while I, however, was due to be with the King of Bavaria at 5.30, I drove back from Flers to Douai in a car belonging to the divisional staff and thence straight on to Lille. The king and Crown Prince were both very nice to me and talked to me for a long time. They were particularly interested to learn that I had brought down another. My ninth gave me special pleasure because he came as such a prompt answer to the 'Pour le Mérite.'

Now comes the reverse side of the medal. Everybody is congratulating me, I am invited everywhere, and they all ask me the same questions—if most of the questioners weren't big bugs, there is nothing I would like better than to print another sheet of questions and answers.

This was the period when not only the whole army but all the civilians at home followed the competition in victories between Boelcke and Immelmann with joyous excitement. From the mass of rhymes which appeared in the press at the time the whimsical verses which "Gottlieb" (Professor Overbeck, of Dessau) published in the "Tag" seem to be worthy of preservation.

*THE FLYING MATCH*

Immelmann, the trusty flier,
Daily screws his plane up higher.
Boelcke, too, delights to roam
In the clouds where he's at home.
If a foe comes downward hurling,
Boelcke's gun has sent him whirling;
He's an insult to the Frenchies,
Who bolt and vanish in the trenches.

Victims five had Boelcke outed;
Read the papers if you doubt it;
Immelmann refused to slumber
Till he got the selfsame number.

Another foeman Boelcke scotches
And so his round half dozen notches;
"Oh," thinks Immelmann, "what tricks!"
And brings his total up to six.
The seventh—ah, but there's no knowing!
Perchance to Boelcke he is going;
Yet Immelmann may chance to slay him;
Competition's bound to pay him.

Whereupon Pastor Karl Boelcke, Oswald's uncle, replied
two days later with the following verses:

Gottlieb, both our gallant aces
Occupy the foremost places;

With his seventh Immelmann
Neck and neck with Boelcke ran.

And then, how glorious to relate!
Both these fellows got an eight;
And Falkenhayn reports with zest
That 'Pour le Mérite' adorns each chest.

But Boelcke, out to give a shocker,
Promptly climbs up in his Fokker,
And, leaving Immelmann to pine,
Romps ahead with number nine.

But Gottlieb finished the rhyming in the "Tag":

### THE RECORD

The record in that daring sport
Our airmen play in heaven
Was held by Immelmann, who fought
And vanquished victims seven.

But Boelcke was a valiant wight,
Who did not sit down sighing;
He quickly put the balance right,
As so one should in flying.

But who'd be first with number eight?
That left us all surmising.
The answer "Both," I'm bound to state,
Was really most surprising.

They dished up two on one same board—

'Twas quite an innovation—
And each received as his reward
A noble decoration.

Then one day later—you'll avow
It's rather hard to swallow—
Friend Boelcke shouted: "Nine! How now!
I've nine, I've licked you hollow!"

And thus these busy airmen climb,
Each day new laurels storing,
The ladder of fame to heights sublime—
And business still is roaring!

*Douai, 20.1.16.* I have to leave here to-morrow—I cannot tell you on what errand, as it is a dead secret. Also I don't know where I am going to; first of all I am travelling to Montmédy. I am sorry to leave Douai, especially as I have just got such a splendid lot of customers here.

Immelmann and I were summoned to lunch again with the Crown Prince of Bavaria on the 17th. Before the meal he gave us our orders with some very nice words and helped us to pin them on properly with his own hands. I sat on the prince's right hand at table; he is very nice to talk to. Yesterday we were invited to H.Q.; the general nearly killed himself with affability and expressed the wish that we might soon return to his corps.

I enclose a couple of the new photos. If the "Woche" is absolutely determined to have one, send it along as far as I am concerned—as a knight of the 'Pour le Mérite' I can no longer keep myself out of the press. But Herr Scherl had no luck when he made his offer for a book.

## BEFORE VERDUN

The new mission was connected with the great Verdun offensive, which was still a dead secret at that time and eventually started on Feb. 2nd. As in September, 1915, Boelcke was again transferred to the Metz 'pigeons,' who had meanwhile received the name of "Fighting Squadron 2" and were led by Wilhelm Boelcke, the latter having been promoted to captain in the summer of 1915. But Oswald did not go to Metz; having being advanced to lieutenant, he was sent from Montmédy direct to the artillery flying section, No. 203 at Jametz, north of Verdun, to act as escort to machines engaged on artillery spotting.

From Jametz he complains on 12.2.16, "Nothing doing here on account of the bad weather—my chief activity still consists of addresses, poems, etc. On many days I have to write between twenty and thirty letters; Fischer always drives me to the work with his 'We must answer this one, sir.'

"I have only flown four or five times since I have been here. It is not worth while to take off, as the French do not come across any more. Once I managed to have a go at a Farman biplane over the lines, but he bolted pretty quickly. Here in Jametz we are really too far behind the lines for scouts.

"Life in the section is quite tolerable. Captain Vogt is a very sensible man, and my brother officers are a nice lot. But the village possesses no charms; it is a filthy hole, especially in these rainy days. There is hardly any civilian population left."

When the offensive began at last, Boelcke was in hospital at Montmédy, whence he wrote on 27.2.1916: "Everything is going off well and according to programme here on the Verdun front. So now you know why I am here. I could not enlighten you before, because everything was a dead secret. I was not sent here to recuperate my nerves, as you believed. If only mother would stop worrying about my nerves! I have none—so I cannot suffer from them!

"But all the same I am writing to you from the hospital. I had the bad luck to get some stupid intestinal trouble a couple of days before the offensive started; as the doctors are now very careful on account of the constant danger of typhus, they stuck me in hospital here. The whole thing, however, has now turned out to be quite harmless; I have not had a temperature for the last four days, and I got up for the first time today. I am furious at having to be in bed just on these fighting days instead of at the front where I could have helped a bit."

The way in which Boelcke took his departure from the hospital is characteristic of him. We have an account of it from Fischer, his batman. The latter was allowed to visit his ailing master in the hospital and told him one day that every morning and evening a French airman, nicknamed the 'Farmers' Terror' came across from Verdun and shot up the environs of Jametz in general and the aerodrome in particular, flying at a low height all the time. Boelcke knew this daring Frenchman from of old; his logbook told him that he had met the 'Farmers' Terror' on Jan. 21st, 1915, when he was at Pontfaverger, and on June 9th, 1915, in the Douai area. It is of course doubtful whether the 'Farmers' Terror' was the same person in each case or whether it was a general nickname coined by our soldiers—who naturally did not appreciate such bombardments from a low height—for enemy airmen that attacked them in this fashion.

But the news made Boelcke restless. Now that he was capable of dealing with such a foeman and no longer defenceless against him, as formerly, he felt that he had to punish the disturber of Jametz's peace for his impudence. He forthwith requested his discharge from the hospital and a car. Both were refused him. So then: "Make a bolt for it!" he decided. He disappeared in the early hours of the following morning without a word to anyone at the hospital, obtained a lift on the first passing lorry and arrived at his section's mess at 7 a.m., much to the astonishment of his captain but just in time to eat with his brother officers the breakfast he had missed in the hospital. While they were still at table, the arrival of the 'Farmers' Terror' was reported. Boelcke ran out, jumped into the private car of an officer of high rank, ordered the bewildered chauffeur to drive him to the aerodrome, took off at once, had a tussle with the 'Farmers' Terror' and shot his machine up so badly that he only just managed to get across the lines with a desperate effort and make a forced landing behind the French trenches. He never repeated his visits to Jametz.

When Boelcke returned to Jametz, he made continual efforts to get moved to an aerodrome nearer the front. His initiative was rewarded with the confidence which the staff officer in charge of the air forces on the Verdun front placed in him, for the latter gave him permission to establish his own aerodrome in a meadow on the banks of the Meuse, close to the village of Sivry. He had selected this site himself, and was also allowed to take with him Lieut. Notzke, whose work he had learnt to value.

Thus Boelcke became the leader of an independent though diminutive 'group' of scouts which was detached from the section and solely responsible to the staff officer commanding the air forces. The significance of these 'groups', which were first established in the neighbourhood of Verdun, and their connection with the development of scout-flying has already been discussed; they represent the first stations on the road to the organised Jagdstaffels. Special mention should also be made of the fact that of the three 'groups' formed Boelcke's was the one to occupy the most advanced post: the aerodrome he chose himself was only twelve kilometres behind the lines, whereas the group stationed at Avillers was about twenty-three kilometers away from the front.

His task was now to intervene aggressively in the struggle for the supremacy of the air taking place over Verdun. His achievements there receive due recognition in the book written by General von Hoeppner, the commander in chief of the air forces, who is always so sparing in his mention of names and praise of individuals: "We owe it mainly to Boelcke's ability and sense of duty that the enemy's numerical aerial superiority did not become a crushing burden upon us. His Fokker always proved itself the master of all enemy aircraft."

Boelcke arrived at Sivry on March 11th. As early as the 12th and 13th he won his tenth and eleventh victories; on the 19th and 21st of the month followed his twelfth and thirteenth.

*Sivry, 16.3.1.6.* I have been here since the 11th. As the front lines have been pushed forward everywhere, we were too far back at Jametz. We could not see enemy airmen over the lines; reports of their presence arrived too late for us to get there in time to deal with them. I therefore begged permission to establish an aerodrome at a more advanced site. For that purpose I chose out a beautiful Meuse meadow near Sivry. I am so near the lines here that I immediately catch sight of any enemy airman who comes across; this means that I am independent of the reports of others and can always take off in time.

It is very nice for me to be completely independent here and in a position to act on my own account. I have a lorry and a car, a corporal and fifteen men. Lieut. Notze was the only officer to accompany me; the other Fokker pilots are still in Jametz. We have made ourselves quite comfortable here; we have joined in a mess with four other officers—the commandant of the village, two from the armoured cars and one from the transport. My address is simply: "5th Army, Sivry Aerodrome."

I started doing good business on the very first days of my sojourn here. The French are now flying more keenly and in larger crowds; moreover there has been good weather so far. So there was and still is plenty of work to do.

I took off on the 12th about 11 a.m. to chase away two French Farman Biplanes that were cruising round the 'Mort Homme,' which we subsequently captured on the 14th. But when I got up, I found four of them there. I waited till two crossed our lines and then promptly attacked the uppermost. A merry fight developed. The two Frenchmen stuck together like pitch and brimstone, but I refused to let go my grip of the one I had attacked and blazed away behind him, while the other Frenchman tried to get behind me. It was a regular game of cat and mouse. The one I was attacking wriggled like an eel to escape me, but finally we dropped down to five hundred metres. Then I managed to get on to my opponent beautifully from behind; I flew quite close up to him, wondering why he did not go into any more turns, and was just about to finish him off—at that moment both my machine guns suddenly jammed. In the excitement of the fight I pressed the trigger-button too hard, and then that stuck too. As the second Frenchman was on to me, I did a quick bolt.

The final stages of the fight took place over our lines on the Côte de Talou (the bend of the Meuse). As my investigations and the reports from the front showed, one of the Frenchmen got his packet. He just managed to reach the further bank of the Meuse in a glide and landed, as some say, or crashed, as others report, somewhere east of Marre. I believe the former version; probably he did not make a good landing but smashed up his machine. After the landing one of the inmates ran into the nearby village, returning in a little while with a stretcher party to carry the other one away. The truth is therefore probably as follows: I wounded the pilot severely, but he got his machine down somehow; then they had to fetch a stretcher for him. The machine was destroyed by our artillery fire.

On the following day (13.3) there was also a lot of business in the air. In the morning I arrived on the scenes just as an 'avion de chasse' attacked a German machine over Fort Douaumont. I went for the former at once and chased him away—it was magnificent to see the hurry in which he went off.

About I in the afternoon I saw a French squadron near the Mort Homme, flying frontwards in the direction of Dun. I picked off a Voisin Biplane flying somewhat apart from the others on the right of the squadron and dived down on him. As I was high above him, I came down quickly and shot up well before he grasped the situation. He turned tail at once and bolted for his lines. I attacked him vigorously again; then he heeled over by the right and disappeared under my wing. I thought he had gone down, but went into a turn so as to get a sight of him, and then I saw to my astonishment that the machine was flying level once more. I naturally went for it again—then I saw a most amazing sight. The observer had climbed out of the machine and was sitting on the left wing, holding on to a strut. He stared up at me in terror and waved his hand. It was such a pitiful spectacle, and for a moment I hesitated to fire at him because he was completely defenceless. I must have shot away the controls and caused the machine to heel over; then the observer climbed out and sat on one of the wings to restore the balance. I sent just a few shots at the pilot so as to force him to go right down; then my attention was diverted by another Frenchman coming to his comrade's aid. As I had only a little ammunition left and was already over the trenches, I did a quick bolt. The other machine then went down for a short stretch in a glide, but finally crashed from a low height. It is on the ground in front of one of our outposts, to the east of Malancourt village. We can see it quite distinctly from our lines.

Those are the two airfights, of which you will have read in the official communiqué.

On the 14th I came to grips with another 'avion de chasse' over the Côte de Talou, but he was in a great hurry to remove himself from my neighbourhood. I accompanied him a bit of the way, and my machine-gun provided the music. As the 5th Jaeger reserves reported, he went down behind Fort Marre. But that will not be credited to me as a victory, because we cannot tell whether he was hit or merely escaped from further attacks by a hurried landing on his own territory.

So I have had a lot of success with my 160 H.P. machine in the last few days, but a lot of trouble too. I got quite close to French machines behind our own lines on several occasions, but they escaped me because my engine was not in order. I am to have a new machine within the next few days—I hope business will be better then.

*17.3.16.* As my letter did not go off yesterday, I can let you know that I was invited to dinner with the Crown Prince at Stenay last night. It was very nice and jolly. The prince is very natural and sets no store by etiquette. He 'sucked me thoroughly dry,' as he put it. We had a long talk, and when I left, he wanted to hold my thumbs so that I should soon get my dozen.

This is the only time that Boelcke—who disliked all forms of boasting—mentioned his relations to the Crown Prince in his letters to his parents. As commander of the 5th army, to which Boelcke belonged when he was on the Verdun front, the prince had his headquarters at Stenay, which was not far from Sivry, and a close acquaintanceship developed between the two men in the course of this month. The Crown Prince came frequently to Sivry aerodrome, while Boelcke was often summoned to Stenay or taken there in the prince's car. Whenever a couple of days passed without news from or about Boelcke, a telephonic enquiry from Stenay invariably followed.

The photograph showing the Crown Prince with the three youngest knights of the 'Pour le Mérite' Order— Boelcke, Lieut. von Brandis, the capturer of Fort Douaumont on Feb. 25th and Lieut. Rackow who led the storm on Fort Vaux on June 6th (see photo section) was taken at Stenay in June.

A proof of the esteem in which the Crown Prince held Boelcke and the gratitude he felt towards him may be seen in the large oil portrait which he commissioned the artist Hans

Schultze-Görlitz, who was paying a visit to the front, to paint after Boelcke's death. It was based on a portrait procured from Boelcke's brother, and shows Sivry aerodrome in the background; at Christmas 1916 he sent it by an officer of high rank to Boelcke's parents in Dessau. The inscription on a silver plate on its frame states: "To the parents of our unforgettable Boelcke. Wilhelm, Crown Prince. Christmas, 1916."

*Sivry, 21.3.16.* Today I received the following letter in the Emperor's own handwriting: "It has been reported to me that once again you have emerged victorious from a fight with enemy aircraft. I have already shown you not long ago by the bestowal of my highest war order, the 'Pour le Mérite,' what importance I attach to the results of your daring courage. But I cannot let the occasion of your twelfth victory, whereby you have now put out of action the strength of two enemy flying sections, pass without expressing to you anew my fullest appreciation of your excellent achievements in aerial warfare. General Headquarters, March 20th, 1916. Wilhelm R."

Isn't that nice? Who would have thought it possible a couple of years ago, when I was a little wireless sublieutenant in Darmstadt?

But now I will tell you how I managed to get my twelfth. I was flying in the neighbourhood of Douaumont about noon the day before yesterday and wanted to go for two Farmans that were tooting about behind their own lines. Then about 12.45 I saw shellbursts over away to north on the west bank of the Meuse. I just got there as an enemy machine was re-crossing to its own side and thought it had escaped me. Then I suddenly saw it turn back and fly at a

German biplane. The Frenchman got into trouble then, because I came down on him from above. As soon as he saw me, he attempted to get away in a steep spiral and tried to fire at me at the same time—but when a fellow is in such a funk and going into turns as well, he can never hit anything. I, on the other hand, always waited for the favourable moments and put in a few well-directed shots. Suddenly I saw my opponent turn over; shortly afterwards a wing broke off, and the aeroplane slowly went to pieces. As there was a south wind blowing, we drifted over our lines in the course of the fight, so that the machine fell into our infantry positions south of Cuisy. (The official communiqué wrongly states Forges Wood.) Both the inmates were dead; I hit the pilot several times, so that he must have died before the machine crashed.

That, then, was No. 12. Yesterday Immelmann rang me up and congratulated me, but said it was a violation of our agreement and that I should wait for him to catch me up before going on to No. 13. I told him I would wait a week, but was unable to keep my promise as No. 13 fell today.

There was really no fight with him, just a bit of quick shooting. About 11 a.m. I saw a German biplane fighting a Farman biplane away to the west of Ornes. I naturally charged down on the latter, got on to him from behind and opened fire from close range, about eighty metres away. As I came down diagonally from above, I got to him in a very few seconds. At the very moment that I was pulling my machine up to clear the enemy, I saw him explode—I got a black pillar of smoke in my face. It was a spectacle of ghastly beauty to see the machine break out in flames and then fall like a huge torch. Its remains are on the ground to the east of Les Fosses Wood.

Loerzer—a Fokker pilot in my old section at Jametz—
shot a Farman down in flames not long ago. They catch fire
so easily because their engines are located aft, with the petrol
tanks over them; if a tank gets hit, the petrol runs out on to
the hot engine, and then the catastrophe occurs. That cannot
happen with our machines. By the way, that Farman had a
3.5 cm. cannon on board—that is the second machine armed
with a cannon that has fallen into our hands.

About an hour before that victory I had already had
another fight, which was really only a chase. I would not
have told you anything about it, if it was not for the fact that
it will show you some of the nonsense that is so often reported about the results of our flights. In this case I went for one
of two Farmans that were nearing our lines; one of our anti-
balloon batteries was firing at him too. The Farman tried to
dodge my attack by a gliding turn, which the gunners of the
aforesaid battery mistook for a fall after a hit. I followed the
Farman down, and also opened fire on him, but was compelled to break off the fight as I found myself over enemy
positions at two hundred metres.

Thirsting for a victory, those gunners reported: "The
anti-balloon artillery hit a French biplane at 10.10 a.m. and
caused it to crash. (!!) Thereupon a Fokker attacked the
falling (!) machine, which landed (if the machine is falling, it
cannot land!) on the Côte de Talou (occupied by our troops)
and flew off as soon as it had been readjusted (!!!). The Staff
officer commanding our air forces has just rung me and is in
a terrible state of excitement at the idea of an enemy
machine being able to land on our side and fly off again. I
have calmed him with a report to the effect that the enemy
machine neither crashed nor landed on the Côte de Talou.
Poor old anti-balloon gunners!

## A "PRACTICAL REPORT"

We have already alluded to the importance of the reports on his technical, tactical and organisation experiences that Boelcke continually supplied to the chief of the air service as well as to the regrettable fact that these reports are no longer available. By chance, however, one at least of them has remained in existence in the form of a pencilled draft found with his correspondence. A perusal of it will give us some notion of the nature of these reports.

The report in question deals with the 160 H.P. Fokker, which is the cause of Boelcke's complaints in his letter of March 3rd, 1916. Its two machine guns were mounted experimentally at an elevation of fifteen degrees instead of parallel to the long axis of the machine, as was the general rule, because it was considered necessary that the lines of flight and fire should coincide.

Sivry, 24.3.16.
REPORT ON THE 160 H.P.E. MACHINE
(1) Aero-technical qualities:

(a) The speed of this 160 H.P. Fokker Monoplane is sufficient for the requirements of the front, especially in a straight flight; the machine loses much speed in climbing, so that several Nieuport Biplanes escaped me in consequence.

(b) The climbing capacity falls off considerably at great heights (over three thousand metres). This defect could probably be avoided by bringing out a light biplane.

(c) The manoeuvering power of the 160 H.P. machine is considerably inferior to that of the 100

H.P. and 80 H.P. types, because of the difficulty in counteracting the active force of the heavy engine. A quick steep turn can only be achieved by shutting off the engine; as this is bound to entail loss of height, a turning fight is very dangerous for the pilot of a 160 H.P. machine matched against an opponent flying higher or at the same height.

(2) Engine. The achievements of the 160 H.P. engine were good at first, even at greater heights, although the engine dropped quite a number of revolutions (about forty to fifty) in comparison to the static radial engines. After long use the engine drops up to one hundred and more revolutions at great heights.

(3) The machine-guns work perfectly when carefully handled. In my opinion, however, the mounting of the guns at an elevation of fifteen degrees is unsatisfactory. The purpose of the device is to facilitate an attack on an opponent from below, but this occurs less and less in actual practice. This mounting is a direct obstacle in a normal attack (from behind or from above and behind). Quite apart from the fact that it is much simpler and more comfortable to take aim with a gun that points directly in the line of flight, because the gunner then keeps the target continually in sight, the line of fire in the 160 H.P. type is faulty. When the machine is flying in line of flight a, the bullets do not proceed in the line of sight b, but in a line c passing somewhat below this and and so miss the target. Therefore the gunner has to make calculations accordingly, and naturally in the excitement of the fight they

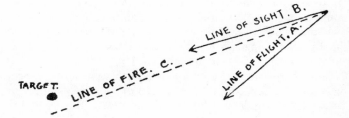

are inaccurate. Consequently shooting is more a matter of hits by bullets spread over a wide surface that accurate aiming at a single point, as in the case of the 100 H.P. type, and thus the expenditure of ammunition is bound to be greater with the 160 H.P. than the 100 H.P. type. The difference is especially noticeable to me, now that I am flying a 100 H.P. type again.

There are three possibilities of obviating this fault: (a) to mount both machine-guns in the line of flight; (b) to leave one gun mounted at the elevation of fifteen degrees and to mount the other in the line of flight; (c) to make the machine guns adjustable. Two positions only would be needed; the basic position should be one which is parallel with the line of flight, but in the matter of an elevated mounting I should advise a greater angle than fifteen degrees. The change of position must be effected by means of a lever that is easy to manipulate.

Subsequent developments justified Boelcke's criticism of the angle at which the guns were mounted as well as his proposal for a light biplane. The experiments with slightly elevated guns soon ceased, and the construction of scouting biplanes was taken in hand. Biplanes were the only machines flown in Boelcke's Jagdstaffel 2, while later in Richthofen's squadron triplanes were actually used.

But the immediate consequence of this particular report was that a few days later Boelcke was despatched to Schwerin to confer with Fokker. Exhausted by the discussion of many hours' duration and innumerable trial flights, he proceded thence to his home for a brief visit.

When he returned to the front, he wrote in his letter of 11.4.16: "Business gets worse every day. The French never come across to us now; they only take the air a long way behind their own lines. Nevertheless our service is not light—this continual lying in wait without results is a greater strain than a jolly scrap." These words imply that the German Fokkers achieved the supremacy of the air on the Verdun front.

In his next letter, dated 17.4.16, Boelcke gives us a delightful picture of his life:

"I went to Charleville several days ago to discuss service matters with the chief of the air forces. On this occasion Falkenhayn asked me to dinner. It was very interesting to get a close view of this man who is moving the scenery in the theatre of the world. We all sat at little tables; I sat with Falkenhayn, General Tappen and the Quartermaster General. I have already told you that the Grand Duke of Saxe-Weimar visited my aerodrome lately and that I dined with him that evening.

"Mother really need not be anxious about me going short here. I get butter, ham, sausages, cakes and even more of the otherwise rare eggs than I can eat. All these are obtained for me by my good Fischer. He need only mention my name to get everything he wants, including even fresh rolls every day from the field bakery. The magic words "For Lieutenant Boelcke" open all doors. The other officers in our mess reap the benefit; if they want anything, they can get it from the hardest-hearted commissariat uncle with the help of my name. When Wilhelm wanted a new car a few days ago, I went with him to the car-park in Margut to soften its boss's heart. The good folk there really opened the doors of their secret storehouse; not only did they bring out the car Wilhelm wanted, but also a brand new 45 H.P. Benz for me—a car which was really supposed to be reserved for some general.

"That is all very well—if only I had not to answer such a terrible lot of letters. Not long ago the German Automobile Club sent me their special gold and diamond tie-pin of honour, and the other day I was made an honorary member of the University Airship Association—I really do not know what I am going to do about all these new honours."

The consequence of the discussion with the air chief mentioned at the beginning of this last letter was that Boelcke was sent to confer with the engineers of the Oberursel Motor Factory. On this occasion there was an amusing incident in the Frankfurt Opera House, which he relates in the following letter, along with the loss of his comrade Notzke and his first meeting with the emperor:

*Sivry, 29.4.16.* First of all some very sad news: Lieut Notzke, who was my business partner here, had a fatal accident on Good Friday. After we had returned from the morning patrol. Notzke, who had experienced several jams, flew off to the 'shooting pond' to test his machine gun. He flew two rounds there; when flying a third, his right wing touched the cable of the captive balloon, which they had sent up over the Consenvoye road for the first time. The machine turned over straight away and crashed; Notzke was a corpse when we got him clear of the wreckage. On Monday we took his body to the railway station at Stenay. He was an only son, and his father is a colonel somewhere at the front. I am very sorry about Notzke, for he was one of our best, keenest and most ruthless airmen as well as a dear, faithful comrade to me.

In his place I have got Lieutenant von Althaus—already once mentioned in the communiqué—and Sub-Lieut. von Hartmann. Captain Haehnelt, the staff officer commanding the air forces in Stenay, asked me to lunch with him on Easter Sunday, so that I should not be all alone. Now it chanced most happily that H.M. was lunching with the Crown Prince. So Captain Haehnelt promptly dragged me off to the castle, where I reported myself to H.M. It was very nice to have an opportunity of seeing our emperor at close quarters and speaking to him.

The Emperor talked to me for a long time, questioned me about my fighting tactics and made me tell him all about my last few fights. He looked quite sprightly—not at all done up, as he appears on his latest photos. He was in a very good humour and roared with laughter when I told him how the French observer sat on the wing of his machine and looked at me with such a terrified expression. Then he gave it as his opinion that 'old Fritz' would hammer away with his stick inside his coffin if he heard there was now an aerial 'Pour le Mérite.' I stayed to lunch, where the Emperor drank my health. Afterwards I had a long talk with Prince Oscar, who was also at table.

Then on Monday evening I went off to Oberursel, near

Frankfurt, where the representatives of the air chief's inspectorate had a conference with the engineers of the Oberursel Motor Factory. As I had nothing else to do on Tuesday evening, I went to the Opera, where they were giving 'Undine.'

In those two days I learnt by experience how conspicuous a young officer with the 'Pour le Mérite' appears at home— it is worse than having a warrant out against you. They stared at me all the time in the streets, both in Frankfurt and in Wiesbaden, where I was on Wednesday afternoon. Also the people in the Opera crowded round me in each interval—it was terrible.

But the worst was yet to come. When the opera-singer Schramm sang the well-known aria "Father, mother, sisters, brothers" he was loudly applauded and encored. At last he reappeared to start his encore. But just imagine—I could hardly believe my ears—the fellow did not sing the proper words but a verse in my honour which they had hastily strung together behind the scenes—it sounds like it. The singer himself sent me a copy round:

> Listen, friends, our airman glorious,
> Lieutenant Boelcke's here to-night.
> Many times he proved victorious,
> Made the foeman feel his might.
> May this hero go on winning,
> Send another hundred spinning,
> And how lovely if we may
> Greet him here another day.

But then you should just have seen the audience going raving mad; they clapped, shouted and tramped their feet. In the next interval I was the target of all opera glasses—then I saved myself from further ovations by speedy flight.

I travelled back on Wednesday night because I wanted to start work again the next day. I arrived in Sivry at 9 a.m.; at the very moment I entered the village, two Frenchmen appeared—for the first time for four weeks. But I took off too late and only arrived in time to see a German biplane shoot one of them down—the other escaped. I then flew off to the eastern part of the Verdun front and arrived just in time for another scrap. Three Frenchmen were promptly attacked by a Fokker as soon as they crossed the lines, but the latter got into difficulties. So I hurried to his help, took off one of his opponents and gave him a twisting. Thereupon the whole lot of them flew back home, but I was not going to let my customer escape. I hung on to him; he turned about like an eel and proved himself a really skilled flier. I got him three times from behind and once when I cut across his nose diagonally; finally his machine went into a steep turn, rolled on to its back so that for a while it was flying with its wheels upward and then went down wing over wing. As several other Frenchmen came up and I was well over the enemy's lines, I then beat a retreat. According to a report from the 14th reserve division the machine turned two more somersaults and then crashed vertically into wooded country to the southwest of Vaux. That was No. 14.

*Sivry, 9.5.16.* I have not yet told you about my fifteenth. On May 1st towards evening, I saw an enemy biplane approaching when I was on the aerodrome. I took off at once and found the fellow cruising round at about five hundred metres. Apparently he failed to see me, otherwise he would have bolted. I dived down on to him from behind and sent him my usual greetings. Then he quickly went into a turn and—just think of his cheek—shot back at me. But he did not go on for long, because I soon had him taped—the business was short and snappy. He did a couple more turns; then he heeled over and fell behind the French lines, whereupon I flew home satisfied. The whole business was over in two minutes.

Since that time I have twisted the tails of four other machines, without, however, scoring a complete victory. At noon on May 2nd three Frenchmen were flying over their lines and four German biplanes over ours; I was flying above the latter. The two opposing squadrons sniffed at each other for some considerable time—about a quarter of an hour—then they approached each other over the bend of the Meuse to the north of Verdun, and finally a Frenchman attacked a German. I had just been waiting for that; I charged down on him at once. The poor fellow got such a shock that he nearly crashed down before I started shooting. I only got within range of him when we were down to one thousand metres—we begun at three thousand five hundred and then I hammered away with my machine guns until I fought him down to five hundred. He must have certainly got a packet, for he promptly landed on a meadow to the south of Charny; the machine stood there for hours and was bombarded by our artillery.

Then I twice caught a Farman over the Côtes Lorraines. Both of them got something, but neither crashed; they managed to get down in a glide.

Finally I 'nearly' brought down a Caudron Biplane on the 6th. The fellow was spotting for his artillery at Hill 204 (north-west of Verdun) and was careless enough to drift up close to our lines in a south wind. That pleased me mightily, because the chance of catching a Frenchman over our lines grows rarer every day. He seemed to be a raw beginner, for he made no turns, but just bolted straight ahead. I was rubbing my hands with glee. Then—I had fired about two hundred rounds—my gun jammed! I was furious to see him escape me. He then landed somewhere to the south of the Bois de Hesse. Perhaps I managed to hit him—he certainly did not do any more spotting that day.

That was my last week's hunting. Althaus flies very decently and goes for his man well; it is great fun flying with him. Unfortunately he is still a bit nervous. He is a very nice brother officer. Yesterday we went to Charleville together to visit the chief; we also met Buddecke there, who flies in Turkey. He told some very interesting tales. To go and see Turkey—that would be a most attractive idea to me.

The date (June 2nd) of the next letter is misleading, because its contents deal with the events from May 17th to 21st. Immediately afterwards Boelcke went home on leave. As his parents had expressed the wish to have a written description of these experiences which he related to them verbally, he wrote them down on the return journey from Dessau. The letter is headed "In the Train" and was posted at Trier on June 2nd. Its contents are as follows:

As I promised, I shall now give you a short description of my flying experiences.

May 17th was a strenuous day. One of our artillery machines wanted to photograph the Côte Marre (to the west of Verdun) and asked me to come along as escort. On the homeward flight I saw shellbursts near Douaumont and went to have a closer look. I found four or five German biplanes there, along with several French scouts. I kept in the background for a while and watched the enemy. Then I saw a Nieuport get cheeky and attack one of our biplanes. I dived on him and thought my victory was certain as I managed to get within close range unobserved. But there was too much way on my machine, so that I shot over him. He speedily bolted, and I followed close behind. I got several good shots at him, but I was up against an able opponent, who flew brilliantly. I followed him for a while, but retreated behind our lines when several of his companions came to help him and watched out for the enemy that were still about. One that was flying much higher than I was came along and attacked me—we went into several joyous turns, and then he cleared off.

This little joke brought me down from my fine height of four thousand metres to two thousand. Then suddenly—I could hardly believe my eyes — eight double-engined Caudrons made their appearance over the lines between Douaumont and the Meuse, flying in pairs at four thousand four hundred. Such a low trick—I now had to climb right up to this height to get at them! But as those fellows flew so uncannily high and took not the least trouble to come down to me, I did not come to grips with them. I tried to give one of them a dose from below, but they punished me with cold contempt and flew homeward without troubling themselves about me.

All this took fifteen to twenty minutes, and once more I reached a considerable height. Then—I was over Douaumont—I saw two more Caudrons coming up over the Côte de Talou and noted with great joy that they were at a lower height than I was. So I flew after them, but meanwhile they had recrossed the Meuse. Then, just in time, I saw another Caudron and a Nieuport diving down on to me. I

engaged the most dangerous opponent first and flew straight
at the Nieuport. We slipped past one another, firing as we
went, but the total sum of our combined flying speeds prevented either from hitting the other. I went into a turn at
once and rattled away behind the other machine. But then
the Caudron came along too and encountered me with the
same manoeuvre as the Nieuport, but did not execute it as
well. I promptly put my machine behind him and was about
to dust him up a bit when another Fokker came to my help
and got in first. He dived on the Caudron, who bolted at
once. The Nieuport saw him and came to help his comrade
in distress. I saw him and came to help my comrade. The
result was the following funny sight: down below was the
bolting Caudron, with the Fokker after him; behind the
Fokker was the Nieuport, while I was behind him. There
was some bright shooting. Finally the Fokker broke away
from the Caudron because meanwhile we had unfortunately
flown over the French lines, while the Nieuport, who was
fed up with my shooting, gave up his pursuit of the Fokker.
I fired off my last round and flew home.

The whole show lasted about an hour. I worked like a
horse that day—unfortunately without any visible success.
But the other Fokker—who afterwards turned out to be
Althaus—and I were at least masters of the battlefield.

My Number 16 arrived on May 18th. I took off in the
evening, but found the air over the Verdun front most offen-
sively full of our biplanes. I considered myself superfluous
and therefore went off for a bit of a trip—I wanted to see the
Champagne again. I flew as far as Aubérive; perfect peace
held sway over the whole Champagne, both on the ground
and in the air. Then I had the luck to run right close up to a
two-engined Caudron south-east of Massiges on my return

flight. The Frenchman had not caught sight of me; he was flying home without a thought of any harm that might come to him. As he made no effort either to attack me or bolt, I flew nearer without shooting. I did not start my steady, well-aimed fire until I was about fifty metres away and the two men in the enemy machine could see me plainly. My opponent banked at once and tried to escape in a downward turn, but it was too late. I was too close to him and could shoot him up at my ease. It did not last long. After firing about one hundred and fifty rounds I saw the left engine emit thick smoke and then explode in a lurid red flame. The machine turned upside down and caught fire. I watched it fall like a log into the enemy's second line, where it went on burning. I am specially pleased at the thought that you will have read of this victory on my birthday.

On May 20th I went hunting in the Champagne again and caught a Farman north of Varennes. I attacked him behind his own lines, but he went down at once. Nevertheless I tried to get on to him because I could see no other machine about anywhere. I hung on to his tail and kept on shooting, but he refused to fall—the Farman pilots are very well protected by having their engines behind them. But in this case I thought I had wounded the pilot, because the machine seemed to be out of control. As, however, the fight took me too far behind the enemy's lines, I flew home again. When I was over our lines, I dropped down to one hundred metres for a lark and waved to the men in them, who went mad with delight.

The next day (21.5.) I had a tangible success once more. I was flying a barrage patrol along both sides of the Meuse about noon. Two Nieuports were flying at a great height on the far side of their lines, but I did not attack them. I wanted to fly home again and went down in a glide over the Mort Homme; then I saw two Caudrons that had hitherto escaped my notice wandering about below. When I went for one of them and began to shoot, I saw one of the Nieuports diving down on me. I was only too pleased to give him something to remember me by, so I broke away from the Caudrons and bore to northward, with the Nieuport behind me in the belief that I had failed to notice him.

I kept a sharp eye on him until he was within two hundred metres of me—then I suddenly went into a turn and flew at him. You should have then seen the fright he got! He wrenched his machine round and bolted southward. I had gained one hundred metres by my attack, so that I could shoot him up from that distance; he made my work easy by flying straight ahead. He soon began to wobble, but I was unable to follow him down and see him crash. It was not until the evening that I learnt from our staff officer that our infantry on the Mort Homme had seen the crash.

That same evening I went off hunting again on my own account and scored after two hours of vain efforts. I was flying north of the Bois de Hesse and suddenly sighted a Frenchman flying about over the wood. I pretended to fly away, and lo! the Frenchman fell into the trap and pursued me beyond our lines. Then I dived on him at terrific speed— I was much higher—he turned away at once, but did not escape me. I caught him just behind his own lines and began to hammer away—a long, steady fire,—and he was stupid enough to fly straight ahead. I made up my mind to get the fellow. I hammered away until this machine too caught fire. I was still shooting when I saw it explode, break up and fall in pieces. One of the wings came off on the way down, and fluttered after him to fall into the Bois de Hesse.

When I arrived home, I could hardly realise that I had got another. To my great joy the confirmation of my morning victory was there. So that is how I got Nos 17 and 18 on one day.

On the night of that victorious day and evening Boelcke started for home on a leave that had been granted some time previously. It began with a most joyful surprise. When he reached Köthen on the following afternoon, he had to wait for a connection to Dessau, and went for a stroll in the street he read the latest communiqué in a shop window: "Lieutenant Boelcke shot down his 17th and 18th opponents south of Avocourt and the Mort Homme respectively. His Majesty the Emperor has shown his appreciation of this superb flying officer's services by promoting him to captain."

Although, having learnt wisdom from previous experiences, he wore his overcoat collar turned up, so that the 'Pour le Mérite' was hardly visible, he was soon recognised in the streets. All the young people from the various schools surrounded him and escorted him back to the station, where he had to listen to a speech before the train left for his native town to the accompaniment of thundering cheers.

Those days in Dessau formed a zenith which gave him ample experience of the joys and drawbacks of being a famous national hero. The news: "Boelcke is here!" spread through the town with the speed of the wind. Deputations made their appearance; his old headmaster came, accompanied by the 1st form, the band of the 93rd reserve battalion serenaded him in the morning, he was invited to lunch with the duke and tea with the duchess, the 'young guard' marched with flags flying and music playing to his home, which became the goal of a daily general pilgrimage of persons anxious for a sight of their distinguished fellow-citizen. Although generally averse to such demonstrations, Boelcke showed much pleasure at them this time, because the honour paid to him came from the home of his childhood. All the same he would have preferred to wander unrecognised through wood and meadow with his parents and Ibi.

When he returned to the front, he wrote on June 12th: "Not much doing here; always clouds which only clear away for a bit occasionally in the evening. If I could have known that in advance, I might have stayed with you a bit longer without missing anything."

In the same letter there follows a passage, which is fraught with significance for German scout flying. "Next week I am to have a Staffel composed solely of Fokker single-seaters here, and shall be its leader. I am to have six machines and shall be an independent commander. I made no efforts to get this; they pushed it on to me almost against my will. But now that I have taken the job on, I find it great fun and I shall take care to make it into a very special Staffel. I am busy looking round for billets, etc., and mean to establish my own mess as well. The only snag is that my Fokker Staffel is not on the regular establishment and so can be disbanded again accordingly."

The Staffel established by Boelcke at Sivry in June, 1916, was not a permanent formation like the Jagdstaffels that came into existence at the end of August, but it was a more regular type of unit than the loose 'groups' of Fokkers that had hitherto been formed. It marks a step on the way that finally led to the establishment of the Jagdstaffels. This development was not a consequence of theoretical considerations but took place under pressure of military necessity.

When the French airmen on the Verdun front proceded from solitary flights to patrols and even to large-sized squadrons, the Germans were forced to oppose them with stronger formations instead of single fliers. As we learn from Boelcke's letter of June 12th, the initiative did not come from him but from the military aviation authorities—either the chief of the air service or his staff officer on the Verdun front — who decided to expand the small force of single-seater fighters into a larger and more regular body of scouts, and entrusted the task to the man who had made good. Other Fokker Staffels came into existence in similar fashion at the same time.

Although Boelcke's Sivry Staffel was an irregular formation and consisted of six machines only, in contrast to the 12 or 14 of the later Jagdstaffels, it was at least one that would have developed into a fighting instrument with a very forceful thrust if inspired by the true Boelcke spirit. But after he had nearly completed the organisation of this Staffel, which was to start its official existence on June 30th, he was not allowed to lead it because only a few days before this date the chief of the air service, acting on direct instructions from the Emperor, forbade him to fly. He was sent on an official mission to the East to console him for this disappointment.

This veto was occasioned by a realisation of the fact that Boelcke's influence on scout flying in general was too great to allow his life to be exposed to the chances of a single combat of minor importance. The authorities wished to safeguard the man whose skill in pilotry they had learnt to recognise.

When the veto was issued, they naturally could not divine that as soon as Boelcke had left for the East the Somme Offensive would see the enemy putting up strong reinforcements of airmen, armed with exceedingly superior types of machines, so that the German scouts, numbering about thirty at the time, were doomed to impotence. The July and August of 1916 are the blackest days in the history of German war aviation, for these enemy squadrons raged unhindered over and behind our lines. The enemy wrested the unquestioned supremacy of the air into his own hands.

This was fraught with momentous consequences for the battles of the ground troops. Our infantry were defenceless against the machine-gun fire of low-flying enemy fighters; no German airman could give them any protection. The activities of our artillery were crippled because no machines could be sent over the enemy's lines to reconnoitre or watch the effect of their shells. Above all, our leaders were deprived of the army's eyes' through the impotence of the German airmen. The great lesson taught by the first battle of the Somme is that all fighting on the ground is dependent on the fighting up above and the supremacy of the air.

Looking back on the situation on the Somme front at that period we are forced to the following conclusion. It was a great mistake to send Boelcke travelling in the East when he ought to have been at the front. If he had gone to the Somme with his new Staffel in July, and if this Staffel had been inspired with his fighting spirit and will to victory—as was later his Jagdstaffel No. 2—he would certainly have made a breach in the strong position of the enemy airmen and at least have broken the completeness of their supremacy of the air—which his and the other Jagdstaffels then did in the September and October of this year.

Herewith another question arises automatically: why were the regular Jagdstaffels not formed in July when they were so sorely needed by the German working machines instead of at the end of August? The fact that the Fokker Staffels already in existence were not considered regular formations has no influence on the answer. It is true the War Office did not give official recognition to the Jagdstaffels until the last week of August, but their formation was only authorised at the beginning of the month. The authorities in charge of military aviation, however, are in agreement that bureaucratic considerations never prevented them from giving the speediest satisfaction to the needs of the front as soon as they were recognised as justified and necessary.

The question why such a delay took place in the formation of the Jagdstaffels that were so badly needed on the Somme front must therefore remain an open one. There is a temptation to answer it with the almost incredible suggestion that the authorities preferred to wait for Boelcke's return.

Not until July 4th did Boelcke write down his highly dramatic experiences of the month of June in a letter which he composed in the form of a report during the journey that commenced his travels in the East:

*M. [Metz?] station, 4.7.16.* Because it is such a long time since I was last able to write to you in detail, I shall utilise the wait at M. station to start my recapitulation.

As I wrote you some time ago, I was nearly through with all the preliminary work in Sivry for my new Staffel. I had made arrangements for Lieut. Hess—formerly with me in Douai—who was seconded to the Staffel to come and help me. Since all the authorities (at the aircraft park, base, etc.) supported me in the most responsive fashion, I soon collected all my equipment, so that I was ready to start work on the 30th. But imagine my bad luck—that was just the day when

I had to make my exit from the scene! That came about in the following fashion:

There was not too much going on in the flying line on the Verdun front, because my customers were all badly scared. There was only one day on which I found any business. I had taken off twice in the morning and was sitting on the aerodrome, thoroughly bored. Then I suddenly heard machine-gun fire in the air and saw a German biplane being attacked by a Nieuport. The German landed on our aerodrome soon afterwards and told me in breathless excitement: "The devil's loose at the front. There are six Americans up aloft. I distinctly saw the American flag on their fuselages. They're damned impudent fellows; they came right up to the lines and crossed them." Well, I did not think it was quite so bad as all that and took off to say how-do-you-do to the six "Americans"—that was the least they could expect, and courtesy required it of me.

As a matter of fact I met the fellows when they were still over the Meuse bend. They were flying up and down pretty impudently in close formation. I flew up to them and saluted the first one with my machine-gun. He appeared to be a fairly raw beginner; in any case I got to close range of him without any difficulty—about one hundred metres—sat on his neck and started work on him. As he was pretty helpless and flew nearly straight, I had good hopes of settling him. But Fate was unkind to me. I was using my machine for the first time after it had come back from the factory and got jams after twenty shots with the left gun and fifty with the right one. I vainly tried to remove them. While I was still struggling with my guns, the other five Americans approached. As I could not fire, I thought it best to retreat, and when the whole mob came chasing after me, I hastened my homeward flight by a sideslip down over the left wing. After a drop of about a couple of hundred metres I caught my machine again, but repeated the manoeuvre when I found the swarm still trying to get behind me. (The consequence was that the English wireless service reported on the following day: "Adjutant Ribière shot down the famous Captain Boelcke in an air fight over Verdun yesterday.") I caught my machine again at about eight hundred metres and flew,—not very pleased, but at least untouched—homeward. I saw that the Americans were still flying their barrage patrol along the front. That made me wild; I jumped into my other machine and flew off again. But I was not destined to achieve anything that day. I was barely fifteen hundred metres up when my engine broke down with a great row and I had to make a forced landing on a meadow near Consenvoye.

But there was another quite decent show that day. Section 203 of the artillery fliers had orders to photograph all the French artillery positions at Belleville and west of Verdun. Captain Vogt wanted to cross the lines in squadron formation and asked two other Fokkers and myself to come along as escorts. I was only too happy to help him. I flew across with their squadron, and as I kept pretty close to them I was on the spot when two French scouts attacked the squadron. The first did not get to grips, but the second dived straight on to the biplane containing Captain Vogt. As the latter was scanning the ground below through his glasses, he did not notice the Frenchman coming down; moreover his pilot only caught sight of him at the last moment and went into such a steep turn in his fright that Vogt was nearly jolted out of the cockpit. Then I came to the rescue and engaged the Frenchman. My word, how suddenly he cleared off! I hardly got him in my sights—he zigzagged about, with me behind him. I gave him a good burst when we were down to eighteen hundred metres and then left him alone—he did not worry my squadron again. As one of my ignition wires was torn and the engine stopped running smoothly, I then flew home. The squadron did its photography in peace and was very satisfied with my success. The machine I attacked was first reported as crashed by our infantry, but later news told me that the pilot caught it and continued his flight.

Then came Immelmann's very sad affair (18.6.1916). One evening the word suddenly went round that he had crashed. I thought it just one of those familiar rumours at first, but unfortunately our staff officer confirmed the report that evening; he also told me that Immelmann's body was to be taken to Dresden. I then asked permission to fly over to Douai.

The ceremony was most impressive. Immelmann lay in state most wonderfully in the courtyard of a hospital. All around him there were obelisks, with torches on them. Various princes were present, including the Crown Princes of Bavaria and Saxony and over twenty generals. The only member of the family present was his brother, who is very like our Immelmann in both appearance and character; we spent the evening together in the mess.

Immelmann lost his life by a silly chance. All that is written in the papers about a fight in the air, etc. is rot. A bit of his propeller flew off; the jarring tore the bracing wires connecting up with the fuselage, and then that broke away. Quite apart from the sad personal loss we have sustained, in my opinion we must not underestimate the moral effect on the enemy and the reaction on our own people.

In Douai I made good use of my chance to fly against the

English again. I was so pleased with it, that I kept on putting off my return to Sivry. One evening I flew one of the new Halberstadt biplanes—it was the first appearance of this type at the front. As it looks somewhat like an English B.E., I managed to spring a complete surprise on an Englishman. I got within fifty metres of him unrecognised and gave his jacket a good dusting. As I had dived on him a bit too quickly and had not the same control of the machine as of my Fokker. I had to pass out underneath him. He promptly went into a turn and came down. I chased him, but my ammunition belt jammed and I had to break away. By the time I discovered the cause of the stoppage my opponent had vanished.

The next day I had two more scraps with Englishmen. The first affair was with a squadron of six Vickers machines over Liétard. I took off with the other Fokkers from Douai. As I had the fastest machine I was the first to come up with the enemy. I engaged one of them and set about him properly; I must have hit him because a great yellow column of smoke came out of his engine—he must catch fire any moment, I thought. But he escaped me and got across the lines in a glide; according to the report from our infantry he landed near Loos, about two kilometers behind the front. I could not quite finish him off because my left gun jammed when I had shot away all the ammunition in my right.

Meanwhile the other Fokkers had got to grips with the Squadron. I saw another 160 H.P. machine (Lieut. Mulzer) set about an Englishman in fine style. As the latter soon received reinforcements and the other Fokkers were all busily engaged, I found I could at least give Mulzer some help by taking on an Englishman and drawing him away—my opponent did not know that I could not fire a shot. Mulzer saw and recognised me and started a most cheeky attack; unfortunately he only scored a half-victory, like the one I had got earlier on. I hung on there until I saw Mulzer fly back. The team-work of these Fokkers still leaves much to be desired. That will have to be changed.

But at last I had to stop my special shows in Douai and return to Sivry. Our staff officer rang me up several times and the Crown Prince also called me up from Stenay. I kept on saying that I wanted to wait for better weather. Then at last they said that if the weather was bad I must come back by train. Well, it was no go—so I flew back to Sivry the next morning.

There I found a telegram: "Captain Boelcke to report at once to the chief of the air service." Great was my joy, because I firmly believed I was going to get transferred to the 2nd Army, where the English offensive was just beginning.

I reported myself to the Crown Prince that afternoon, but doubts about that transfer to the 2nd Army began to creep in because he left me quite in the dark about my further work. These doubts were strengthened when I heard shortly afterwards that after Immelmann's death the Crown Prince said he would not let me fly again under any circumstances.

The next day I reported to the chief in Charleville and lo! my anticipations were exceeded in every respect. The chief made a long speech, the purport of which was that I was to sit in a glass case in Charleville; I was not to fly at all for the present, because my "nerves" must be rested, but I could organise a Fokker Staffel in Charleville. Well, you can just imagine my rage! I was to sit in a cold water sanatorium in Charleville, stare up at the sky and take over the job of leading a crowd of weak-nerved pilots in need of rest! The chief tried to make me say that I would be willing to take over the post 'provisionally' on the strength of the reasons he had adduced. But I could only protest vigorously and then, knowing no better counsel, took my leave.

When I got outside I cursed the adjutant and other pen-pushers in a most offensive fashion, which only, however, provoked mirth from all concerned. One of the fellows gave me a wise lecture to the effect that I was no longer a private individual who could play with his life at will but the property of the German nation, which still expected much from me. Finally Captain Förster told me that for the present I was not to fly any more—there was nothing doing there because it was a direct order from the Emperor, who had continually kept himself informed about me through the air chief. But if I had any other wish, I had only to express it; for example, I could go to Turkey and have a look at the other fronts.

It dawned on me that in any case that would be better than sitting idly in Charleville. After I had rung up Wilhelm—even he was pleased instead of pitying me—the business was put into official form: "Captain Boelcke has been sent on an official mission to Turkey, etc., by the chief of the air service." Although that is no substitute for an airman's life, at least it is some sort of plaster on a throbbing wound.

Then I went off back to Sivry at once to pack my things and thoroughly exploit the two days flying left to me. I flew twice that same evening (June 27th)—I had to use the time somehow. In spite of the bad weather I was lucky enough to meet five Frenchman over the lines on my second flight. One came within striking distance, and I went for him. He was fairly low down and over his own trenches, but I was so furious that I did not care about that. I flew at him, pounded at him with both guns, then passed out over him, went into a turn and meant to attack him again, but failed to find him; it was then fairly dark. When I got home, I made enquiries all round as to whether the fellow had crashed, but no one knew anything definite. I did not report this combat to the staff officer in case he might positively forbid me to fly during my remaining day and a half.

There was bad weather the next day; I therefore only flew across to say goodbye to Wilhelm. In the afternoon I read in the wireless report—you may imagine my astonishment;— "A French machine was shot down over Douaumont yesterday evening." It could only be mine, because I was the only German to take off in that bad weather. So I rang up our staff officer to enquire.

"Yes, it was a Fokker yesterday evening," he replied, "but no one knows who the pilot was." Then I gave him time, place, etc., of my fight, whereupon he showed great astonishment and forbade me to fly any more—he also promised to make the necessary enquiries about my victory.

Its confirmation came the following morning. That was very nice for me. Now that I have definitely brought a machine down after my promotion to captain and thus given the lie to all the false news published about me by the enemy, my departure from the front is only half as bitter. But to prevent me indulging in any such further escapades, they ordered me to report at Charleville that same day. I was very pleased to be able to promote all my four mechanics to lance-corporals and give three of them the Iron Cross before I left.

The only thing I did in Charleville was to make brief preparations for the journey, get my passport, etc., and now I am on my way to Dessau and Berlin. On the day of my departure I was invited to lunch with the Emperor who greeted me with the words: "You see, we have put you on the leash now!" I had the high honour of sitting next to His Majesty—with the exception of the usual court spooks the only other person present was the minister for war. When I left, I met His Excellency von Falkenhayn in the courtyard; he also gloated over me—they are all pleased to have me sitting in a glass case.

The worst of the whole business is that I am put out of action just at the very moment when on account of the English offensive the enemy's flying activity is more intensive than ever before and my experience and ability might have been able to help our lot a bit!

Boelcke only passed over or concealed one thing from his parents in this letter which reveals so much vigour and lucidity even though hastily written in the train. When he was safely housed in Charleville, his last days there were by no means devoted entirely to preparations for the journey. He also took part in most important conferences with the chief of the air service and his staff.

To the lively interest evinced by Colonel Thomsen in the publication of this book we also owe the following statement:

"Boelcke then spent several days with my staff in order to co-operate closely with our experts in establishing the basic principles of scout flying and making preparations for the further development of this new arm. At my request he drew up the following summary of the principles which should govern every air fight; briefly composed and simply expressed, they were also to serve as a source of success for the younger scouts. These principles established by Boelcke remained in force until the end of the war."

They are:

Try to secure advantages before attacking. If possible, keep the sun behind you.

Always carry through an attack when you have started it.

Fire only at close range and only when your opponent is properly in your sights.

Always keep your eye on your opponent, and never let yourself be deceived by ruses.

In any form of attack it is essential to assail your opponent from behind.

If your opponent dives on you, do not try to evade his onslaught, but fly to meet it.

When over the enemy's lines never forget your own line of retreat.

For the Staffel: Attack on principle in groups of four or six. When the fight breaks up into a series of single combats, take care that several do not go for one opponent.

The subject of the discussions in Charleville was the formation of the new Staffels. Boelcke emphasised the opinion—which his recent experiences at Douai had strengthened that it would not suffice to merely form a number of pilots into a company of single-seater fighters; on the contrary it was most essential to train all members of a Staffel to co-operation by strict discipline and thus organise aerial warfare. Hitherto the scouts—including Boelcke himself—were generally left to scour the air on their own account; in future they were to be welded into a homogeneous fighting-instrument in the Jagstaffels.

Not until the late summer were the findings of the Charleville discussions transmuted into action. Boelcke received his own orders to organise a Jagdstaffel on August 8th. When he set out on his long journey, the prospect of leading such a Staffel was probably held out to him, but he knew nothing certain about his future employment. The only thing definite was that the Emperor had forbidden him to fly. During his journey he was therefore dominated by the feeling of being an exile from the front—this, however, did not prevent him from absorbing with much pleasure all the beautiful or interesting impressions his tour afforded him.

At this point it becomes necessary to correct a certain inaccuracy. A writer whose information is otherwise the best possible informs us in his outline of the history of the Boelcke Jagdstaffel that "the memorandum Boelcke wrote in the summer of 1916 on the exploitation and organised development of Jagdstaffels is an eloquent testimony to the clearsighted view which enabled him to recognise the significance of this weapon and foresee its possibilities."

This is the only reference we have to such a memorandum. There are no signs of it in the state archives, where it would naturally have been deposited with the other papers of the chief of the air service, but what is even more convincing proof is the fact that Colonel Thomsen himself cannot recall ever having received a memorandum written by Boelcke and considers it impossible that such a work could have vanished from his memory. Therefore it would seem as if the writer in question has made a mistake; possibly the document he has in mind is the pamphlet printed by the inspectorate of flying under the title of "Experiences of air fighting. Jadgstaffel Boelcke."

This work indeed contains a highly interesting compilation of Boelcke's experiences in air fights and his instructions for the use of scouts, but it was not published until a considerable time after his death, as in shown by the name "Jagdstaffel Boelcke," which was bestowed on Jagdstaffel 2 by the Emperor on Dec. 17th, 1916. The original manuscript, which I found in the state archives along with the papers of the Staffel, is signed by Captain Wolz, who led it from Nov. 29th, 1916 until June 9th, 1917. But Boelcke wrote no memorandum himself.

# CHAPTER VII

# *In the East*

BOELCKE'S long, enforced holiday trip—on which he was accompanied by the faithful and now indispensable Fischer—is only an episode in his flying career and a joyous intermezzo between two phases of heavy fighting. The welcome he experienced everywhere he went is a proof of the universal significance his personality had already assumed. To him, mildly receptive as he was of all external circumstances, which however failed to leave any permanent impression on him, it was (at least as far as its second portion was concerned) more of a hardship than a recreation. The time he spent in Kordilio, the seaside resort near Smyrna, comprises the last peaceful happy days of his life.

Boelcke described his experiences in daily entries into a diary, which were then sent off as instalments of letters to his parents. These jottings begin with ample details, but finish as mere keywords. It is easy to recognise the sections into which this informal diary is divided. The first cleavage occurs towards the end of his sojourn in Constantinople, when the grave news from the Somme front reached him along with a summons to return as soon as possible—from that point the journey becomes more hurried and his notes on it shorter. This stage comes to its end with the news he received in Teschen and the order to form a Jagdstaffel, which reached him in Kovel—after which his journey is a hasty rush and the jottings consist solely of keywords.

213

Boelcke was then actuated by one sole idea, to complete his journey as quickly as possible and then: "Back to the front, to my Staffel!

*Vienna, 10.7.16.* My grand tour has begun with a breakdown. I intended to travel direct to Constantinople with the Orient Express on Saturday. The train was due to leave the Zoological Gardens station at 8.6 a.m. Half an hour before this time I noticed I had not got my 'Pour le Mérite,' without which I could not possibly show myself on the journey. As a matter of fact the order had remained on the coat of the suit of mufti I wore when visiting Aschenborn the previous evening; the suit was in the trunk which Fischer had packed and left with some friends of mine. So while Fischer was finishing packing I hurried there and got the order out of the trunk, but the consequence was that I arrived at the Zoo station just as the train was steaming out; meanwhile my batman was wandering about with the luggage at the Friedrichstrasse station. After several fruitless journeys we met again in our pension—Fischer trembling like an aspen leaf because he thought he was to blame for all the trouble.

Now I promptly changed my plans—I had to make some use of the days until the next Balkan train left. So I decided on Vienna and Budapest. I got the inspectorate of flying to report me to Vienna and shipped off that evening from the Anhalt station. My sleeping companion was a certain Herr Petschek, a Bohemian coal-king—he has only subscribed for thirty millions of war loan, but quite a nice fellow. The journey passed off quite well except for a few raids by autograph collectors. At the frontier station in Teschen the kindness of an Austrian officer belonging to the passport department relieved me of all frontier formalities—to the great woe of my sleeping companion who had to pass the barrier in spite of all his letters of introduction from the Foreign Office, etc., whereas I could go to bed unmolested.

At Vienna I was welcomed by brother officers of the Austrian Air Service, who drove me straight away to the commander of the air troops. The latter most graciously placed a bear-leader in the person of a certain Captain von Mandel-sloh and a car at my disposal. In the morning I drove out to Fischamend, where a reserve flying section was quartered, but as it was Sunday I could do nothing of a military nature in the afternoon. So I had a trip through Vienna with my escort; in the evening we dined in the Hotel Imperial, where Prince zu Fürstenberg, the friend of our Emperor, talked to me for a long time. He gave me the impression of a typical Austrian—nice-looking, with easy manners and a flow of affable conversation—in short a charming companion.

Today, Monday, we went off in the morning to Aspern aerodrome, which corresponds more or less to our Aldershof. I saw some interesting machines there; I had my first sight of an Italian Caproni and also saw the French machine in which a mad chap made an effort to fly from Nancy to Russia via Berlin. He nearly succeeded; he is said to have got as far as the eastern front where he was shot down after a flight of nearly ten hours; he is supposed to have flown over Berlin at 12.20 a.m. Then there were various Austrian machines, most of which looked rather exotic.

At noon I called on the commander again, who advised me to be sure to go to Trento on my way back from the Balkans and have a look at the mountain flying. I cannot tell whether I shall do so or not; it all depends on circumstances.

In the afternoon I went to the Kahlenberg to have a look

at Vienna from above. On my way back I was caught by my first reporter. The poor fellow had heard of my presence in Vienna and followed me about for two days until he ran me down—it was great fun to keep him on tenterhooks. As he could not get anything out of me, he was nearly in despair, but finally he admitted his satisfaction at having at least spoken to me.

I went out for another stroll in Vienna in the evening. The town gives one a much quieter impression than Berlin; one has the feeling of being in a comfortable sort of residential town rather than a modern capital. Another difference from Berlin is that you can buy anything you want for money. There are certainly bread and meat cards, but you buy everything without them. Fischer said at once: "We'll have to lay in a good supply of thing for our parents on the way back, Herr Captain."

*11.7.16.* To save a tedious railway journey I travelled in a mail-steamer to Budapest, where I am to catch the Balkan train. In this way I enjoyed the country more and got a better impression of it. It was a wonderful trip, even though not to be compared with the one on the Rhine. The finest part of it is the actual entrance into Budapest. In is most impressive; on your right there is the royal palace and the fortress, while on your left you see the hotels and the principal buildings, of which the Houses of Parliament are the finest.

On the trip I was recognised by a twelve year old youngster, who refused to let me go. He was a queer chap—he knew all the dates of my victories. He told me that his worst experience was having an aunt who did not even know who Immelmann was.

The moment I entered the Hotel Hungaria, a reporter fell

on me—I have never yet experienced such obtrusiveness. I spent the evening with the officers of the German Control Commission.

*12.7.16.* At last I have had my sleep out. Then I tramped up to the castle to enjoy a view of Budapest. In the afternoon an officer took me in a car, and we had a trip through Ofen to Margarete Island and then past the Houses of Parliament to the Stadtgarten, where I fairly gorged myself on cakes at Kugler's. I spent the evening again with the German officers. Budapest makes a very modern impression; the women (including many Jewesses) are supermodern.

In the Balkan train: slept through Belgrade. Woken up by music at a station in the middle of Serbia. From Nish the train went through a narrow valley between high rocks, alongside the Bulgarian Morava. From Pirot onward the country assumes the character of a tableland with mountain peaks rising out of it. The ground is fairly stony and sparsely cultivated. The nearer one gets to Sofia, the larger are the cultivated areas, until at last the country becomes a huge plain, with the Balkan mountains in the background. From the railway Sofia hardly gives one the impression of a capital; there are low houses and a small station. Darkness is coming on behind Sofia.

*14.7.16.* On the way through Turkey. The railway is now a single line, with very few places for trains to pass one another. This makes railway traffic in war time very difficult; very long waits at the stations. We passed a military transport; the fellows sat packed like herrings. They had rugged brown faces, and their entire equipment seemed to be of German origin.

I saw my first caravan of camels when we reached the Gulf of Kuchuk. Then came the sea—brown, greenish, violet, shimmering with all colours. On the shore there were bathers disporting themselves and two anti-balloon guns of the oldest pattern.

St. Stefano. Nice little European houses—this is the Turkish Johannistal, with wireless station, etc. Then comes Constantinople. There is not much to be seen when you enter the station, and what you do see is not particularly beautiful—dirty old houses that you could blow over with a breath.

## CONSTANTINOPLE

I was met at the station by our German airmen; spent the evening with Major Serno, who is the local air chief, Major Gratz, who is in charge at St. Stefano, and several gentlemen from the German War office.

*15.7.16.* Morning trip to G.H.Q. Called on Enver Pasha, who invested me personally with the Iron Crescent. Enver comparatively young and makes a sympathetic, energetic impression. In the afternoon I went out with Serno to the 'General,' which is the ship where the German naval officers are quartered. In the evening we went to the Petit Champ, which is a garden café with a German military band.

To keep things simple I have moved into the pension where Serno lives. I get great fun out of my batman, who is thoroughly miserable because he cannot get into the swim of things here and is continually swindled by the natives. He had imagined Turkey to be quite different. He is horrified at the row the people make in the streets at three a.m.

when they bleat out their goods.

On the 6th I visited His Excellency von Bronsart, the chief of the staff, who is an almost exact likeness of his son (leads a Staffel on the Verdun front); he also was not particularly edified with the Turks. Then I drove out to the 'General,' because I wanted to see a U-boat at close quarters. On the 'General' I was hauled along first to His Excellency von Usedom, the commander of the Straits, then to the commander of the fleet and finally to Captain Deckert. The last-mentioned was very nice; he invited me to lunch and a trip through the Bosphorus next day. Then I went with Lieut. Heller to see the U.38; she is one of the most up-to-date submarines.

In the afternoon I strolled round Galata in a borrowed suit of civilian attire and caught sight of the Sultan, who was just coming out of a mosque.

*Monday, 17.7.16.* At last I was able to see a bit of the air service; hitherto Major Serno was too busy with the commission sent out from the German War Office. We drove through Stambul in a car, past the old Byzantine town wall, the old cemetery and several barracks; then we crossed a stretch of waste land to St. Stefano and saw the air station there. Serno has made himself a fine kingdom out of nothing here—everything that is done here comes up against tremendous difficulties through the failure of local industry, which at present is nothing more than a pious aspiration. I was invited to lunch with the naval officers on board the 'General,' and in the afternoon I crossed the Bosphorus with Deckert and other gentlemen to Therapia, where the German war cemetery lies in beautiful surroundings. Then we went out to the 'Goeben' and the 'Breslau,' where we had a really charming welcome. After seeing over both ships and dining on board the 'Goeben' I listened to a concert on deck in the glorious summer night. When I left, Captain Ackermann, the commanding officer of the Goeben, called for three cheers for me, and the sailors hoisted me on their shoulders. What a lot of things they do for me! Who would have thought it all possible a few years ago!

*18.7.16.* I spent all today trotting about the Sea of Marmora in a motor-boat with Serno's adjutant, who is a Turk; we went past the Sultan's palace to Scutari, and then to the Princes's Islands, where we landed in Prinkipo. To the people of Constantinople Prinkipo is what Grunewald or Wann-see is to the Berliners—it is a wonderful mountanous island, full of pines, in the middle of the sea; the well-to-do people have their summer residences there. We drank our coffee in the Casino garden, where we had a view over the sea and neighbouring islands. We then cruised round the neighbouring islands—on one of which the captive defender of Kut-el-Amara lives in a beautiful villa—but I got home in good time because Serno and I were entertaining Major Schlee to dinner; he was attached to the 3rd Telegraph battalion for a long time and is now head wireless officer of Turkey.

## SMYRNA

*19.7.16.* Left for Panderma with Serno at 9. With the exception of a few officers practically all the passengers on board were peasants. Lt-Col. von Frese took us into Panderma in a small government steamer, while all the others had to land in lighters. After a snack of lunch in the mess we started our journey in the saloon coach belonging to His Excellency Liman—the train was a special one for us. Fairly barren country as far as Maniyas Goel; a few fishing boats on the lake and a lot of storks by the wayside. The scenery changes in the Susurlu valley; more villages, with fruit trees and huge herds of sheep and oxen. Then it grew dark; I slept well after a jolly dinner.

*20.7.16.* Woke up after passing Akhissar. Very pretty country and well cultivated, many herds. Camel caravans, each headed by a donkey who leads the beasts. After Magnesia vegetation became more luxurious, though only in the plain—many stones on the mountains, not much bread there. Wonderful view of Smyrna on the slope of a hill. Buddecke and others met us at station. I am put up in the Hotel Krämer, close to the shore—I have a view over the whole Gulf of Smyrna from my balcony.

Lunched with Excellency Liman von Sanders, who was very nice and had his photo taken with Buddecke and myself. Strolled through the bazaar in the afternoon; not as large as the one at Stambul, In the evening big dinner at Buddecke's; present Liman von Sanders, Colonel Kiasim (chief of staff), Count Spee, the German consul, etc.; after the meal the Austrian, Dutch and Swedish consuls came along with their ladies. A very nice evening.

On the 21st I went out with Faller, my old instructor at Darmstadt in August, 1914, to Sevdi-köi aerodrome, south of Smyrna. We rode from the Station to the aerodrome. The Turkish soldiers make a good impression, but their officers—pilots and observers—not so good.

In the afternoon I called on General Trommer, who spoke his mind about the rotten state of things in Turkey. Then went to station to say goodbye to Excellency Liman, who was going back to Panderma. All the bigwigs there—lot of fuss. Spent evening with Count Spee in Sporting Club, where there is a wonderful view over the Gulf of Smyrna.

*22.7.16.* Went bathing with several ladies and gentlemen in Kordilio, where Buddecke came for us with a yacht. Glorious! The view of the surrounding mountains and Smyrna is wonderful. In the evening we went to tea with the Austrian consul and met all sorts of people. Conversation carried on in ever so many languages.

Boelcke originally intended to return to Constantinople with Major Serno on the 22nd. When he was making up his mind to stay on, the gay society in which he found himself exercised a strong influence on his decision; on the other hand he also speculated on the possibility of flying to the Dardanelles, his next destination, from Smyrna in a few hours, thus eliminating the twenty-six hours' railway trip to Pandermaas well as the further journey from Constantinople to the Dardanelles.

And so he spent the next three days in Kordilio, enjoying the yachting parties and the gay society there; once more he tasted the innocent pleasures of his youth. Even his former youthful exuberance awoke once more. When his batman Fischer, who accompanied him on a yachting trip, succumbed to sea-sickness, Boelcke tried a new remedy on him; giving the sailors a hint, he simply threw his faithful Fischer into the water, then quickly jumped in after him, rescued the patient whose complaint had speedily vanished and handed him over to the sailors.

But his plan of flying to the Dardanelles did not materialise. On July 25th he wrote in a somewhat humble strain: "I now have to go the long way round by Constantinople to the Dardanelles. I could have been there in two and a half hours in an aeroplane, but Buddecke will not let me have one. He gave me a thousand reasons why it was impossible, but I believe he received instructions from the air chief or even from G.H.Q. that I must not fly here either." On the 26th he therefore left beautiful Smyrna "only one and a half hours late. After endless whistling, waving and screaming our little train set itself in motion. Luckily we (Schüler and I) had a compartment to ourselves. At the stations the chief thing is to make as much row as possible. The obtrusive begging there is horrible. We had three to four hours' wait in Soma—reason not apparent. About 1.30 a.m. we were disturbed by the former governor of Samoa, who boarded the train.

## THE DARDANELLES

At 10 a.m. on the 28th I went down to Chanak on the Dardanelles in a little gunboat that was towing a 'Malone.' There was not much new to be seen on the trip; Gallipoli is just a little country town with big barracks. As we steamed at the terrific speed of five knots, we took twenty-six hours over the trip and did not reach Chanak until about midday on the 29th.

There Schüler, Commander Landsberg of the sea planes and I reported at once to Merten Pasha. In the afternoon I visited the aerodrome of Lieut. Kroneis, the Fokker expert of the Dardanelles. I then had a very fine flight in the biplane of Lieut. Meinecke, who came across from Galata. He took me all round by Troy and Kum-kalessi to Sedd-ul-bahr and

the English positions on the Dardanelles. The islands of
Imbros, Tenedos and especially Samothrace looked wonderful when I saw them rising from the sea; we could plainly see
the English warships lying in Cephalo Bay at Imbros. Also
we got a very clear view over the barren hills of the peninsula where so much fighting took place. We dined with Merten
Pasha in the evening. I shall never forget the night in the
Sailors' Home on account of the bugs there.

On Sunday, July 30th, Kroneis, Schüler and I went over
to Sedd-ul-Bahr in a little steamer. We got out just before
reaching the place, and were met by a naval officer, with
whom we rode right across the peninsula alongside the old
trenches. It is all in a frightful mess now, but there is a conspicuous difference between the English and Turkish positions—the English were able to work with much better
materials. Then I also looked at the English landing-places,
where they simply put a couple of steamers on shore to cover
the landing.

After a hasty lunch I flew to Chanak with Meinecke, who
came to fetch me; then we went back to St. Stefano along the
northern coast of the Sea of Marmora. It was a fine flight as
far as Rodosto, after which it became boring. But in this
fashion I got back to Constantinople in three hours instead
of the twenty-six taken by the steamer.

*31.7.16.* My last time with Serno, who is off to Baghdad today. I have decided to leave to-morrow, my immediate desti-
nations being Sofia and Uskub, but presumably I shall only
stay a short time there. I am all impatience to be back at the
front.

On his return from the Dardanelles Boelcke received news of

the state of the terrific struggle on the Somme and the superiority maintained by enemy airmen there, together with an express request from the chief of the air service to come back soon, although his enforced leave was originally intended to prevent him reappearing on the western front before Sept. 1st. These tidings induced him to cut down his journey very considerably. He had only time to write these reports for his parents in the train. Consequently we find the next written on the journey from Uskub to Hudova.

## BULGARIA

*1.8.16.* Left Constantinople after farewell meal with Schüler. Great excitement at the station as Enver Pasha travelling by the same train. The whole place so heavily guarded that even Schüler in uniform not allowed on to the platform. The train even left punctually to the minute. Enver sent for me to come to tea in his saloon coach. In addition to his staff I met von Lossow, the German military plenipotentiary in Constantinople. Enver was very nice and a lively talker; our conversation was almost entirely in German.

About 11 a.m. on Aug. 2nd I reached Sofia after a pretty trip through the well cultivated parts of Roumelia; I was met there by Captain von Steinwehr and other airmen. Called on Lt-Col. von Massow in the military chancery, after which Steinwehr gave me a talk about conditions in Bulgaria. In the afternoon a stroll through Sofia, which gives the impression of a central German residential town. Steinwehr gave a big dinner in the evening.

*3.8.16.* Visited the cadet school; the military smartness made a very good impression. Then with Lieut. Haase, Steinwehr's

adjutant, to the aerodrome close to Sofia, where the Otto
was the type of machine mainly represented. In the afternoon I drove out with Steinwehr to the Boschurishte Flying
School, where Captain Petroff, the commander, showed me
his 1913 Blèriot as something very special; the school is only
in its infancy as yet. Then to Banja hydro, which is in very
pretty country. Dinner with military attaché, von Massow, in
the evening; Prince Cyril was present. He interested me very
much and asked all sorts of questions, some of which were
quite clever ones.

*4.8.16.* Called on Bulgarian War Minister, General
Neidenoff, who speaks quite good German and had a long
talk with me. Then I was shown a cavalry barracks, where I
saw the new cavalry machine-guns. I spent the afternoon
strolling in the Boris Garden and seeing the Sofia 'beauties.'
Invited to the club by Lt-Col. von Müffling in the evening.

*5.8.16.* An audience with the Bulgarian commander-in-chief,
General Shekoff. Then off to Uskub in a car lent by the
Ministry of War. Broke the journey at Keustendil, where I
lunched with Shoikoff, the Bulgarian chief of the staff, at the
mess. Then an interesting trip to Uskub, which I reached
about 9 p.m.

On the morning of the 6th I chanced to meet Colonel
Schroeder, my former C.O. at Coblence, in the streets—great
joy! At noon I called on Excellency von Mackensen, whom I
also sat next to at lunch. Mackensen has an interesting,
striking appearance, but does not look anything like as
severe as his portraits make him out; he had a long talk with
me during and after the meal.

In the afternoon I caught the train to Hudova, where I

reached the headquarters of our 66th section, who put me up in most hospitable fashion. All our airmen here are quartered in wooden huts; their aerodrome is all stones and withered bushes—not exactly a pleasant station for a long time, especially as they have had very little to do for months.

*7.8.16. (Written on the journey from Sofia to Teschen).* Called on Excellency von Winckler in command of 11th army, and stayed to lunch; then visited Section 28, who live in much the same fashion as No. 66. In the afternoon went for a flight with Captain von Eberstein, of 66, along the Greek front, returning thence direct to Uskub, where I spent the evening in the aircraft park.

*8.8.16.* After a short visit to Colonel Schroeder returned to Sofia in my Bulgarian car. We had several breakdowns en route. that were most funny affairs as I could only talk to my Bulgarian chauffeur in the language of gestures. Not far from Kumanova I saw a Macedonian fair, which interested me greatly; the peasants wore white costumes and executed a strange but very beautiful dance to the music of bagpipes. In the evening dined with von Gröbitz, the representative of the German War Ministry; there were several other German ladies present in addition to his wife—a pleasure that has long been lacking!

*9.8.16.* Shortly before I left, the War Minister's adjutant handed me the Bulgarian "For Valour" medal, together with a portrait of the Minister. Colonel Loloff, the chief of the Bulgarian flying corps, came to the station with several of his officers to say goodbye to me—which gave me great pleasure.

Boelcke appears to have left a deep impression behind him on the occasion of his visit to Bulgaria, so far as we can judge by the number of congratulatory telegrams found among his papers and messages of condolence received by his parents. One of the most original in the former category is a long telegram dated 10.10.16, in which the "Pupils of the upper classes of the first Sofia Grammar School" congratulate him on his 30th victory.

The memories of him cherished by the Turks are shown by the gigantic dimensions—nearly a metre in diameter and weighing a hundredweight—of the wreath of artistically wrought gold bronze shaped in the likeness of their pilot's badge that the Turkish airmen sent through their Embassy after his death.

While these last letters give some sort of picture of his sojourn in Bulgaria, even though hastily written on the train, his further communications shrivel into mere jottings. The haste of his journey is shown by the fact that he did not spend as much as twenty-four hours in the Austrian G.H.Q. He reached Teschen about 2 p.m. on August 10th and set off for Kovel at 11 a.m. the following morning. There he only paid the most unavoidable calls; on the evening of that day he paid his respects to General Conrad, "who received me very jovially (without a collar), while on the following morning he called on General Cramon and the Archduke Friedrich, "who received me in the garden and does not exactly look as if Mars stood godfather at his christening."

In Kovel he met his brother Wilhelm, who had been transferred thither with his fighter squadron in July. There he received the decisive telegram from the chief of the air service: "Return to west front as quickly as possible to organise and lead Jagdstaffel 2 on the Somme front."

Equipped with full power to pick out the most suitable pilots for his Staffel, he started by enrolling two officers particularly recommended to him by his brother in Kovel—a young Uhlan lieutenant named Manfred von Richthofen who had already made good on the Verdun front and a reserve lieutenant, Erwin Böhme, a gentleman already in his 37th year who had resided for many years in the Kilimanjaro district but whose iron will and youthful vigour rendered him the equal of any of his juniors. Richthofen developed into Boelcke's most famous pupil, while Böhme became the best of his friends. Both were his comrades in battle and eyewitnesses of his death-flight. Richthofen carried the cushion for his orders at the funeral; later Böhme followed his master and friend to death while leading the Boelcke Staffel. Thus their destinies were linked.

Boelcke's ample collection of war pictures contains two photographs from Kovel, the purport of which can only be intelligible to those who are familiar with Erwin Böhme's letters.* On August 3rd, 1916 Böhme wrote that his machine had been decorated with a fearsome dragon as a talisman, which 'at least made a terrifying impression on the Russian peasants.' At the close of this same letter he refers to the terrific storm that swept over Volhynia: "Our tame squadron stork 'Adolar' was scared out of his wits and crouched on the lee side of my car beside his friend, the jackdaw. [see insert] we find illustrations of both, as the upper one shows the dragon machine, together with Böhme and his observer Lademacher, while the lower one is a picture of the squadron-stork with his jackdaw friend perched on his back.

* *"Briefe eines deutschen Kampffliegers an ein junges Mädschen"* (Letters of a German fighting pilot to a young girl). Edited by Johannes Werner, Leipzig, 1930. 5th edition 1932.

These two photos appear under the heading of "The Humours of War" in Boelcke's collection.

The Kovel entries in the travel-diary make no reference to the urgent summons from the air chief, but merely note briefly that Boelcke called on General von Linsingen on the 12th and dined with him that same evening, that he met two old acquaintences on Sunday, the 13th, i.e., Gause of the war academy and Kohlhauer of the telegraph battalion, that he went up to the lines on the 14th and that he spent the same evening with Section 4b, which had been formerly in Douai.

The entries for the final days are still more laconic:

*15.8.16.* Noon (still in Kovel). Lunched with Staffel 7. Then a trip to Brest Litovsk, which is quite burnt out. Spent the evening with Baltzer.
*16.8.16.* Called on Excellency Ludendorff. Introduced to Field Marshal Hindenburg before lunch, sat between Hindenburg and Ludendorff at the meal. Afternoon: flew to Warsaw to visit experimental park.
*17.8.16.* Travelled to Vilna. Met Martin.
*18.8.16.* Travelled with Martin to Kovno, then on to Berlin.
*19.8.16.* Various business at inspectorate and Johannistal.
*20.8.16.* Travelled to Dessau.

Thus ended the six weeks' tour in the East, which was begun in ease and comfort and finished in impatient haste. The news from the front and the new great task that awaited him left him no rest. He was burning with impatience to help with his Staffel. "The Somme calls me!" And so he said only a brief farewell in Dessau—"there was no holding him"—and then hurried off to the Somme front, towards the zenith and end of his flying career.

# CHAPTER VIII

# *The Master Scout*

THE nine weeks on the Somme constitute Boelcke's heroic epoch. We need only compare one of his latest photographs with the reproduction of the painting copied from a photograph taken in May 1916. This last is the portrait of a serious-minded, energetic man, but still retains a youthful, frank, carefree expression. The former shows the fixed look—as if directed upon a foeman of the air—of one whose sole objectives are fighting and victory. All other interests fell away from him—even his letters to his parents grew scantier. He had now no thoughts for anything but his Staffel, which he resolved to develop into a model of its kind in order to achieve victories and break the enemy's aerial supremacy. With these supreme efforts of his taut will and his entire strength his character assumes heroic proportions.

But the impression conveyed to the reader by Boelcke's reports of his victories, which followed hard upon one another with such an incredible rapidity, resembles that of a thunderstorm in the mountains when it discharges its fury in one blow after another. Spellbound by the magnitude of the events taking place, one can think of nothing else; one can only await the next blow.

When Boelcke reached Bertincourt, where his Staffel was to be organised, he found there nothing but an aerodrome in the Vélu aircraft park with four permanent hangars previously used by Section 32 and some of the aircraftmen

231

assigned to him. Whereas Jagdstaffel 1, which was due to come into existence simultaneously, was formed out of a large single-seater fighting unit already serving with the 1st Army and consequently its organisation was so far advanced when Captain Zander took over the leadership that he could even give some aircraftmen and Lieut. Höhne (on August 29th) to Jagdstaffel 2, Boelcke had to create his formation out of raw material. "I am now hard at work, and my first job is to get hold of everything I want; there are still many things lacking, above all, the most important—the machines," he complains to his parents in his first short letter from the Somme.

The entries in the "War Diary" of the Staffel—which is preserved in the state archives—begin on August 27th, 1916, which date may therefore be reckoned its birthday:

*27.8.16.* "Jagdstaffel 2 assembled under the leadership of Captain Boelcke. Effectives: three officers (Lieuts. von Arnim and Günther in addition to Boelcke), sixty-four N.C.O.s and men. Quarters: Officers to be billeted in Bertincourt, men to live in huts. Machines: none to hand as yet. Activities: preparation of aerodrome."

Lieuts. Reimann and von Richthofen joined on September 1st, in addition to Sergeants Reimann and Max Müller, while Lieuts. Viehweger and Böhme came on the 8th, As Lieut. Höhne arrived on August 29th, the Staffel had seven pilots on September 8th for its fourteen allotted machines, because the Lieut, von Arnim counted in the strength of the effectives on August 27th received his transfer to the Staffel on that date, but fell the following day while still flying for his old section.

The Staffel received its first machines on September 1st—an Albatros Biplane that Sergeant Reimann brought from

Jagdstaffel I and two Fokker Biplanes, one of which Boelcke fetched himself from the army aircraft park. This Fokker, the official designation of which was D.III.352/16, was subsequently presented by the Emperor to the armoury museum in the Berlin Zeughaus in memory of Boelcke and is still on exhibition there.

On the following day (September 2nd, 1916), which in addition to being Sedan Day was the second anniversary of Boelcke's first arrival at the front, he secured his twentieth victory on this Fokker:

*Bertincourt, 4.9.16.* You will have been astonished to read of my "twentieth," because you will have imagined me as organising my Staffel but not yet flying.

Several days ago Fokker sent two machines for me, and I made my first flight on one of them the day before yesterday. There was a fair amount of enemy aerial activity at the front. Those fellows had grown very impudent. One of them tried to have a go at me when I was flying peaceably behind our lines, but I refused to let myself be drawn—he was flying much higher than I. Somewhat later in the day I saw shell-bursts west of Bapaume. There I found a B.E., followed by three Vickers single-seaters, i.e. an artillery plane with its escort. I went for the B.E. But the other three interrupted me in the middle of my work, and so I beat a hasty retreat. One of those fellows thought he could catch me and gave chase; when I had lured him somewhat away from the others, I gave battle and soon got to grips with him. I did not let him go again; he did not get another shot in. When he went down, his machine was wobbling badly, but that, as he told me afterwards, was not his fault, because I had shot his elevating gear to pieces. The machine landed north east of

Thièpval; it was burning when the pilot jumped out and beat his arms and legs about because he was on fire too. I then flew home and took off again with fresh supplies of ammunition because other Englishmen had appeared, but I did not score any further successes.

Yesterday I fetched the Englishman I had forced to land—a certain Captain Wilson—from the prisoners' clearing depot, took him to coffee in the mess and showed him our aerodrome, whereby I had a very interesting conversation with him.

My aerodrome is gradually getting ready. I still have no machines for my pilots. I have now sent several of them to Germany to hurry up delivery, but I also have my hands completely full here. Still I hope to be ready in about a week.

Owing to pressure of work I forgot to tell you that I visited our little Max on the way here. He positively beamed all over when he saw me. He was quite proud of the fact that he is the closest to the front of all us four brothers and lives in a dugout like a real 'field-grey.' It would be hard to find anyone so heart and soul in it as he is. By the way he took me for a walk that lasted half the afternoon because he wanted to show himself in the company of his 'big brother.'

The communiqué that announced Boelcke's new victory when the public had not heard anything about him for two months had the effect of a clarion call. On the Somme front, in all the dug-outs and trenches the tidings ran from mouth to mouth: "Boelcke is back again! Boelcke will do the job!"

We have an interesting description of this last fight from the other side in the person of Captain Robert Wilson, of the R.F.C. The version of it appended below is a combination of a letter which he wrote home from the prison camp at

Osnabrück and his own personal statements made there:

"It is some consolation to me that I was brought down by Captain Boelcke, the greatest German airman, and that my life was preserved in a fashion that is almost miraculous.

"As you know, I fly a fast Vickers Fighter. When out on reconnaissance work I saw a German scout intending to polish off one of our slow old B.E.s and came just in time to rescue it. After I loosed off a couple of shots at the German, he went into a turn and flew home. I was fool enough to chase him and failed to spot that he only wanted to lure me further on to his territory. When I had followed him about fifteen miles behind the German lines, he turned round and attacked me by climbing above me at a fabulous speed—he flew a machine I never saw before, and I had no idea of its speed and climbing capacity. I hardly let off a couple of shots before my gun jammed, so that I could not fire a single round more.

"Under these circumstances I did the only thing left to me and fled to get out of the way of a better machine and a superior pilot. I tried to shake him off by all sorts of tricks, but he followed all my movements magnificently and sat on my neck the whole time. He shot away all my controls, with the exception of two that were jammed, shot holes in my machine, shot the throttle away when I had my hand on it; then he put some holes in my tank and a couple in my coat when it was soaked with petrol. Naturally I lost all control over my machine, which whizzed down in a nose dive—a most uncomfortable sensation! I sat there, pretty dizzy and waiting for the crash when I hit the ground below, but when about fifty feet up I made a desperate tug at the stick and somehow obtained enough control at the last moment to dodge the crash and bring off some sort of a landing, which however set the machine and my coat on fire. I managed to jump out and pull my coat off without getting burnt. The German came down quite low and flew away as soon as he made sure I was settled.

"Next day Boelcke invited me to his aerodrome and entertained me in his mess. We were also photographed together. (see insert) I got a very fine impression of him both as a pilot and a man, and this fight will remain the greatest memory of my life, even though it turned out badly for me."

After Boelcke's death Captain Wilson sent a laurel wreath for his conqueror.

As the new Albatros biplane destined for the use of the Staffel had not yet arrived, only individual hunting expeditions could be undertaken in the few available machines. The War Diary records nine such flights up to September 14th. On them Boelcke achieved a series of five victories during the week of September 8th to 15th.

From this period when he had to fly without his Staffel originates the following delicious anecdote which was found in a memoir on him written by one of his faithful followers and deposited with his papers:

"Whenever Boelcke returned from a flight, we asked him while he still sat laughing in his machine: 'Well, got another, captain?' whereupon he replied with another question: 'Have I got a black chin? (i.e. from the smoke of the machine gun). Well, that's all right, then.' In which case he had brought down another victim."

We may also state from these personal recollections that Boelcke was extremely moderate in his mode of life. He was never a smoker; the most he ever did was to light a cigarette in company when courtesy required it of him, but he always laid it down after a few whiffs. He was a very moderate drinker and lived almost abstemiously, but he was too natural a personality to ever make a principle of this abstinence or refuse to take a glass of wine on suitable occasions in the company of friends. His chief recreation seemed to consist of going to bed as early as possible. When the weather was good for flying, nothing existed for him except the service.

The new Albatros biplanes reached Cambrai at last on September 16th and were fetched by the pilots of the Staffel. That very same evening Lieut. Höhne secured his first victory on one of them at 6 p.m. The entry for the 17th then records the following details: "thirteen flights, five fights, of which four were successful." At 7.45 a.m. Böhme scored a a victory; of the pilots who started at 10.45 Richthofen, Lieut. Reimann and Boelcke each secured a victim.

This Sunday, September 17th, 1916, is the real birthday of the Boelcke Jagdstaffel. Boelcke relates his own experiences in the following letter:

*Bertincourt, 17.9.16.* You have come off rather badly in the last few days, but I have really had no time to write letters. But early this bright summer morning I must manage to give you a report.

First in reply to father's questions: Our quarters are quite decent; I have a nice room and a good bed. The Staffel is not quite up to strength yet, as I am still without about half of our machines. But yesterday at least six arrived, so that I shall be able to take off with my Staffel for the first time today. Hitherto I have generally flown Fokker biplanes, but today I shall take up one of the new Albatroses. My pilots are all passionately keen and very competent, but I must first train them to steady team-work—they are at present rather like young puppies in their zeal to achieve something.

Yesterday my officer for special purposes (office work) arrived; he is a certain Lieut, von Zastrow whom I met in Jametz when he was with the artillery section No. 203. He cannot fly in consequence of a severe wound, but he will relieve me of a lot of work. Nevertheless my time is very fully occupied when I am not flying. It takes a lot of work to build up a section from nothing, so to speak. But it gives me great pleasure to see things gradually got going.

There is a lot of flying going on here; the English always come over in large numbers. Meanwhile I have completed my quarter century.

No. 21, a Vickers biplane, I got to grips with over Flers. The fight did not last long, as these machines are almost defenceless against a skilled single-seater. I got on to the Vickers obliquely from behind (that is the best position; if you attack him directly from behind, his engine protects him like a thick armour belt); he tried in vain to wriggle out of the situation. Soon his machine took fire. My attack had brought me so near to him that his explosion splashed my machine with the oil that ran out. The machine then went down in spirals, throwing its occupant out, and was completely consumed by the flames.

No. 22, another Vickers biplane, fell to me in similar fashion the next day. He and four others were cruising about most impudently on our side over Bapaume, where he attacked some German machines. He suffered for it, as did also one of his companions who was shot down by a couple of Rumplers. After I had fired off a few rounds, the machine was wrapped in bright flames and went into a glide. He reached his lines, but crashed there.

Nos. 23 and 24 followed on the 14th. I took off about 9

a.m. with two other machines of my Staffel (Lieuts. Böhme and von Richthofen). North of Bapaume we barred the homeward way of an English squadron coming from the east. As the first of these machines bolted, I engaged the second, a Sopwith Biplane. The third attacked Lieut. von Richthofen, but was soon involved with both Richthofen and Böhme. Immediately after my first attack my opponent spun down for several hundred metres. As I know this trick, I followed hard behind, and then the fellow actually caught his machine and tried to escape over his lines. He did not succeed, but crashed near Morval. The machine shed its wings and broke up in the air.

Shortly afterwards I saw several Englishmen whirling about to the north of Peronne. When I approached, they wanted to attack me. But as I merely intended to go for an innocent little stroll—as a matter of fact I was flying lower than they and could do nothing—I sheered away. Then I saw one of these fellows attack another German machine—naturally I could not stand that. I engaged that lad in single combat, and he had to pay for his impudence. I shot his petrol and oil tanks to pieces in a series of fighting turns; he was forced to land at Driencourt, where he was taken prisoner.

No. 25 had to give me best the next morning. A squadron of seven English Sopwith Biplanes flew over our aerodrome on their way home. I took off at once and chased them. I came up with them near Hervilly, eastward of Peronne, but could do nothing for the moment because I was flying below them. The fellows took advantage of this to attack me. Impudence! I soon turned the tables on them and got one in my sights. I came nicely up to him and gave him about fifty rounds from close range—about twenty to forty metres. Then, having had enough, he went down—after Lieut. von

Richthofen had also given him a few superfluous rounds—into a wood near Hesbécourt and crashed.

About half an hour later I saw an enemy squadron dispersing northward of Peronne and flew there quickly with Richthofen. When I attacked one—they were Sopwith Biplanes too—he promptly put his nose down and tried to escape me in a steep dive. As he was as fast as I was, I did not manage to get close to him, but hung on about one hundred and fifty metres away. We whizzed along as far as the lines in this fashion; I was behind him all the time, putting in a shot every now and then. As we were only about two hundred metres up over the front, I gave him one good final burst and then broke away. He crashed about five hundred metres behind the enemy's lines.

*17.9.16. Afternoon.* Meanwhile the status quo has altered once more. This morning I ran into an enemy squadron with two of my pilots (Lieuts. Reimann and Richthofen). We cleaned them up thoroughly; each of us got one. I engaged the leader's machine, which I recognised by its streamers, and forced it down. My opponent landed at Equancourt and promptly set fire to his machine. The inmates were taken prisoner; one of them was slightly wounded. The pilot had to land because I shot his engine to pieces. So that was No. 27.

The Staffel is making itself! We have got five English machines since yesterday evening!

In view of these many 'numbers' mother will be saying again that it is not right to number our victims in this unfeeling way. But we don't really do it—we do not number the victims who have fallen, but the machines we have brought down. That you can see from the fact that it only counts as one victory when two inmates are killed, but that it still remains a 'number' when both the inmates escape unhurt. We have nothing against the individual; we only fight to prevent him flying against us. So when we have eliminated an enemy force, we are pleased and book it as one up to us.

*Lagnicourt, 8.10.16.* I have had a lot of work again with the Staffel. At last everything was shipshape at Bertincourt; the aerodrome was in working order, the machines were in the hangars, the mess and officers' huts on the aerodrome were ready. Everything was fixed up, in fact—then the English streaked in to Bertincourt and we had to go on our travels.* The whole business had to start again from the beginning. I have not yet been able to put up sheds for our machines, which must therefore be accommodated in tents at present, as we have not the men for the work. My first aim is to get huts built for my officers so that they can be accommodated on the aerodrome instead of living in the village and always be ready to take off. What a lot of work it all means.

Besides that I have to give my pilots some training. That is not so simple because they are all inspired with such fiery zeal that it is often difficult to put the brake on them. They have certainly all learnt that the main thing is to get the enemy in your power and beat him down at once instead of arguing with him. But until I get it into their heads that everything depends on sticking together through thick and

*The transfer of the Staffel to Lagnicourt took place on the night of Sepember 22nd under the supervision of Lieut. Viehweger because Boelcke was so badly smitten by his asthmatic complaint in consequence of the wet autumn weather that the faithful Fischer was hardly able to move him across to the new aerodrome. He absolutely refused to leave his Staffel and go into hospital. The war diary reports six fights and three victories for September 23rd, the first day on the new aerodrome. These were credited to Böhme, Richthofen and Lieut. Riemann. Boelcke was able to resume flying on September 27th

thin when the Staffel goes into battle and that it does not matter who actually scores the victory as long as the Staffel wins it—well, I can talk myself silly, and sometimes I have to turn my heavy batteries on to them. I always give them some instruction before we take off and deal out severe criticism after every flight and especially after every fight. But they take it all very willingly.

You will certainly have read of my "Thirtieth" in the official communiqué, but that is now ancient history. No. 31 followed his predecessor yesterday.

No. 28 fell on the evening of the 19th. Six of us rattled into a squadron consisting of eight or ten F.E.s and several Moranes—the fat lattice-tails down below and the Moranes above as a cover. I engaged one of the latter and pranced about the air with him—he escaped me for a moment, but I got to grips with him again west of Bapaume; one of my guns jammed, but the other shot all the better. I shot up that monoplane from close range until he broke up in flames and fell into the wood near Grévillers in fragments.

I met another five Englishmen in the Bapaume area about midday on the 27th. I was on a patrol with four of my gentlemen; when we reached the front, I saw a squadron which I first took for a German formation. But when we met to the south-east of Bapaume, I recognised them for enemy aircraft. As we were lower than they, I turned away to northward. The Englishmen then passed by us, crossed our lines, circled round a bit behind our captive balloons and then wanted to go home. Meanwhile, however, we had climbed to their height and cut them off. I gave the signal to attack, and the fun started. It was a mighty scrap. I got to grips with one and basted him properly, but came up too close and had to pass out below him. Then I went into a turn, in the course of which I saw the Englishman go down and fall like a sack somewhere near Ervillers.

I engaged another immediately—there were plenty of them. He tried to get away from me, but it did not avail him—I hung on close behind all the time. Yet I was surprised at this opponent's tenacity—I thought I really must have settled him some time before, but he kept on flying round and round in the same sort of circles. At last I could stand it no longer—I said to myself that the man must be dead and the controls are jammed so as to keep the machine in a normal position. So I flew quite close up to him—then I saw the man sprawling over in the cockpit, dead. I left the machine to its fate, having noted its number—7495. When we got home, it came out that Sergeant Reimann had also shot down a machine that bore the number 7495. To avoid doing either of us an injustice the staff officer acted on my suggestion that the victory should not be credited to anyone.

After leaving No. 7495 I took on another. He got a good dose from me, but after a series of fighting turns managed to escape behind his own lines. When I had to pass out under him, I saw how my bullets had cut his fuselage about. He will remember that day for a long time! And so shall I, for I worked like a nigger and sweated like a reserve officer.

No. 30, who fell on October 1st, was much easier. I surprised him at the front, over Eaucourt l'Abbaye, to the north-west of Flers; he was an artillery flier. He heeled over and disappeared after I had given him two hundred rounds.

The fall of No. 31 yesterday was a magnificent but awesome spectacle. I was over the lines with five of my gentlemen; we amused ourselves by attacking and chasing away all English and French machines we found in order to test our machine guns and practise on living targets. But they did not seem to like it—and would not let us do business with them. Then all at once I saw one pottering about alone low down east of Morval. So I went down, got on to his tail, came up to close range and then took good and steady aim. My opponent—a Nieuport double-seater—did not make matters too difficult as he flew straight ahead. I kept within twenty to thirty metres of him, until he exploded close before me in livid yellow flames and crashed down in pieces. It can hardly be called a fight, because I took this enemy completely by surprise.

You will be interested to know that the official report of our activities which I have drawn up for the Staffel's September work includes one hundred and eighty-six front flights, in the course of which sixty-nine fights took place and twenty-five victories were won. This in spite of the fact that we did not really begin operations until our machines arrived on the 16th.

Lucid as all these descriptions of fights may be, they do not give a complete picture of Boelcke's life and Staffel. We are shown the climaxes and successes, but there is no mention of the enormous expenditure of energy that represented the many—sometimes five or more in a day—unsuccessful flights carried out under the tension of expected action. The heroic upward curve of achievement under Boelcke's leadership can only be fully appreciated by those who bear in mind that in the winter of 1914–15 some of the officers of Section 13 could not reconcile their nerves to more than two hours flying a day, on mere reconnaissance work, as no fights took place in the Pontfaverger area at that time!

Here are a few of the Staffel's October achievements, as shown by their war diary:

*10.10.16.* 31 flights, 18 fights, 5 victories. 9.50 a.m.
Böhme, 11 a.m. Sergeant Müller, in the afternoon Lieut.
Imelmann (the youngest in the Staffel, not to be confused
with Immelmann), Richthofen, Boelcke.

*16.10.16.* 6 victories. 2.5. p.m. Sergeant Reimann, 2.30
p.m. Boelcke, 5 p.m. Richthofen, 5 p.m. Lieut. Sandel, 5.45
p.m. Boelcke. 5.50 p.m. Sergeant Müller.

*22.10.16.* 33 flights, 17 fights, 6 victories, of which 2
each fell to Boelcke and Sergeant Reimann, and the other 2
to Böhme and Immelmann.

It is quite comprehensible that Boelcke did not inform his
parents about the losses these victories involved. Four pilots
fell up to October 1st. The first of these casualties occurred
on September 22nd, the victim being the youthful Uhlan
officer, Lieut. Winand Grafe, from Elberfeld, whom Boelcke
had known from Jametz days and therefore asked to join the
Staffel. Winand Grafe was killed on his fourth flight that
day, after having scored his first victory in the morning. The
next was the keen Lieut. Hans Reimann on the evening of
the 23rd; he also gained a victory on the morning of his
death. Then followed on September 30th and October 1st
the deaths of Lieuts. Ernst Diener and Herwarth Philipps. As
mentioned previously Lieut. Joachim von Arnim, who heads
the Staffel's roll of honour, only belonged to it formally but
did not meet his death in it.

But these sacrifices and the zeal that was willing to make
further sacrifices were not in vain. Even in October it was
clear that the enemy's high spirits were broken. "If then"
writes General von Hoeppner, "the enemy's superiority in
the air that was so oppressive at the beginning of the Battle
of the Somme was broken at its end, the merit is due in no
slight measure to Boelcke and the Jagdstaffel he led. Their

joyous, vigorous thrustfulness and exemplary teamwork rendered them a model for all German Jagdstaffels. Eighty-seven victories won during the fighting on the Somme testify to their activity. Our Jagdstaffels forced the enemy who had hitherto been so sure of himself to adopt a cautious reserve, the effects of which were gratefully noted by the troops on the ground."

Captain Hans Ritter also writes in his excellent work, "Der Luftkrieg," of which we have made such frequent use: "Under the leadership of a Boelcke the German Jagdstaffels accomplished the wonderful feat of gradually checking the activities of the enemy aircraft to such an extent, despite their numerical superiority, that our own reconnaissance machines were eased of their burdens and could work again; at the same time they had sufficient forces left to put a very perceptible check on the activities of the enemy artillery planes that had hitherto worked practically unmolested.... The attacks of the Entente lost a considerable amount of thrust when their unconditional supremacy of the air was abolished. In the late autumn of bloodstained 1916 the Battle of the Somme slowed down to its end."

Boelcke's letters also show the enthusiasm which he gave to the training of his Staffel. His skill in the air, his mastery of the tactics of aerial warfare and above all his inspiring and yet tranquil steady personality made him a leader and instructor who remains second to none. He picked out his pupils with unfailing discrimination, grounded them thoroughly in all technical details, imbued them with the spirit of unselfish teamwork and welded them into a fighting unit with thrusting powers that had never before been seen in the air. Through this foundation of a 'school' which turned out a large number of brilliant scout 'aces' Boelcke rises above his personal masterly achievements to grow into a figure of historical importance in war aviation. From a master of aerial single combat he developed into a masterful instructor of organised teamwork in scout flying.

What Boelcke taught his pupils was no blind, headlong thrustfulness but a combination of daring and deliberation. He held that an attack should only take place after a careful deliberation of the circumstances which might motivate an avoidance of combat or even a direct retreat; once an attack had been decided upon, however, it was necessary for the leader to carry it through with an impetuous obstinacy while still keeping a cool head. That is the principle which Boelcke adopted from the very beginning of his war flying—the combination of vigour, audacity and prudent restraint with which his firm, resolute, balanced nature endowed his entire personality.

As an instance of the extent to which he trained his pupils in technical details, we may state that he attached great importance to a thorough knowledge of the individual types of enemy machines, their strong points that threatened danger and their weak ones that gave opportunity for attack. In the brochure entitled "Experiences of air fighting" which reproduces the essential points of Boelcke's teaching and completes it by virtue of later experiences, there is a brief summary of all the types of enemy aircraft. As, for example:

Vickers Single-seater. Very agile, somewhat slower than the Albatros, generally loses height in steep turns. Generally armed with only one machine gun, pivotable in an upward direction (can also fire obliquely upward), but sometimes with two parallel guns. Defenceless in the rear, where the pilot's view is obstructed. Best attacked from behind; can also be very effectively attacked from behind and below by means of a zoom.

Vickers Double-seater. Not so agile or fast. Two pivotable machine guns for observer sitting in front, one of which can be inclined upwards. Can shoot well forward, upward or sideways, but rear fire limited by necessity of shooting clear of propeller. Should be attacked from behind on same or slightly lower level; when going into turns, always try to get on its outside for brief intervals.

Both Vickers types can stand a lot of bullets because the inmates have their backs well covered by the engine. Nevertheless attack from above inadvisable. The Vickers machine seldom falls vertically, even when the pilot is disabled, but goes down in a flat glide and wide turns.

Nieuport Single-seater. Very fast and agile. Armament and shooting possibilities very similar to our own scouts. Generally loses height in prolonged turning action. Attack from behind if possible and at close range.

These examples show the wealth of experience on which such instruction is based and the cool deliberation with which he reviewed the special features of every opponent he fought.

Among our illustrations will be found a photograph of a Vickers single-seater, with Boelcke and Richthofen standing in front, while Höhne is sitting in the machine. This Vickers played a great part as a practical demonstrator for Boelcke's instruction courses. The photograph was taken by Lieut. Böhme, but he did not send it to Boelcke's parents—with whom he was then on terms of friendship—until the summer of 1917, when he led Jagdstaffel 29 and was soon to take over the leadership of the Boelcke Jagdstaffel. We quote from his accompanying letter of July 11th, 1917:

"One of the photographs is valuable because it shows the two greatest heroes of our air service, Boelcke and Richthofen, standing side by side. The background is provided by an English single-seater which our master used to say he had manoeuvred down intact to serve as a 'means of instruction' for all of us, including Richthofen, who were raw beginners at the time. I visited Richthofen in hospital at Kortryk yesterday and from his latest flying activities in the Ypres area our conversation drifted back to the Somme and the way in which Boelcke roused in our air service that spirit of attack which made our great swing-over possible."

As shown by the forceful way he expresses himself about his pupils in the letters of September 17th and October 10th, Boelcke was anything but an easy-going superior. Ruthless in all service matters, he demanded and enforced an iron discipline. All the more remarkable is therefore the love and adoration given to him by all officers and men of his Staffel. The reason is that he set an example in everything that he demanded from others in addition to showing them a personality that was not merely impressive but won all hearts by reason of its constancy and enlightenment, its honesty and kindness, and its combination of affability and dignity.

Manfred von Richthofen writes in his book, "The Red Air Fighter": "It is remarkable that everyone who knew Boelcke imagined himself to be his one and only friend. I have met about forty of these 'one and only friends,' and each of them was convinced that he was the only one. This is the one remarkable phenomenon that I noticed in him. He never had an intimate personal friend. He was equally amiable to everyone and neither more nor less to anyone. The only person, perhaps, who was on a slightly more intimate footing with him was the man who participated in the accident I have just described (Erwin Böhme)."

Moreover Hellmuth von Zastrow, the adjutant who managed his office business for him, wrote in a letter:

"It is difficult to express in words the love and adoration that we who were in the more intimate circle of his comradeship felt for him, and no outsider will understand it. The German nation may adore him as its hero, but to us it was always a special happiness and a proud pleasure to have lived and worked with and under him. When in my capacity of office-superintendant I came to report to him every evening in his room and when sometimes our conversation would shift from service to personal matters as we sat round the fire, I felt that I not only admired and adored him but had learnt to love him with my whole heart and so gave myself double pains to carry out his orders and requests in the way he would have them done. Never was a comrade so loved by his comrades or a superior so loved by his subordinates as he was."

The most striking testimony, however, that originates from the Staffel is to be found in the words written by Erwin Böhme on October 18th, 1916—i.e. ten days before Boelcke's death—in a letter to his friend:

"You admire our Boelcke. Who would not? But you admire in him only the successful hero; you can know nothing of his remarkable personality. That is known to only the few who are privileged to share his life. This simple young man, who is very far from having his head turned by his fame, has a mature, enlightened nature that is most remarkable in view of the fact that he underwent no particular experiences in the course of his brief pre-war life. I assure you that not only do I admire Boelcke as my master, but—

astounding as it may seem considering that he is only 25 years old—I honour him as a man and am proud that a friendly relationship has grown up between us. He may have been influenced towards this friendship because he sees in me an older and more mature man and is delighted to find me serving the cause he has at heart with an ardour that is quite youthful.

"It is most remarkable how Boelcke inspires everyone of his pupils with his own spirit and carries them along with him. They will go wherever he leads them; none will leave him in the lurch. He is a born leader.

"No wonder the Staffel flourishes. Victories are mounting up. And yet in spite of many fights and many daring deeds we have suffered no loss in the last two weeks."

*Lagnicourt, 19.10.16.* The development of my aerodrome has profited much of late by the bad weather we have experienced. I have allotted all my officers small rooms in the new huts I have built in addition to their quarters in the village. So now we are all warmly and comfortably housed on the aerodrome, close to our machines. Also Lieut. Kirmaier, my technical officer—a splendid Bavarian and a very fine pilot who joined the Staffel two or three weeks ago—has put up some fine large workshops, etc.

My flights have been quite remunerative.

When flying with six pilots of my Staffel on October 10th I encountered west of Bapaume a squadron of Vickers biplanes of about the same strength. The enemy did not see much fun in a fight and so tried to sheer off as quickly as possible. We dived down on them. I singled one of them out, but then saw that Kirmaier was going for the same man and so picked out another, with whom I came to grips over Pys.

Twice I gave him a real good dose, but I came down to four hundred metres in the course of the fight and so broke away as two others were trying to sit on my neck, which is a proceding I do not particularly relish. The fellow I attacked got home over his lines and landed somewhere near his own artillery positions at Pozières. His machine was photographed there by Section 32. If it is credited to me as a victory, it will be my 32nd.

There was a lot of flying activity again on the 16th. As of late the English were very impudent after lunch, between 2 p.m. and 3 p.m. when they thought we would be enjoying our forty winks, we took off at 2 and tackled all the fellows we found flying round the front. We swept the board between Thiepval and Sars, i.e. we attacked and chased away every Englishman we found, no matter whether he was flying high or low. Unfortunately only one of them crashed (Acting-Lieut. Müller shot down his fourth); the rest got away.

Shortly afterwards I spotted an artillery flier amusing himself over the lines. I polished him off at the first onslaught—apparently I must have killed the pilot at once. The machine went into a spin and crashed into the foremost English trenches with such a violent impact that we saw a cloud of dust as high as a house.

On our next flight that same afternoon we ran into a squadron of six Vickers single-seaters south of Bapaume at 5.45 p.m. We went into some fine turns. The English leader—with streamers on his machine—came just right for me. I settled him with my first attack; apparently the pilot was killed, for the machine spun down. I watched it down until it crashed about a kilometre east of Beaulencourt and then looked round for a new customer. Meanwhile the others were scrapping with several Englishmen. One of the enemy was actually obliging enough to come quite close to me; I gave him a good shaking up until we got quite low down, and then he escaped across the lines by some very skilful flying.

This was also a very good day for my Staffel. In addition to Müller, Lieut. von Richthofen (his fifth) and Lieut. Sandal each got one, so that the Staffel scored five victories altogether. The total since September is thirty-seven victories, although we have had a lot of bad weather lately. They are really splendid, clever gentlemen—my Staffel!

No. 35 came the next day (17th). After a long and useless flight over the lines I again caught sight of six Vickers Biplanes in our territory. I flew after them with Lieut. Böhme. Three machines from Jagdstaffel I also turned up. Lieut. Leffers, of Jagdstaffel I, tackled one first and forced him down—his eighth victory—whereupon the other Englishmen left their harassed comrade in the lurch and flew on in close formation, evidently well scared.

I picked out the lowest of them, attacked him and forced him away from the others. So then I had him to myself. His machine took fire the second time I attacked him; it fell and was burnt up completely on the ground, about five hundred metres west of Bullecourt.

It is strange that my opponents catch fire so often. The others swear it is due to suggestion on my part; they put it down to the power of my eye, with which I fix my opponents—I have only to attack and then the enemy either catches fire or at least sheds his wings.

I shall bring you the portrait of the Emperor, signed and inscribed with his own hand, which he sent me on the occasion of my 30th victory. I hope to spend at least a couple of days with you at Christmas.

By the way, mother need not paint such a ghastly picture of the circumstances and dangers in which I live. She only need think of the extra experience and routine with which I go into action, quite apart from all our technical advantages in flying and shooting gear!

That was the last letter written by Oswald Boelcke to his parents. The only accounts we have of his further activities are those taken from the combat reports he sent in to the staff officer of the air service.

20.10.16. About 10.30 a.m. five gentlemen of my Staffel and I attacked a Squadron of six F.E. Biplanes coming from Douai. The machine I engaged went down after a fight, in the course of which the observer fell out, and crashed behind the enemy's lines. The wreckage of the machines lies about five hundred metres west of Agny.

22.10.16. At 11.45 a.m., flying with several gentlemen of my Staffel, I cut off two enemy biplanes on their way from the east, meeting them south of Bapaume. Both were brought down. The machine I attacked broke to pieces under my machine-gun fire and went down in flames. The wreckage of this machine lies close to Beaulencourt.

22.10.16. At 3.40 I saw an English scout diving on two German biplanes over Bapaume. I immediately attacked him and forced him down when he tried to make for the lines. The enemy landed in a shell-hole south of Grévillers Wood and wrecked his machine. The inmate was hurled out in a high curve. Salvage impossible on account of drum fire.

25.10.16. This morning I shot down an English B.E. over Miraumont. The machine fell near Battery 381, east of Puisieux-au-mont. Its two machine guns were recovered by Jagdstaffel 2.

## THE "FORTIETH"

Report on the English B.E. Biplane which I shot down at 4.45 p.m. on October 26th south-west of Serre.

About 4.45 p.m. I attacked several English biplanes with seven machines of my Staffel in the area west of Puisieux-au-mont. The observer of the machine I attacked did not return my fire after my first attack; the machine began to smoke heavily the second time I attacked it. Both inmates seemed to me to be dead. The machine sideslipped, fell into the second English line and remained burning on the ground. As I was attacked by a Vickers scout at about two to three hundred metres, I could not watch it any longer. According to the evening report from Group A. of H.Q.1 a B.E. attacked by a scout at 4.45 fell into trench section 34.

Testimony of Lieut. König: I saw an enemy biplane attacked by Captain Boelcke catch fire at about six hundred metres up and fall to earth.

On October 28th, 1916 Oswald Boelcke took off for his last flight at precisely the same time that he won his fortieth victory two days before.

# CHAPTER IX

## *The End and the Inheritance*

ON a dismal autumn day, when the clouds and mist let hardly any sunlight through, the sunny Oswald Boelcke met his end.

"My captain kept on growing thinner and more serious," states Fischer, his faithful batman. "The superhuman burden of seven take-offs a day for fights and the worries about his Staffel weighed him down. General von Below, the commander-in-chief of our army, wanted to send him on leave because he was overworked, but he would not go. 'I'm needed here,' he said. He was always cheerful when he came back from a victory with the Staffel, but otherwise he was often in a very depressed mood in the last few days. When he came home from a flight a couple of days before his death, he said to me: 'Fischer, I found an opponent who was a match for me today. There'll be hard fighting in the next few days. But no bullet will ever hit me,' he added, as he so often did. That was neither pride nor superstition—he did not believe in any charm that made him proof against bullets like some of the others—but just his firm determination to win. And no bullet did hit him.

"The last evening he soon left the mess and came back to his room. 'There's too much noise for me,' he said. He sat down by the hearth and stared into the fire. Then he said to me: 'Fischer, put on the gramophone record: Father, Mother,

Sisters, Brothers, have I in the World no more.' Then Lieut. Böhme came in and asked: 'Can I keep you company for a bit, captain? There's such a row in the mess.' They then sat talking a long time by the fireside, until at last I said: 'It's time we went to bed, sir, now.' 'Who's on duty tomorrow?' he asked, and then he said 'Good night,' and that was all.

"The next morning we had muggy weather again, with rain and sleet at intervals. It was hardly seven o'clock when a report came through from the aerodrome: 'Aircraft overhead.' 'We can do what they can,' he said, and in ten minutes he was up. An hour later he came back with his chin black from the powder gas; 'Well, I've showed them I'm still on the spot,' he said. I had hardly brought him his breakfast before he was off again, and so it went on all through the morning. He was up four times that morning. We were meaning to go to Douai by car after lunch—then another six of those fellows came over, and the captain took off again. Not long after the gentlemen came down I wanted to take the captain his chocolate, but at 4.30 there came a message for help from the front. We wanted to keep the captain back because everyone was dead beat, but he jumped into his machine. 'All ready?' he asked. He took off in spite of the bad weather, with the Staffel after him as if they meant to say: 'Where you go, we follow!'

"About a quarter of an hour later we saw the captain fighting. It went on for about ten minutes, then we saw the enemy bolting. Then all of a sudden there was a German machine and another one—and then they went into a spin. Lower and lower they dropped—oh Lord! A quarter of an hour went by; then Lieutenant Höhne came up to me and said: 'Where's your captain?' I stared at him open-eyed. 'Come,' he said, 'he's crashed—dead!' 'That's not true; I don't believe it,' I replied, 'because he never believed himself that it could happen.' But it was true all the same. When I saw Lieutenant Böhme and his face and his machine, then I had to believe it."

We must also include the report of the catastrophe given by the nearest eyewitness. Erwin Böhme wrote in his letter of October 31st, 1916:

"On Saturday afternoon we were standing by in our little house on the aerodrome. I had just begun a game of chess with Boelcke—then, about 4.30 p.m., we were called to the front because there was an infantry attack going on. We soon attacked some English machines we found flying over Flers; they were fast single-seaters that defended themselves well.

"In the ensuing wild battle of turns, that only let us get a few shots in for brief intervals, we tried to force the English down, by one after another of us barring their way, a manoeuvre we had often practised successfully. Boelcke and I had just got one Englishman between us when another opponent, chased by friend Richthofen, cut across us. Quick as lightning, Boelcke and I both dodged him, but for a moment our wings prevented us from seeing anything of one another—and that was the cause of it.

"How am I to describe my sensations from the moment when Boelcke suddenly loomed up a few metres away on my right! He put his machine down and I pulled mine up, but we touched as we passed, and we both fell earthwards. It was only just the faintest touch, but the terrific speed at which we were going made it into a violent impact. Destiny is generally cruelly stupid in her choices; I only had a bit of my undercarriage ripped, but the extreme tip of his left wing was torn away.

"After falling a couple of hundred metres I regained control of my machine and was then able to observe Boelcke's, which I saw heading for our lines in a gentle glide, but dipping a bit on one side. But when he came into a layer of clouds in the lower regions, his machine dipped more and more, owing to the violent gusts there, and I had to look on while he failed to flatten out to land and crashed near a battery position.

"Men came running to the rescue from the battery's dugout. My attempt to land close to my friend was impossible on account of the trenches and shell-holes there. So I flew quickly to our aerodrome. They did not tell me till the following day that my machine turned over on landing—I certainly knew nothing about it when it happened. I was absolutely distracted, but still cherished hopes.

"But when we arrived at the scene of the accident in a car, they brought the body along to us. He must have been killed outright at the moment of the crash. Boelcke never wore a crash helmet and never strapped himself in tight in an Albatros—otherwise he might have survived the crash, which was not too bad a one."

Richthofen, who was another eyewitness, writes: "I looked round and caught sight of Boelcke about two hundred metres away, jockeying his intended victim. A good friend was flying at his side. It was an interesting fight. Both fired—every moment I thought the Englishman must fall. Suddenly I saw both machines moving unnaturally. 'Collision' flashed through my head. I had never seen a collision in mid air and imagined it would be quite different. It was really no collision, but just a touch. But with the great speed at which such machines fly, a gentle touch is a terrific impact."

It is idle to discuss who was to blame for the catastrophe. While Captain Bolle writes in his sketch of the Boelcke Staffel's history: "Evidently Böhme's undercarriage touched the upper wing of Boelcke's machine," the official report drawn up by Lieut. Kirmaier as acting-leader of the Staffel says: "In the course of the turns Captain Boelcke pressed hard on his opponent and thereby touched another German machine (flown by Lieut. Böhme) that was also trying to get behind the Vickers." The actual occurrence must have tallied with what Böhme wrote to his friend on November 12th 1916:

"I have now regained a superficial control of myself. But in the silent hours my eyes see once again that ghastly moment when I had to watch my friend and master fall from beside me. Then the torturing question comes up once more: Why was he, the irreplaceable, doomed to be the victim of this blind destiny—for neither he nor I bore any blame for the calamity!"

The news of Boelcke's death flashed round like an electric shock, filling with dismay all hearts in the army and throughout the whole of Germany. At first everyone refused to believe it; all were so firmly convinced of the invincibility of the unconquered champion. His personality had grown into an incarnation of victory and the will to victory, an incarnation of the promise of Germany's final triumph. Our allies sorrowed with us, while the enemy, relieved of his most dreaded opponent, breathed freely once again. It would not be too much to say that in view of the value attached to Boelcke's name in the army and at home, in the minds of both friend and foe, his death counted as much as the loss of a battle.

Captain Wilberg, the staff officer for the airmen of the first army, issued the following:

> ORDERS OF THE DAY
> A mighty hero, a noble warrior,
> A pure soul, our Boelcke has fallen.
> His deeds are immortal!
> His name is imperishable!
> May his spirit be our spirit!

Some years later General von Stein, who was quarter-master-general at the beginning of the war and afterwards Minister for War and general commanding the 14th Reserve Corps on the Somme, wrote in his "Experiences" (Leipzig, 1919): "Boelcke was my Staffel-leader. Anyone who knew this calm, modest man will judge of my anguish when a general staff officer reported to me with tears in his eyes: 'Boelcke is dead!' Not long before he had been my guest. The contrast between life and death was too great for me, and I was not ashamed of my tears."

In his letter of October 31st, 1916, Erwin Böhme depicts the impression in the intimate circles of Boelcke's bereaved Staffel:

"A harder blow could not have befallen us. Everything seems so empty here. Only very gradually do we realise what a gap our Boelcke leaves and how the soul of our entity has departed with him. In every respect he was our unique master. He exercised a forceful influence on all who came in contact with him, including his superiors, purely by virtue of his personality and the naturalness of his character. He could lead us anywhere he pleased. When he was with us, we never felt that anything could possibly go wrong, and so we succeeded in practically everything we did. In this last month and a half he has enabled us to put over sixty enemy machines out of action. The superiority of the English waned daily. Now we others must look to it that his triumphant spirit does not depart from the Staffel."

This letter was written on the evening after the funeral service in Cambrai. On the morning of this day Boelcke's parents, who had arrived with his three brothers on active service to take charge of the body, visited the Staffel at Lagnicourt in order to view the scene of their son's last activities and press in sympathy the hand of the friend who was involved in his death. "His parents are splendid folk—for all their sorrow they face the irrevocable most valiantly," writes Böhme. The fact that a heartfelt friendship grew out of this first meeting of the parents with the man who was associated with their son's death-flight is a beautiful testimonial to both parties. Destiny sealed this friendship when Erwin Böhme, the leader of the Boelcke Jagdstaffel, followed his friend and master to his death exactly one year, one one month and one day after Boelcke's fatal flight.

The funeral service for Oswald Boelcke took place in Cambrai on the afternoon of October 31st. The coffin lay in state before the altar of the mighty cathedral. It was the first time that one of the large cathedrals of northern France was the scene of a memorial service for a German hero, and it did not take place without some opposition from the archbishop.

Deep silence reigned in the vast building, while at the same time heavy fighting took place on the near-by front. The generals present were headed by Crown Prince Rupprecht of Bavaria, while the Emperor was represented by General von Below, the commander of the 1st army. A poem composed by General von Stein, that had been set to music, was sung; then Pastor Stelter, the divisional chaplain to the 4th division of foot guards took as his text the heroic words of chapter IX, Verse 10 of the First Book of Maccabees: "If our time has come, so let us die in knightly fashion for the sake of our brethren and not let our honour be shamed."

"From a soldier's point of view," he continued, "our Boelcke's life could have found no more beautiful ending than this death in the air for his country. No foeman may ever boast of having overcome him. He remained unconquered, even in death. He has not merely achieved temporary greatness, for he will always remain great. Nothing can now trouble the radiant vision of him that all we Germans bear in our hearts. Every child knows his name and loves him as a German national hero.... He was not actuated by personal ambition or desire for fame, but by love of his country, an iron sense of duty and the noblest valour. Despite his high fame he always remained the modest, reserved comrade who was so kind to all around him. In him there was a combination of outward heroism and the true inward simple German greatness of character. That was what welded him at such an early age into a complete and harmonious personality that radiated a mysterious magic force, that carried all hearts with it and fired them to emulation."

Just as the coffin was carried out of the cathedral and hoisted on to the gun-carriage drawn by six black horses, the sun broke through the clouds. Bathed in rays of light, the procession—Manfred von Richthofen walked before the coffin, bearing the cushion on which reposed Boelcke's various orders—passed onward to the station through a long lane formed of lancers and footguards, while German airmen circled round in the sky above. Then the coffin lay in state once more before the draped railway carriage, while General von Below delivered an oration in the name of the Emperor and Lieut. Kirmaier spoke on behalf of Jagdstaffel 2. A company of guards that had only been brought out of the trenches that morning fired the funeral volley, and then, to the strains of the "Good Comrade" Oswald Boelcke began his last homeward journey.

Greeted by solemn military music when it reached Magdeburg, saluted by comrades of the air in Halberstadt, the coffin reached Dessau the following evening. Despite the lateness of the hour, its coming was awaited by the leading officials of the town and a vast crowd. It was taken to St. John's Church to lie in state before the altar where Oswald Boelcke had knelt for his confirmation. N.C.O.s, all of whom were pilots that had won the Iron Cross First Class, furnished the guard of honour.

On the next day, November 2nd, the whole town wore mourning. At an early hour of the afternoon a short memorial service took place in the church, the officiating clergyman being Pastor Finger who had confirmed Boelcke. The Emperor's representative was General von Lyncker, who reminded the congregation of the pleasure given to him in the summer of 1911 in Coblence by the gymnastic feats of Aspirant Boelcke which he witnessed as inspector general of the communications troops.

Here, as in Cambrai, airmen circled over the church. When the coffin was carried out, they glided down silently with motionless propellers to greet their master who had ruled the ocean of air only a few days before and now lay confined in his narrow coffin.

The Reigning Duke of Anhalt awaited the endless procession at the entrance to the new war cemetery in the southern quarter of the town. After addresses had been delivered by the officiating clergyman, the mayor of Dessau and Pastor Karl Boelcke, Oswald's uncle, Lt-Col. Thomsen spoke in the name of the air service. His forceful words will be long remembered by German airmen and the German nation:

"Boelcke has fallen. When the sad tidings reached us, his comrades, our hearts were crushed. Boelcke has fallen! After a war career of incredible successes, after forty glorious victories in the air Boelcke, our friend and master, has departed from our midst as an invincible hero.

"The German air service has indeed sustained an infinite loss through his early death, but the gains it has achieved through his life and deeds are likewise infinite.

"Today there is no vigorous, active German lad in our country whose heart does not burn with the secret desire: 'I want to be a Boelcke!' And out yonder, at the front, there is not one among our youthful German airmen, who does not glow with the fervent aspiration: 'I will be a Boelcke!'

"This is a proud consolation that we all, friends, comrades, parents and relations, may take away with us from the grave of our comrade whose name will never be forgotten.

"And so I lay as a farewell greeting on the grave of our dear friend those words which must constitute a solemn vow for every one of our German airmen:

"'I will be a Boelcke!'

"As long as these words remain our guiding star, as long as Boelcke's spirit and Boelcke's prowess remain alive in our air service, so long may our dear fatherland remain untroubled."

It would be contrary to what Boelcke would have wished if we quoted in detail all the various telegrams and messages of condolence that came from the Emperor, the Crown Prince and other Prussian royalties, the rulers of the other German states, Hindenburg, Ludendorff, the Imperial Chancellor, etc. The value of each and all lies in the fact that we find in none of them the accomplishment of an empty formality but genuine esteem of the deceased and heart-felt sympathy.

In addition to the manifestations of sorrow emanating from those who knew Boelcke personally there were countless letters, poems, etc., from individuals who were never acquainted with either him or his family. Anyone who examines this mountain of letters gains the overpowering impression that our whole nation mourned for Boelcke in those days.

Among them there is a letter from Countess von Spee, who lost her husband, the victor of Coronel, and two sons at the Battle of the Falkland Islands on December 8th, 1914. She writes to Boelcke's mother:

"In these days when the memories of Coronel and the Falkland Islands are still fresh, I sympathise with you from the depths of my heart. You too have trod the proud path that leads from victory to doom. I give you my hand in warmest sympathy."

Next to this there lies the touching letter sent by the school-children of a distant Pomeranian village with the wreath of oakleaves they had twined with their own hands. From Pomerania also came the letter of eight year old Dete von Schaumann:

"I loved Boelcke very dearly. That is why I am sending him a wreath. I made it myself, and the ribbon on it is my harvest ribbon. Please lay the wreath on his grave."

Beside the letter from an Italian airman who was taken prisoner in Bulgaria there lies that of a French pilot from a

Würzburg prison camp; both express their admiration for the daring flier. The knightly spirit of the English airmen is manifested in a wreath dropped behind our lines, together with a letter addressed: "To the German Flying Corps" (see insert). The message inside it runs:

> "To the memory of Captain Boelcke, our brave
> and chivalrous opponent.
> From the English Royal Flying Corps."

And in the funeral procession in Dessau was carried a huge laurel wreath sent by four captive English airmen in Osna-brück for 'the opponent we admired and esteemed so highly.' Among these was Captain Wilson, the victim of Boelcke's twentieth victory.

After the fifth anniversary of Boelcke's death had passed, the town of Dessau erected a beautiful memorial. On the tombstone over the hero's last resting-place is carved an eagle, under which is inscribed in mighty letters the single word: "Boelcke." It was, however, a geneial idea of the sculptor, Professor Albinmüller of Darmstadt, to surround the memorial with a wide semicircle of twenty-two flat pillars on which are engraved the names of more than two thousand sons of Dessau who fell in the war. Thus even in death Boelcke remains in close contact with the German brothers, for whom and with whom he fought and died.

Great is the inheritance that Boelcke left behind him in the form of after-effects.

The second portion of this work has shown the permanent influence he exercised on scout flying. He was a pioneer, because his genius made him the first to grasp the significance of his new weapon, because he was the first to recognise and employ the aggressive tactics for which it was created and because he was the first to discover the battle technique it required and develop it to such a pitch of perfection that his tactics of aerial warfare became a general standard and remained so until the end of the war. Thus the pioneer became a master of aerial warfare.

Boelcke was one of the leaders on the road travelled by scout flying from its beginnings as a series of single combats to the teamwork of the organised Staffel. By training Jagdstaffel 2 into a pattern and example for all the others the master of aerial warfare showed himself to be the perfect instructor for scout flying. But neither his supremacy as flier and fighter nor his organising capacity can serve to give a satisfactory explanation of the effect he produced. The essential factor is rather to be sought in the spirit with which he inspired his subordinates in his lifetime and the entire body of German airmen after his death. This is made up of his will to conquer and his high sense of duty. For him 'duty' was never a mere fulfilment of service orders; his conception was the higher ethical one which made it incumbent on him to sacrifice his person and the last particle of his strength willingly and ruthlessly for the cause he had at heart.

Yet these words do not suffice to depict the 'Boelcke spirit.' 'Spirit' is something that cannot be comprehended and defined in words; it cannot only be perceived by those whose hearts and minds are open to it. Still less do we know how the spirit is transferred from one person to another; the explanation must be finally sought in the secret of the effects produced by personality. Sceptics may deem this an illusion and psychosis, but we know that the something which exercises an inward compulsion on human beings to sacrifice their lives gladly and willingly is a real force and power. It is something sacred to those who believe and follow it. Boelcke's true heroism is to be found in this 'Boelcke spirit' rather than in his external triumphs. This heroism begat other heroes.

The greatest and most valuable inheritance left us by Boelcke is the transmission of his spirit to German aviation. Thus he was not merely the pioneer, master, leader and instructor of scout flying, but the 'good genius' of German war aviation. That is the deep inner significance of the vow laid by Thomsen on Boelcke's grave in the name of all German airmen.

These German airmen cherished Boelcke's inheritance as something sacred and faithfully fulfilled the vow made in their names. Apart from the foolish jealousies at Pontfaverger Boelcke never found anyone envious of his triumphs and honours, and in similar fashion no one ever disputed his title to fame after his death. Manfred von Richthofen, his most successful pupil who won double the number of his victories, always acknowledged that he owed his position to what he learnt in Boelcke's school. Once when he received congratulations on a new victory, he said: "If Boelcke had lived, his score would be over a hundred by now." And an another occasion he remarked: "I am only a fighting airman, but Boelcke was a hero." In all the works that have been written on war flying we continually find Boelcke designated the 'pastmaster.'

In the days immediately following his death his value grew greater with every fresh manifestation of the effects of his spirit and his achievements, Evidence of this is afforded by the ceremonies that took place at his grave on October 27th, 1917, the first anniversary of his death. They were attended by Lieut. Böhme, who then led the Boelcke

Jagdstaffel, and a deputation of twenty-five airmen sent by the General commanding the air forces; Captain Steffen, their spokesman, deposited a laurel wreath in the name of the German air service with the words:

"Let this be a token of our inexhaustible gratitude to the mighty hero and victorious genius of aerial warfare." Since that day Boelcke's grave and memorial have become a holy place for old war pilots who have a particularly high regard for their traditions and are often the scene of pilgrimages and solemn ceremonies, the import of which is: "We will guard the inheritance left us by Boelcke."

Boelcke also exercised a strong influence in Germany in the days that followed his death. The heroic figure of the triumphant youth whom the younger generation loved so fervently and tenderly and the older one so proudly lived on in all hearts after he had fallen for his country and roused them to loyalty and sacrifices. The fact that Thomsen's words: "I will be a Boelcke" became widespread as the theme of numerous poems and kindled a sacred flame in the hearts of young and old cannot be regarded as a mere emanation of war psychosis.

But those were days when manliness and the heroic spirit still counted for something, when the idea of self-sacrifice was still a live one and a sacrificial death was felt to be something sacred. It was the time when the German nation was not yet vitiated by the poisons of doubt, discontent, despondency and treachery, but still believed in its country and the victory of its just cause and was ready to make any sacrifice, trusting in God and this cause.

There is one consolation for those who look back. Happy is the man who was inspired by such faith to give his life for us all and did not need to live through all the sadness of the bitter end and its sequel. Such a heroic life could only end greatly and worthily with a heroic death—a death in which he fell as the conqueror and not the conquered.

And today, yes, just in these days when the time seems at hand for the errant German nation to find its way back from the wilderness, when patriotic sentiments and German resolution flood all hearts like a vast tidal-wave, Boelcke's spirit seems called upon to exercise the influence that it did in the time of our need and crisis. "A nation perishes without heroes and hero-worship," says Heinrich von Treitschke. Wakened to new life from the letters he has left us, the vision of Boelcke's patriotic figure now stands before us in all its genuine radiance. His spirit speaks to us from those letters that reveal his personality.

May the vision of this youthful hero who ripened to manhood in the service of his country fire the youth of today to emulate him and become what he was—true German to the core, devout in heart although he never made a show of it, spotless in character, faithful to death in duty, of a cheerful and joyous disposition in life, resolute and vigorous, conscious of his power and value and yet modest withal, a friend to everyone but always mindful of his own dignity, and always faithful to his principle: "Reality rather than appearances."

# APPENDIX

# *The Victories of Oswald Boelcke*

| VICTORY | DATE | TYPE | NOTES |
|---------|------|------|-------|
| 1915 | | | |
| 1 | 4 Jul | Morane Parasol | Lt. Tétu & Lt. de la Rofoucauld, of MS.15, both KIA. Crashed near Valenciennes |
| 2 | 19 Aug | Bristol Biplane | Force-landed front lines, evening. British? |
| 3 | 9 Sep | Morane Saulnier Two Seater | Crashed near French Front trenches, Douai; evening. Two killed. (No French casualties recorded.) |
| 4 | 25 Sept | Voisin ? | Crashed in front lines near Pont-à-Mousson. (MF.29 lost two Farmans on this date.) |
| 5 | 16 Oct | Voisin B1 | Crashed near St Souplet, am. (VB.110 lost one aircraft on this date.) |
| 6 | 30 Oct | 2/seat pusher ? | Crashed near Tahure, am. (MF.8 lost a Farman on this date.) |
| 1916 | | | |
| 7 | 5 Jan | BE2C (1734) | 2 Sqn RFC, 2/Lt W.E. Somervill, Loyal North Lancs Regt/RFC, WIA/POW. Lt G.C. Formilli Royal Garrison Artillery/RFC. WIA/POW. Near Harnes, Henin Lietard. |
| 8 | 12 Jan | RE7 (2287) | 12 Sqn RFC, 2/Lt Leonard Kingdon, Worcs Regt & RFC, KIA. (Aero Cert No.1533, 4 Aug 1915). Lt K.W. Gray, 3rd Wilts Regt/RFC, WIA/POW North East of Turcoing, am. |
| 9 | 14 Jan | BE2C (4087) | 8 Sqn RFC, 2/Lt Justin Howard Herring, RFC (SR), wounded by three bullets in small of back. From Surrey. Aero Cert No.1430, 13 July 1915. Capt Ralph Erskine, Royal Scots Fus/RFC, from Glasgow, wounded in the leg, but died in captivity 1 Jan 1918. Force-landed in front line trenches near Flers. Aircraft destroyed by artillery fire. |

| VICTORY | DATE | TYPE | NOTES |
|---|---|---|---|
| 10 | 12 Mar | Farman | Force-landed in front trenches E of Marre, am. No French aircraft reported lost but several airmen were wounded on this date. |
| 11 | 13 Mar | Voisin | Crashed 1 pm, Malincourt, Verdun. One crew of BM.113 wounded this date. |
| 12 | 19 Mar | Farman | Crashed near Cuissy, 1 pm. MF.19, Lt Libman & Sgt Galiment, both killed |
| 13 | 21 Mar | Farman | Force-landed Fossers Wood, 11.15 am. From either VB.109 or VC.111 Escadrille. |
| 14 | 28 Apr | Caudron | Crashed, Verdun front, nr Vaux. No French two-seaters reported lost |
| 15 | 1 May | Biplane | French front lines, evening. Two French airmen wounded this date. |
| 16 | 18 May | Caudron 2-eng | Force-landed, evening nr Ripont. C.56 lost one aircraft this date. |
| 17 | 21 May | Nieuport | Crashed, am. near Morte Homme. Two French Nieuport pilots wounded on this date. |
| 18 | 21 May | ? | Crashed, evening at Bois de Hesse. AL.209 & C.42 each lost and aircraft this day |
| 19 | 27 June | ? | Crashed, evening, Douaumont. No known French losses this date |
| 20 | 2 Sep | DH2 (7895) | 32 Sqn, Capt Robert E. Wilson, Hamps Regt & RFC. POW. Force-landed on fire near Thiepval |
| 21 | 8 Sep | FE2b (4921) | 22 Sqn, Lt Eynon George Arthur Bowen, RGA & RFC. Served in France with artillery and later as air observer. Aero Cert No.2541, 6 June 1916. Lt Robert McCallum Stalker, 5th Seaforth Highlanders, att'd RFC. Both killed when they fell from their spinning and burning machine, near Flers. |
| 22 | 9 Sep | DH2 (7842) | 24 Sqn, Lt Neville Philip Mansfield, N'ton Regt & RFC. Aero Cert No.2384, 22 Nov 1915. Fell in flames over front lines near Bapaume. |
| 23 | 14 Sep | Sopwith 1 1/2 Strutter (A1903) | 70 Sqn, 2/Lt John Hugh Gale, RFC (GL), from Oxford, KIA. Sapper J.M. Strathy, 2nd Canadian Div, Sig, KIA. Machine fell and disintegrated south of Bapaume, |

| VICTORY | DATE | TYPE | NOTES |
|---|---|---|---|
| 24 | 14 Sep | DH2 (7873) | 24 Sqn, 2/Lt J.V. Bowring, Sth Lancs Regt & RFC. POW after force-landing near Driencourt. |
| 25 | 15 Sep | Sopwith 1 1/2 Strutter (A895) | 70 Sqn, Capt Guy Lindsay Cruikshank DSO MC RFC. French Aero Cert No.1520, 9 Aug 1913. KIA. Lt Rudolph Arthur Preston, MC, Lincs Regt, att'd RFC, KIA. Fell near Hesbecourt, Ypres |
| 26 | 15 Sep | Sopwith 1 1/2 Strutter (A1903) | 70 Sqn 2/Lt Neville Kemsley, RFC. Aero Cert No. 3164, 28 May 1916. Believed killed. 2/Lt Carl John Beatty, RFC (GL), KIA. Crashed in British front lines |
| 27 | 17 Sep | Fe2B (7019) | 11 Sqn Capt David Benjamin Gray, 48th Pioneers, Indian Infantry/RFC. POW. Aero Cert No. 2263, 10 Jan 1916. Lt L.B. Helder, Royal Fus, att'd RFC. POW. Force-landed near Equancourt and crew set the machine on fire. Jasta 2 brought down a total of four 11 Sqn FE's in this fight. |
| 28 | 19 Sep | Morane Bullet (A204) | 60 Sqn, Capt Hugh Christopher Tower, RFC (SR), aged 30, KIA. Aero Cert No.466, 23 April 1913. Fell in flames into Grevilliers wood early evening. |
| 29 | 27 Sep | Martynside G. 100 (A1568) | 27 Sqn, Capt Henry Arthur Taylor MC, Royal West Kent Regt/RFC, KIA. Aged 18 from Wimbledon. Aero Cert No. 2306, 18 Jan 1916. Went down over Ervillers |
| 30 | 1 Oct | BE2d ? | NW Flers. No losses recorded. |
| 31 | 7 Oct | Nieuport 2/Seat | Crashed in flames at Morval. Possibly a Nieuport XII of F.24, lost this date |
| 32 | 10 Oct | Fe2B | 23 Sqn Capt Ralph Newton Adams MC, 7th Royal Fus/RFC. To France Dec 1914. Aero Cert No.1967, 17 Oct 1915. KIA. 2/Lt Ogg, safe. Adams mortally wounded and Ogg landed machine in British lines near Morval but crashed into a shell hole. |
| 33 | 16 Oct | Be2C (6745) | 15 Sqn Sgt F. Barton, KIA. 2/Lt Edward Mervyn Carre, Lincs Regt/RFC, KIA. Carre was 22, served in the artits' Rifles in 1914 and was commissinoed into the Lincolnshire Regt in 1915. Transferred to RFC May 1916. Elder brother killed in 1915. Crashed into front trenches near Hebuterne. |

| VICTORY | DATE | TYPE | NOTES |
|---|---|---|---|
| 34 | 16 Oct | DH2 (A2542) | 24 Sqn, Lt Patrick Anthony Langan-Byrne DSO, Royal Artillery.RFC. KIA. Fell east of Bullencourt. |
| 35 | 17 Oct | Fe2B | One of two Fe2B's lost this am by 11 Sqn, 6965 or 7670. Ltn Leffers of Jasta 1 claimed the other during a fight over Bullencourt. |
| 36 | 20 Oct | Fe2B (7674) | 11 Sqn, Lt Robert Parsons Harvey, 4th Norfolk Regt/RFC. Aero Cert No.2766, 10 Apr 1916, WIA. 2/Lt George Keith Welsford. RFC, KIA. Welsford was 25, educated at Harrow. School champion lightweight boxer. Despatch rider 1915, commissioned June 1916. Crashed inside the British lines west of Agny although Welsford was thrown out during the descent, falling into the German lines. |
| 37 | 22 Oct | BE12 (6654) | 21 Sqn, 2/Lt W.I. Willcox, W. Yorks Regt/RFC. POW. Fell on fire south of Bapaume. |
| 38 | 22 Oct | Sopwith 1 1/2 Strutter (A1903) | 45 Sqn, one of three lost during and air battle this am. A1061, 777 & 7786 all fell to Jasta 2, over Grevillers Wood/Bapaume. |
| 39 | 25 Oct | BE2d (5831) | 7 Sqn, 2/Lts William Fraser (KIA) & Bernard Tarrant Collen (GL), DOW 26 October. Crashed east of Puisieux-au-Mont, mid-morning. |
| 40 | 26 Oct | BE2d | 5 Sqn, 2/Lt Smith, WIA. Lt John Cedric Jervis, RFC. Aged 26, he had previously served with the Royal Fusiliers. Jervis was killed in the air and the BE fell into British second line trenches where it was shelled on the ground. |

Compiled by Norman Franks, 1991

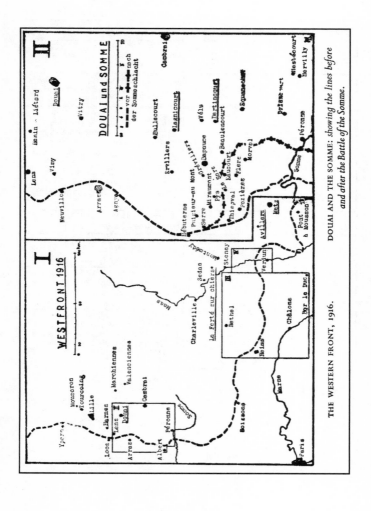

THE WESTERN FRONT, 1916.

DOUAI AND THE SOMME: *showing the lines before*
*and after the Battle of the Somme.*

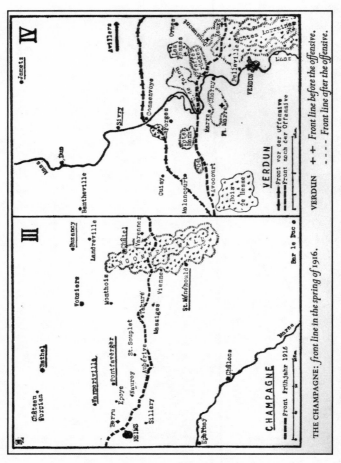

*Maps from the original edition of the book.*